T0006851

TALKING THE TOUGH
STUFF WITH TEENS

Fiona Spargo-Mabbs

TALKING THE TOUGH STUFF WITH TEENS

Fiona Spargo-Mabbs

First published by Sheldon Press in 2022
An imprint of John Murray Press
A division of Hodder & Stoughton Ltd,
An Hachette UK company

1

Copyright © Fiona Spargo-Mabbs 2022

The right of Fiona Spargo-Mabbs to be identified as the Author of the Work has been asserted by her in accordance with the Copyright, Designs and Patents Act 1988.

Illustrations © Bethany Rendell 2022

All rights reserved. No part of this publication may be reproduced, stored in a retrieval system, or transmitted, in any form or by any means without the prior written permission of the publisher, nor be otherwise circulated in any form of binding or cover other than that in which it is published and without a similar condition being imposed on the subsequent purchaser.

This book is for information or educational purposes only and is not intended to act as a substitute for medical advice or treatment. Any person with a condition requiring medical attention should consult a qualified medical practitioner or suitable therapist.

A CIP catalogue record for this title is available from the British Library

Trade Paperback ISBN 978 1 399 80026 6

eBook ISBN 978 1 399 80027 3

Typeset by KnowledgeWorks Global Ltd.

Printed and bound in Great Britain by Clays Ltd, Elcograf S.p.A.

John Murray Press policy is to use papers that are natural, renewable and recyclable products and made from wood grown in sustainable forests. The logging and manufacturing processes are expected to conform to the environmental regulations of the country of origin.

John Murray Press
Carmelite House
50 Victoria Embankment
London EC4Y 0DZ

Nicholas Brealey Publishing
Hachette Book Group
Market Place, Center 53, State Street
Boston, MA 02109, USA

www.sheldonpress.co.uk

To my dear Jacob with love, and thanks for all the years of chats

CONTENTS

About the author   ix

Foreword   xi

Introduction   xv

PART 1: EVERYDAY TALKING

  1 Walking in teenage shoes   2

  2 Understanding adolescence (1) – what on earth
is going on?   27

  3 Understanding adolescence (2) – what on earth
were they thinking?   52

  4 Talking about talking   74

  5 What could possibly go wrong?
(And what to do if it does) – the teenager   102

  6 What could possibly go wrong?
(And what to do if it does) – the parent   127

PART 2: TALKING THE TOUGH STUFF

  7 Talking the tough stuff of sexuality and gender identity   169

  8 Talking the tough stuff of relationships and sex   186

  9 Talking the tough stuff of mental ill health   204

 10 Talking the tough stuff of alcohol and drugs   222

 11 Talking the tough stuff of eating disorders   240

 12 Talking the tough stuff of self-harm   258

 13 Talking the tough stuff of suicide   276

For your bookshelves   293

Acknowledgements   295

Index   297

ABOUT THE AUTHOR

Fiona Spargo-Mabbs has worked with parents and families for more than two decades. Having studied English at the University of Oxford, Fiona met and married her husband, Tim, had her two boys, Jacob and Daniel, qualified as a teacher and began teaching English in adult education as Dan started school. Her first love, and specialism, was Family Learning, which involves working in some of the most deprived areas with parents whose limited confidence and skills are risking their children's progress and achievement. The fundamental premise of Family Learning is that the involvement of parents is vital to the impact and success of children's learning, and that parent–child communication is at the heart of this.

Over the years, as well as her role expanding locally, Fiona took on increasingly high-level responsibilities strategically at a national level within this specialism. Then, in 2014, her bright, big-hearted 16-year-old son Dan suddenly and unexpectedly died from an unintentional overdose of MDMA (ecstasy). Fiona and Tim were left with a passionate commitment to do all they could to prevent any harm happening to anyone else's child from drugs, and in response founded a drug education charity in Dan's name, the Daniel Spargo-Mabbs Foundation.

With her personal and professional lives having collided, as a drugs educator Fiona has worked with tens of thousands of young people, parents and professionals across the United Kingdom and Europe, and less than a decade after setting up the DSM Foundation, she is considered to be one of the leading UK experts in drug and alcohol education. As well as regularly being asked to talk to the media, she speaks across a range of platforms, informing and influencing policy and practice at a national level.

Fiona's first book, *I Wish I'd Known – Young People, Drugs and Decisions: A Guide for Parents and Carers* (Sheldon Press, 2022), weaves Dan's story around a wealth of information, advice and practical tips for parents. It won Gold in the Nautilus Book Awards 2022 in the category of Parents and Families. Supplementary materials to the book, including a guide for parents of neurodivergent children, are also available to download from https://library.johnmurraylearning.com.

About the illustrators

The artwork for this book was produced by final year students (aged 17-to-18-years) at **The BRIT School** in South London, one of the UK's leading Performing and Creative Arts schools. They bring not only their creative talent but also their teenagers' take on the topics and issues themselves. **Anastasija Andriuskina's** design was chosen for the cover. Ana came to the UK from Lithuania with her family when she was nine. She's now studying Illustration and Visual Media at the University of the Arts in London, and hopes to work in illustration and graphic design in the future and do more editorial work like this. **Bethany Rendell** has created all the illustrations for the book. Beth is now at Camberwell Art School in London studying illustration. She said, 'I've always loved drawing and since a young age I've always seen a future in my passion. I plan to get my artwork out there and put it to good use. I love being able to express feelings and emotions through art and I can't wait to involve myself in the industry.'

FOREWORD

by Jeremy Vine

This book is a goldmine of parental wisdom. That struck me at the weekend, only a day or two after I had finished it. There was a sadness about the realisation. I had taken my eighteen-year-old daughter to see our football team. We always have the same ritual: Thai food for lunch, then up to the stands in time for kick-off.

But last weekend was different. Saturday was poignant. My daughter had just got into university. She now has a reading list eight feet high, so this game was probably our last for a while. The ritual felt extra special – we had talked over our food and now we chatted over our football. And as we spoke, I realised the best conversations are the ones which are indirect. "How are you feeling about uni – BLOODY HELL REF ARE YOU BLIND?" is, strange to say, a wonderful formula. When Katsu curry or a foul on Kanté are the main focus, serious conversation about life can be a natural sideline.

My eldest has been going to Chelsea games with me since she was five and Mourinho was in charge. At her first game she was so shocked by the roar when the home fans welcomed an early goal (51 seconds in, against Fulham) that she burst into tears. Later that day she told me she thought the opposition supporters were "quite rude" to sing "YOU'RE GETTING SACKED IN THE MORNING" at Mourinho. Then we talked about other stuff, and we have been talking ever since.

Finishing this wonderful book made me wish I had read it a decade earlier, because it would have crisply explained something I took years to discover: sometimes you need to face away from your son or daughter to have the best conversations. This is the kind of basic rule you feel should have been written down – 'Talk to your child while driving; they are far more open when they're not being stared at' – and the sort of parental principle we only discover by accident. When I think about my football weekend, I realise I only grasped the lesson as my daughter left us. Why isn't there a book to help?

Actually, there is. You're holding it.

What you're about to read is a brilliant corrective to accidental parenting. It could almost have been called 'The Rules'.

I had a happy childhood and was much loved. But my poor parents had been brought up around Jim Reeves and were now sharing house with the Sex Pistols. While the grandpa managers at Radio 1 were banning *God Save The Queen* for the line "…and her fascist regime," my mum and dad were insisting the twelve-year-old me accompany them to the Mall at 5am to give Her Majesty a respectful Silver Jubilee wave, which she was hardly likely even to notice. That's a communication breakdown right there.

I learnt from their mistakes, of course. As soon as my young girls fell in love with Lorde and Taylor Swift I was blasting them from my study so loud that my daughters were asking me to turn my music down. But that creates other problems. It was their music, not mine, and I had nicked it. Bad move.

The generation gap in the seventies meant all children felt like rebels. The responsible teens in my corner of Surrey were few and far between. I used to wonder how they had got their lives together so young while I was all over the shop. One such person was Tim, the kind of older lad who looked sorted, reasonable, unfazeable; he seemed to have a wise head on him. Eventually our generation went out into the world beyond Cheam. Tim had an unusual surname, and many years later my ears pricked up when I heard it during a news item on my Radio 2 show. A father was in agony, speaking about how his sixteen-year-old son had died from an accidental drug overdose. I was shocked when I realised it was my childhood acquaintance on the news. My instant reaction was that if this tragedy had befallen Tim, it could happen to anyone. You could say the same of Fiona, Daniel's mother, the author of this book. If that particular disaster can happen to Fiona and Tim Spargo-Mabbs it can happen to any parent anywhere. This book won't stop it happening again, but it might stop it happening to you.

Although the loss of a beloved son must have given Fiona her professional urgency, it does not dominate the book you are holding. The pages you will read have such extensive tips and lessons, for such a range of situations, I lost count. When I grew up, sex was never mentioned, and technology meant having a fax machine. The comedian Arthur Smith said he was "at such an advanced age, I remember when they brought in cordless pyjamas".

Nowadays, tech is so universal Arthur's joke barely makes sense. As for sex: 'Love Island', anyone? A friend of mine told me, "Your daughters will definitely be watching 'Sex Education' on Netflix. Ours have binged it." When I said no, they were still quite young and I was sure it would not be on their radar, the friend told me how to find 'View History' in the Netflix settings. Sure enough, they only had 22 minutes of the entire season left.

Parents may think they can offer useful advice. Most of us just look at what our own mums and dads did, and reverse it. But unspoken beneath all our attempts to intervene in our children's lives is the question – what gives a generation that torched the planet and trashed the economy the right to tell a fifteen-year-old she needs to be home by eleven?

If you think you need this book, you do. If you think you don't need it then you really, *really* do. Apart from anything else, it is packed with stories and fantastically well-written. Some parental missteps are so glaring they almost made me laugh: I wanted to wrap my arms around the mum who panicked when her teen asked her if it was true that she would bleed from "down there" once a month, and decided the best response was to simply deny it. At the end of this pageturner, like me as the final whistle blew on the weekend's football, you will say to yourself: "I wish I'd known all that at the start."

INTRODUCTION

Connor: Can we have our names on the inside cover, Miss? And our photo?

Me: It's all meant to be anonymous!

Zain: Maybe just the initials then? Or maybe we can use an anagram of all our names? Or maybe, like, a word search on the last page?

Me: Do you honestly want your parents to know what you said about them?

Zain: A hundred per cent!

Connor: Yeah! I snitched them!

As I sit and write, here in a frame on my desk are a couple of notes from my then five-year-old son Dan. They were part of a series that fluttered down the stairs up which he had recently stomped in high dudgeon, having been sent to his room in response to some long-forgotten misdemeanour or other. The first of these says, in his furious five-year-old spelling, 'I hat [hate] you mum.' This was rapidly followed by a shower of others, and I remember the speed and remorse of it well, because it was so touching at the time, and touches me still. The series continued (with some help with translation):

'I love you mum so much'

'I love you to plooto'

'I love you to the nxt galaxe'

'I love you mum evan arand spas [even around space]'

'I love you mum to the nxt wald [world] and on'

'I love you mum and I love you on and on so it goes for evr and evr'

It's these last two that are in my frame, on my desk, and although it may surprise you to learn that I decided, on balance, not to frame that first, furious message of hatred, nevertheless it's tucked in my drawer, along with the others, and I know that it's there. This early record of communication with my younger son, in the special archive I store with my socks, embodies that passionate turmoil of emotions our children can encounter in their experience of their parents – and that, just occasionally, we as parents can experience in our relationship with our children, too, loving them to the depths and heights of forever though we do. I expect I was full of fairly big feelings, and probably not too positive ones either, when I sent little Dan to his bedroom for whatever it was he had done.

This maelstrom of emotions is never more turbulent than in the teenage years, and it can be hard to hold on to the fact that the sometimes painful words that can fly from a teenager's mouth are rooted in the most enormous love and loyalty, as is the fury that sometimes slams the door, and the solid, impenetrable silence that sometimes sits and glowers behind it. You may not see any messages of eternal and infinite love fluttering down your stairs, but those feelings are all there, even if currently buried beneath heaps of rage/embarrassment/disdain. And this makes it all the more confusing all round. Teenagers need their parents, and perhaps more now than ever, as they face stuff of increasing magnitude and seriousness – though they begin to need them differently, which can all be a bit bewildering. Talking our way through these years, however we can, really does help, and really is important.

Communication is key to helping our children navigate their way safely in, around and through to the other side of the many and various risks that can face them in adolescence. There's a lot of tough stuff to get through, it has to be got through together and there's lots to be talked about along the way in order to get out the other side safely. But communication is perhaps never more fragile than during those teenage years. It can be a source of huge frustration and pain, but also great joy on both sides, great amusement all round and great discovery, as we as parents explore the world all over again with them. And a very different world it now is.

The purpose of this book is to provide a handbook for parents, full of information, insights, tips and practical strategies. Its hope is to help both parents and teenagers to communicate more constructively, collaboratively and positively about the issues that are most challenging in young lives, and can cause not only most tension and disruption within families, but also present highest risk to adolescents. These are the conversations that both may prefer to avoid. It's easy as a parent to forget from our own younger days how awkward it can be as a teenager to broach certain subjects at home. You don't want to worry your parents, or disappoint them, or never get let out again. You don't want them to jump to conclusions that are wrong, or to judge you for conclusions that are right. But you really do want (and need) to talk to them.

Talking the Tough Stuff with Teens is born of hours and hours of listening to teenagers and parents telling me what they think works, what doesn't, what they need, what they don't, what would help. And years of working with teenagers and parents in the context of drug education, talking about how to have conversations that help (and lots of other things too). And before that, years of working with parents and children in the context of community education, enabling them to build effective communication within their family (and lots of other things along with that, too). And, to add to the mix, my own experience as a mum to two erstwhile teenage boys.

The book is in two parts. The first explores the context for both parents and adolescents in which communication happens. It lays out the ways the world has changed from a parent's teenage years to now. It looks at the amazing adolescent brain, the role hormones play, the shifting social dynamics between family and friends, and the impact all this can have on conversations at home. It examines the art of communication, what can make it work well, or cause it to break down, what can make something that should have been small grow out of all proportion, and get out of control, and skills that can be brought to a conversation that starts out awkwardly.

The second part tackles the toughest of stuff. It takes a look at some specific issues in teenagers' lives, the ones that present most risk and that cause most concern to both them and their parents: sexuality and gender identity; relationships and sex; mental ill health, drugs and alcohol; eating disorders; self-harm and suicide. As well as an overview of the issues and risks, there are insights into what can lie behind behaviours, signs for parents to look out for, and practical advice for both parents and teenagers, all focused on conversations. There are stories and case studies, contributions from experts in each specialist field and signposting to further information and support.

My hope is that this is a book that's useful for every family, across the generations, bringing insight, understanding and practical strategies so that conversations at home enable pre-teens and teens to live happily, healthily and safely, and grow into confident, independent adults – people who still enjoy talking with parents back home.

Note: The names of all the teens, twenty-somethings and parents who have contributed their conversations to the book have been changed, and any identifying features altered, to make sure their identities are anonymized.

PART 1
EVERYDAY TALKING

1
WALKING IN TEENAGE SHOES

'Yeah, so I suppose there's kind of a lack of
understanding, because they were brought up in
completely different worlds, so they see things
differently, and then it's a little bit difficult to
communicate when you have different
viewpoints and a clash.'

Megan (15)

The world is a very different place for teenagers now than it was when their parents went through their teens. We humans have hurtled through change in the last 30 years at a headlong speed never experienced before in history, and those changes have touched – and transformed – almost every aspect of our lives, including communication.

This book is all about conversations, and making these work when they matter most, and that relies on sharing a language, which is so much more than words. With language – what we say and what we hear, two things in themselves fraught with potential for dissonance – comes worldview, perspective, expectations, experiences, assumptions, prejudice, heritage. All sorts of baggage, in short. So, it's useful to start by walking a little while in their shoes, as well as examining our own, and what we carry along on our shoulders, and exploring some of the ways in which shifting our starting points as parents can help us walk, and talk, more closely with our teenagers, especially when we're talking the tough stuff.

PARENTS TALK

'That's why I think the communication is quite difficult for me, to try and understand where they're coming from. Like, when they are following people, or they are listening to some music and I'm watching, thinking oh my word, what are they wearing?! You know, some of these representations of women? Sometimes you look at the videos and it's just so far away from my world. And that is difficult, 'cos we are different.' **Giovanna**

When the average parent of the average teen was a teenager themselves, there was just a small handful of TV channels, the mobile phone hadn't yet arrived in the UK, and to find something out you had to rummage through textbooks or dig into massive encyclopaedias. Now a teenager streams or downloads their viewing online, binge-watching entire seasons of series, browsing infinite menus of films, and watching television on catch-up, and rarely on an actual television set. Teens touch screens to make calls, message friends, take photos, make films, find things out and scroll social media. The world is, indeed, a different place, or at least their interaction with it is.

TWENTIES TALK

'I'm watching *Seinfeld* at the moment, and it is funny when they're saying, "I need to call George," and I'm thinking, "Well, just call him!" And then I think, "Oh no wait, they need to go to a payphone."' **Flo (20)**

What's remained unchanged, however, is that fundamental human need to be loved, and to love, to be accepted and safe, to learn, to explore, and to grow from a child into a happy, healthy, independent adult, and these remain the biggest, most powerful and most important drivers of everything. There's much that we do know as parents, though we walk and talk with our teens in this very different landscape, surrounded by much that's a bit of a mystery. It's good to hold tight to what we know, and to what's most important, while we learn and digest the rest.

TALKING STUFF

- Have you ever taken a moment to think about how much the world has changed since your parents, grandparents or even their parents were teenagers?
- Do you remember being a teenager yourself? What was going on in the outside world when you were 15? What about in your family? Friendships?

- How do you think this affects the way you see the world now, and the way you interact within your family, especially with your teens, and especially when things get tough?
- What were the worries then, and now? When was it easier to be a teenager? Or is it just different? Can you compare notes with your teenager?

The generation game

Most parents reading this now will be classed as Gen X (born roughly 1965–80), and their teenagers will be Gen Z (born roughly 1995–2012), and while these labels are huge generalizations, they can be a useful way of getting an understanding of some of the things that can shape parent–teen conversations.

Parenting Gen X style

Gen X teens were the first generation of 'latch-key' kids, with freedom to roam the streets unsupervised, in a world of increasing divorce rates, rising numbers of mums out at work and not many childcare options available. As parents ourselves now, we want to be around more for our children, to spend not just quality but quantities of time together, to get work and life better balanced and household responsibilities more fairly distributed. Mobile technology was just arriving as we became parents, and our expectations now are of close and continual contact with our own children, although our own parents had to manage without this. And although we'll always be several miles behind our teens in the nuances of all that technology can bring, it's so deeply embedded in all we do, too, that this common ground, and shared language, can also bring connection in more ways than just the multiple means of communication it provides us with.

5

PARENTS TALK

Andy: I think that's a big difference. There wasn't an app on your phone to check everything. There wasn't a phone! You had to wait and get on the bus when it arrived, and you'd get there and hope your friends would turn up at the time you agreed. And then you'd come home again. You couldn't check in with your parents. I think that's a massive difference, that they can constantly keep in touch – which is good, because it probably would have been much more practical when we were their age to be able to check in with friends en route and know that you're all going to turn up, rather than "Let's meet at three," and everyone leaving and hoping for the best.

Dave: That also creates worry, though, doesn't it, because you know they can keep in touch and then when they don't, you instantly think why aren't they? Whereas with my parents it was, we'll just wait, and if we get a knock on the door from the police, something's happened; otherwise we'll assume everything's OK. And that's kind of what it came down to, wasn't it?

What's so special about Gen Z?

TEENS TALK

'I feel there's kind of like a split between the older and younger generations, because a lot of the time when we try to speak up about issues like climate change, we're told we're too young, we don't really understand, when they're basically the ones wrecking the planet.' **Amy (16)**

Gen Z is a generation that cares, that campaigns, that carries burdens of responsibility for saving the world – burdens that many of them feel their parents don't quite share, or at least, they feel, not with quite the enthusiasm, intensity and vision that's needed if we're not to become beyond hope.

Gen Z is the generation of Greta Thunberg (b. 2003), that inspirational teenage force for change, whose vision drew pre-teens and teens out of their schools and onto the streets.

Gen Z is the generation of Malala Yousafzai (b. 1997), shot by the Taliban simply for being a girl and at school, who survived and became, in her turn, the most famous teenager in the world, speaking out for the right to education.

Gen Z is the generation of #NeverAgain, launched in 2018 by US teens who'd witnessed yet another school mass shooting, this time at their own school in Florida. Enough was enough – both attitudes and legislation had to change to stop this happening again, and their protests are credited with bringing in significant state-level gun control measures.

There are so many more examples, in which change has come through passionate young voices, and teenage tenacity, reminding the generations above them what matters, and doing this now with a digital savviness that taps into their sense of global citizenship and connectedness.

TALKING STUFF
- What does your teenager think the big issues are for the world right now?
- What were the issues that troubled you when you were growing up?
- What were some of the key moments in history that shifted your perception of the world? What are some of the key historical moments in your teenager's life?

Gen Z and difference

This generation is one of greater diversity globally, and one with a greater willingness to embrace all that's different. This encompasses race, religion, gender identity, sexual orientation, body size, disability, mental health, neurodiversity and so much more besides. Although there is so much still to be done to challenge prejudice and dismantle judgements, expectations have changed for us all, and have done so throughout our own Gen X youth and adulthood. It's easy to forget how recently some very big things have changed, even in our Gen X lifetimes – the legalization of same-sex relationships, for example. Attitude change can lag long behind legislation – as well as race ahead of it – but for teenagers who've grown up in an altered climate, though created in part by their parents, the lenses through which they view the world will be different.

TALKING STUFF

Challenge each other to reflect on the stereotypes, assumptions and judgements of your peers (and reflect on your own along the way) by setting each other a series of scenarios and 'How would they feel / what would they think / what would be said if …?' questions. For example, 'How would your classmates/colleagues feel if they heard that the new person at school/work was …? What would they expect? What would they think? What might be said?'

Gen Z and mental health

Mental health is another example of attitude shift. Things have been changing, thanks in part to high-profile, highly respected public figures speaking out loudly and clearly. Teenagers definitely feel they have the advantage over their parents, with a greater degree of understanding, insight and support on offer to them, and they feel sympathy for parents who suffered under the stigma that used to be so much bigger. But thank goodness that stigma has shrunk, and support has grown, because teenage mental health is of great concern, and greater still since COVID-19.

TEENS TALK

'I think there's a lot of difference in the awareness of mental health, and a lot of the stuff surrounding that. We have lessons that help us learn about it, whereas I know back in the day for my parents, they didn't have anything like that, so it would have made them much less able to deal with issues.' **Daniela (16)**

Gen Z under pressure

Rising rates of mental ill health are just one of the pressures our teenagers carry around. There's a seriousness, and a touch of despair, especially for older teens, who can feel they face adulthood disadvantaged compared to their parents.

Chatting with Jacob

My older son, Jacob, and I are both at the upper end of our respective Gen Z and Gen X eras. He's now in his mid-twenties, has various grown-up responsibilities (a home, a job, a pension, a puppy) but he's young enough still to have some interesting insights, and also a bit of useful hindsight, into his own teenage years. There's a lot more chatting with Jacob to come, but for now here's a bit of how he sees things changing for his Gen Z peers.

Me: So, what worries people most in your generation?

Jacob: Existence. Yeah, survival.

Me: Wow, that's a bit bleak.

Jacob: I know, but I don't think a lot of young people see a future, either in terms of the climate crisis, or just economically. The things you need to live, like housing, and increasingly food, and work, are becoming so scarce, and actually unattainable for people my age, and younger than me. And older than me too, but this is the system people my age and younger have grown up with. We've not known anything different. In 2008 I was 13, and that's when I got my first job – I got my paper round then – so I've never been in the workforce before the global crash of 2008. It's almost a given that things can only get worse, because things *have* only got worse, for the entire lifespan – or political awareness, or economic awareness – of people my age.

The earliest years of our current teens were overshadowed by the global economic crisis of 2007–8, and although they're mostly too young to remember this, they've lived with its ongoing legacy, and its impact on their parents. There's no longer much of an expectation of getting and keeping a steady job that will pay the bills, or finding affordable housing, or getting to the end of the student debt gained doing the degree they felt they had to do to get the unattainable job.

TEENS TALK

'I think it's much harder these days to set yourself up in life, because I assume – well, I think – in our parents' time it was a lot easier to get a job, get a house. It was a lot cheaper or whatever. But now you've got to get a degree, you've got to get a master's, you've got to go to uni, do a bunch of things. You've got to get an enormous mortgage. You've got to be massively in debt. It's all this stress that you *have* to do so much to have a good life really, as opposed to before.' **Jamal (16)**

Gen Z and a world at war

And then there's living with terror. The devastation of the 9/11 attacks, which sent a tsunami of shock round the globe, happened before our teenagers were born, but the impact lives on. They've grown up in a world in which random terror attacks can happen anytime, anywhere, and at any scale. Many UK Gen X parents grew up with the hovering threat of unpredictable terror attacks by the Irish Republican Army, with bomb scares and constant vigilance just part of everyday life. But this enemy is of a different order, and it's not just one enemy, with one coherent ideology to try to grasp. And then there are global pandemics, and always the enormity of global warming.

TEENS TALK

'Our generation's had it a lot worse in terms of a lot of things. It's kind of been all of the things that have happened over the course of ten, fifteen, twenty years, that have made it harder for us. The housing situation and everything else. It's all just gone downhill for us, and we have to try and pick up where older generations have not really cared about things – or not cared, but they haven't had to worry about it. We're the ones that have to worry, like especially with something like global warming and climate change. We're the ones who have to make the real difference because they never had to worry about it, or never thought about it.' **Amy (17)**

Online living

_____

Chatting with Jacob

Me: I've just come across this term 'phygital' in relation to your generation. Apparently, it's a marketing thing, something about blending the physical and digital experience to sell stuff, but it's also about young people not having any sense of separation between online and offline. Do you think that's true?

Jacob: The distinction between online and offline is there – people know when they're talking to someone or when they're messaging or video calling – but I guess maybe the meaningfulness of that distinction has been eroded. I guess I'm an older Gen Z. Growing up when I did, the internet was something that was entering people's homes for the first time.

Me: And you can remember it changing?

Jacob: I can still remember dial-up. You used to be able to tell if you were connected or not depending on the sounds it was making, and we used to just have that one computer in the living room, and you used to have to come off the phone to use the internet. So, I can remember going from online being something where you went online for a defined period, and then you went offline. And then probably with smartphones, you started being always online – you were never offline. When I was growing up you'd always come back from school, and log into MSN messenger, and you'd send someone a message on there, and if they happened to do the same thing they'd see it, but otherwise they'd see it when they logged in. Till they did they'd have no idea.

Me: So smartphones were the real game changer in terms of it all being immediate?

Jacob: I think that's what's changed the distinction between online and offline. You're never offline anymore. Being offline

12

is something people can seek out, if they're on a retreat or something. It's something special. Your default is online now, rather than offline. No one's ever offline anymore.

Gen Z have the whole wide world literally at their fingertips, and they move fluidly between online and offline without barriers. They are those for whom the term 'digital native' was coined. The divisions between real and virtual, online and offline, simply don't exist for those who've grown up with life online being normal. And this has had a radical impact on almost everything, in a relatively short space of time.

PARENTS TALK

'I think for me I always feel like I'm one step behind whatever the new things is. So there are certain things I understand – Facebook, Instagram and so on – but then they come home with new things. And I don't want to have to rely on her to say – although she can – what's appropriate and what's not appropriate. She's only fourteen. She shouldn't be having to say that. I'm the parent. For me, the online world does feel a little bit too advanced for where I currently am. I can't be there constantly, following her with a cushion – I feel that's what I want to do, but you just can't.

'And that cut off, when they are and they aren't on it, it is just a constant. Even with school – homework will be researching something online, and then they'll be chatting to friends on another device, and it's just this whole merged world. I find it a bit overwhelming more than scary. Though it's also scary.' **Lauren**

TALKING STUFF

- Below is a very brief timeline charting the arrival of some of the bigger digital changes that have transformed our lives (although for most of us some considerable time after they first appeared).

- Go through this with your teenager and track your own childhood, and on into theirs, against all these dates.

- Can you remember when you first encountered any of these yourself, and when they became part of everyday life? Can you remember the impact it had?

- Were there any surprises looking at this? How do you both think this has changed the way we all interact with each other and the wider world?

Technological timeline

1979 Sony Walkman

1980 *Pac-Man*

1991 Invention of the World Wide Web

1994 Amazon

1994 Yahoo; PlayStation

1995 Commercial dial-up internet

1997 Netflix

1999 Commercial wireless internet

2001 Xbox

2004 Facebook

2005 YouTube

2006 Twitter

2007 iPhone

2008 Android smartphone

2009 WhatsApp

2011 Snapchat

2016 TikTok

How much is too much? The screen-time conversation

We're the first generation of parents having to work out the rules about screens for our children, as we are with all things online, and this can be a continual cause of conflict because there's always a screen around somewhere. And it's not just parents. Teachers also find themselves battling students concealing their phones under tables as they scroll away, oblivious of the lesson at hand (though in our generation how many of us sneaked a book or comic under our desk or inside a much less interesting textbook?). It's complicated by the range of devices available to use, and for a variety of purposes, from research for their homework to chatting on social media, and one can easily morph into another, invisible to the parental eye. It's an issue that gets harder to manage as they get older, because so much more of their lives will be accessed that way – social, educational, recreational – but you'll probably find the worst of any arguments happen in those earlier teenage years, and as they get older they'll hopefully begin to moderate their own online behaviour better.

And we need to check our own habits. Do we sometimes spend too much time on screens ourselves? Are we also sometimes distracted from the conversation in the room by the ping on our phone?

TEENS TALK

Does anyone's parents have a go at them for spending too long on their phone?

'It's more like, if anything happens, it's always: "You just need to spend less time on your phone." It's just kind of an excuse for them to blame it.' **Ali (14)**

'I'm the same. I'll have, like, a headache, and they'll say: "That's because you're on your phone too much." Or I'll cut my finger and it's: "That's because you're on your phone too much."' **Rachel (14)**

'Or if you're struggling with your English: "It's because you're on your phone too much."' **Billy (15)**

'Or they get annoyed with me because I go on my devices but not for educational reasons, just go on social media. Like, I wouldn't go on a device to look at the news or check on politics. I'll just go on to check Instagram ...' **Mahmood (14)**

PARENTS TALK

'I have to say that I think screens haven't helped communication in our house. For me that's such a bugbear. It's caused quite a lot of friction over the years. When they were younger we had rules, like no phones at the table, and you weren't allowed them at night in your bedroom. Things like that. We were really quite strict about it. Obviously, they're adults now, and it's impossible. The youngest, who's 17, gets away with more than the others did at that age, of course, because he's the youngest.' **Sue**

TALKING STUFF

You need to accept that, whatever the boundaries you decide on for your child, or your family, they almost certainly won't go down well, at least not all of the time. And, of course, as with boundaries in general, they'll need to be negotiated and flexed as they get older. There's more on boundaries to come.

We'll come back to screens, but for now, here are some questions to consider, depending on your child, their age, and your family situation. If you can involve your teenager in setting and agreeing the rules, so much the better, but that doesn't always work out.

- *What's the impact?* It can be helpful to start with a focus on how your child's time on screens affects them, and your family, and importantly your communication. Does it have an impact on their behaviour or mood? Does it lead to arguments about other things, perhaps things that don't then get done or get done less well than they should be?

- *What?* What are they spending most time doing on screens, and what screens are they doing it on most? What activities do you feel – for both children and parents, if possible – could be cut back on? You could keep a family log over the course of a week, and perhaps track each other's screen time. There are apps you can use that will log the amount of time spent on certain screens and activities.

- *Where?* Are there places you feel should be screen-free, depending on factors such as their age? For example, some families ban all phones at the meal table, if they share family mealtimes, or at other family times. Some parents hold off screens being used in bedrooms for as long as they can.

- *When?* What are reasonable limits on the total amount of screen time in a day, at a stretch? What about a cut-off time to help protect sleep, homework or valuable downtime? Will any of this be different during the week and at weekends? How will you manage this? Some parents set an alarm for a teenage gamer, for example (though it's rarely the right moment to stop

17

when you're gaming, partly because of the way many games are designed).

- *How?* How will you monitor this? How will you enforce it? What will the consequences be? How will you manage negotiations and different boundaries for different children? And how will you ride out the challenges that may follow?

Chatting with Jacob

Jacob: So, if we're talking about listening, for example when internet gaming became a thing, you'd say, 'Jacob, Daniel, come on, it's time for dinner.' And we'd go, 'But we're right in the middle of a game,' and you'd go, 'Just pause it,' and we'd be, 'We can't pause it – it's an online game!' And you wouldn't get it, you wouldn't listen, you'd be like, 'No, you have to come down!'

Me: Oh yeah, that's true I did! I do understand more now about how difficult it is to just stop – it was all very new then – but I think I'd still think, if dinner's ready, that actually *is* more important than being in the middle of a game.

Jacob: Well, that's easy to say if you're not in the game.

Me: That's easy to say if you've not spent ages cooking dinner!

Jacob: OK, well, maybe …

Too much information?

Being able to open the world at the touch of a screen is a wonder we now take for granted, but most of us agree there is far too much information and that we take it on board to frequently. Both parents and teens can worry about each other in respect of online information overload, though for different reasons.

PARENTS TALK

'They've got access to so much more information, but not all of it right. I mean, I can get them telling me something they've heard on YouTube, that's not always related to anything that's important, but, you know, and I say, "That's not true!" And they say, "But it was on YouTube." It's just factually incorrect, and if they're taking that as that's the thing, or that's the right way, especially if it comes to things like drugs, and sex, and things like that, and they're hearing things, or looking at things, or seeing people's experiences, and thinking that's the norm ... that really worries me, yeah. It feels very out of control ...' **Dawn**

TEENS TALK

'My parents didn't grow up with social media, and the whole media wasn't such a big thing, whereas now media is so big, and stories are constantly put out there, and it's always the bad stories, not the good ones. My mum will panic, like, "Oh, you spoke to someone online!" I met my best friend online, and she panicked for years, thinking I was talking to a creep, because that's always what's in the news. She always thinks something bad's going to happen because the bad stuff's always in the news. People go out and walk all the time at night; it just happens there's a tiny number that do get murdered, or that sort of stuff, and they only see that sort of stuff, and because they didn't grow up with it, they now don't know how to cope with it with their children.' **Rachel (16)**

Social media: the good, the bad and the carefully airbrushed

And then there's all that social media brings. Platforms grow and develop new spaces, new platforms arrive and gain new ground, their use by young people changes constantly, and it's an essential ingredient of almost all teenagers' social lives and evolving social identities. With so much focus on its potential for harm, it's easy to forget that social media also brings lots of good things in the way of connection, affirmation, encouragement, fun, learning, creativity and new ideas, and when COVID-19 locked us all away at home it played a key role in many young people's general wellbeing. But it can also wobble or totally topple the fragile self-esteem and vulnerable sense of identity of the average adolescent,

presented with idealized lives, airbrushed images, the competitive quest for likes and clicks, manipulation, bullying and pressures that now never stop or give them a moment of peace. The social expectations, and personal anxieties, can all be very similar to when we were teens, but with it all being constantly active and forever present on a phone in their pocket, it can now feel relentless. And social media is not going anywhere any time soon. It's something we'll come back to.

PARENTS TALK

Erin: Someone was telling me at work the other day about this A4* piece of paper thing that's going round social media for kids – you know, the one where your waist shouldn't be wider than a piece of paper?

Dawn: No way! Which way round, portrait or landscape?

Erin: Portrait.

---

*UK A4 size paper is roughly the same as letter size in the US.

Nisha: To be honest, either way with my waist …

Erin: So, whereas we're all going, 'What? That's nuts!', young impressionable girls – and boys – are going, 'I need that to happen.' We think it's crazy, but things like that are out there.

Meera: But then there were always those things. I mean, I remember the three diamonds – do you remember?

Dawn: What was the three diamonds?

Meera: You were supposed to be able to see these three diamonds between your legs when you are standing there with your feet together. One between your ankles, one just there, below your knees, and one between your thighs, kind of in the middle. Your legs mustn't meet, in other words. When I was growing up that was the thing, and I was, like, 'My legs will *never* have three diamonds!' It was a really big thing for all the girls in my school. So, although it might be spreading further now, that pressure has always been there.

Dawn: I think that's exactly it. You're right, it's the fact that it gets round so much further and faster. I don't think it's changed but it's more accessible, and more in your face.

Nisha: I know. They can't get away from it, it sort of follows you wherever your phone is. If they get caught in a negative spiral it's really hard for them to get away from it. That really worries me.

The open online door

TEENS TALK

'I'll be on social media and there's this trend going round, and I don't remember the song but at the end you blow out your vape, and my mum saw that and she thought social media was going to influence me to do this because she thinks if I see it I'll be, like, "Oh, everyone's doing it," and think it's kind of cool, and like it's not a big deal because everyone's doing it.'

'And also, on social media drug dealers do shoutouts, for stuff like weed edibles, and my parents will see it and they're, like, "Why are there drugs on your screen?" and I'm, like, "I'm not trying to buy the drugs; they're just trying to sell me the drugs!" My parents obviously think social media's going to influence me to do drugs, but it's not.' **Cate (15)**

What else has slipped through? Without wishing to be too alarmist, teenagers now have ready – and not always sought-after – exposure and access to sex, drugs, violence, and all sorts of things that most of their parents would never have seen, and things many would rather just not think about their child seeing. Growing numbers are accessing porn, at worryingly young ages, and some serious, hardcore porn at that. The sending of self-generated sexually explicit images has become somewhat normalized, and again at worryingly young ages. Gaming involving high-level violence is easy to come by online for free, as well as in games they can buy online, with age limits that can easily get slipped past parents. On social media, drugs are sold openly, self-harm and suicide messages shared, and children and young people can be accessed, groomed and exploited by adult criminals.

And then there's the darknet.

There's no putting the online genie back in the virtual bottle, and we wouldn't want to do this even if we could. The tough stuff for parents is to be as aware as you can of the risks, to decide on appropriate boundaries for your child, and how these should shift as they get older, and work with them as well as you can to protect them online, and to develop the skills they need to protect themselves.

TALKING STUFF

As with the screen conversations above, how you help your teenagers manage risk online will depend on your child and their age. It will also link into all of the more general adolescent risk management and protective factors covered in Chapter 3, and coping with more specific risks that we'll come to later on in Part 2.

Be curious. What do they spend most of their time online doing, and where, and who with? How does it work? What do they love best about it? Can they show you? Would they let you join in or have a go?

Talk about risks. What makes them feel good about themselves online? What makes them feel bad, unsafe or uncertain? What do they feel might be some of the risks they encounter online that could affect them – or are affecting them – offline?

Talk about boundaries. This will depend on what you know about your child and how well they can self-moderate and manage risk, as well as their age. Some parents insist on having their child's password and do random checks. Others, especially as they get older, might agree with their teen they can check their phone if they have concerns. Neither of these might work with your teen, and as they get older their privacy is an important part of their growing independent identity, but keep on talking, being curious and checking in.

Setting parental controls. This is important, wherever you are on this spectrum – on the Wi-Fi, and/or individual devices, apps and programmes, as appropriate to the age of your children.

Do your research. Check out online safety resources, for example in the US the Family Online Safety Institute (www.fosi.org) or Common Sense Media (https://www.commonsensemedia.org/), or in the UK the Safer Internet Centre (https://www.saferinternet.org.uk/). Go onto the social media platform sites and check out their safety guidance and parental advice. Find out about privacy settings and make sure they put these in place. Look out reliable sources for reviews of video games or new apps teens are using. Go through this together.

And finally, what is your conversational legacy?

PARENTS TALK

'In spite of the great modern developments we've made, it still seems there's something slightly suspicious about a man that knows what he feels and is able to articulate it. With my dad, I mean, he's classic 1940s boys' private school environment, and him going, "That's good, well done," is, like, wow! That's like emotional incontinence from him, you know? I think that's not unusual. You think, "Oh I'll be better than that." Every generation tries to avoid the mistakes our parents made but we end up making a load more, don't we?' **Jim**

Each generation has parented the next as well as it could, and they've done this with the legacy left by the parenting they received themselves, just as we do now in our turn. If you jump back through the generations you can quickly see some huge historical events and significant social shifts that will have influenced each family. (This is an interesting exercise to do – and may interest your teen, too – you never know.) In addition to all the external factors, all those individual family dynamics and mix of personalities play their own important roles in shaping parenting styles, and those parent–child conversations.

We each bring a particular model of communication to how we talk to our teens; a mixture of what we've inherited, our reaction to what we've inherited and what we've learned from all that's around us in relation to parents, parenting and communication generally. We'll take some time later to reflect on all of this in more depth, when we come to how we respond and react to our teens in those tough conversations. Taking time to understand our own stuff is a valuable, even vital, exercise in helping those conversations work. But at this starting point, just begin to think about the conversations you had with your parents as a teenager yourself, and to reflect on what you retain, or reject, in how you communicate with your own teenage children. In all self-reflection, be kind and compassionate, and remember that your intention is to be the best you can be – but good enough is generally good enough.

PARENTS TALK

Me: What were the conversations you found most awkward with your parents when you were a teenager?

Clare: I don't think we had them.

Erin: No. They weren't awkward; they just didn't happen.

Kari: Yes, same here. There were just certain things that you didn't discuss.

Me: What were the things you didn't discuss?

Kari: Well, we'd never talk about sex, and we still don't speak about anything like that. If I talk to my sister, she'll say that even when she needed to tell my mum she was pregnant, she had to build up to it over about two hours, because then the implication was that she had had sex. Yeah, so we just never did.

Nisha: We were the opposite: we talked about *everything*, and you couldn't really have any privacy because they wanted to know *everything* – and they're still like that, they want to know every detail. So we'd talk about the most inappropriate things at breakfast. Nothing was private or not talked about.

Lauren: My experience was very similar. Nothing was off the table. My mum was always very keen to share everything she thought I ought to know, or didn't know. I'm trying to think back – it was so many years ago – but I think because of that I can't remember ever feeling embarrassed about it. I don't think I ever did, because it was

25

just a conversation. I don't remember ever feeling embarrassed. Perhaps I did, though – it was a long time ago …

Me: Was there anything you felt you couldn't talk about?

Lauren: No, but it's still the same: my family are a very open family, so even now they still want to know everything. And I remember, you know, first boyfriends, first kiss, first everything was just, 'Oh, so did this happen? Did that happen?' and it was just a sort of an open discussion – probably, actually, my mum being very nosy, now I think about it, rather than anything educational. But it just made it a normal stream of conversation rather than it being a taboo subject, really. But I don't remember having The Talk or anything. I remember periods, though. I remember her coming in and explaining what you should use and how you should use it.

Gina: My parents are closed books. They are complete closed books. Everything gets swept under the carpet. Even now if there's an issue, it's not dealt with. There'll be a big screaming, shouting match about it and then it's never mentioned again, never dealt with. So I learned from quite a young age that there was no point, absolutely no point in speaking to them about anything. And even now as an adult. I love them dearly 'cos they're my parents, but I've got no depth of a relationship with them unfortunately. If I had a problem, I wouldn't go to them. I'd go to my mother-in-law probably before I went there.

Me: Gosh, that's really hard. And has that affected the way you talk to your own kids?

Gina: Definitely. I've got a very open-door policy with my boys deliberately, 'cos I never had that growing up. I've said to them, 'There is absolutely nothing you can do that would make me not love you.' I'll say a million times a day, 'Love you, love you, love you.' You know, just because I think it's important. I think it's important for them to hear that. If I say it a thousand times a day, you know, I'll say it 1001. And, you know, they'll say it back. Like, he's 13 years old, and every night he'll say, 'Night, Mum. Love you.' I say, 'I love you more' at the end. But yeah, I love that.

2
UNDERSTANDING ADOLESCENCE (1) – WHAT ON EARTH IS GOING ON?

'That's the thing with parents. No one has the definitive handbook on how to be a parent. There's nowhere that tells them, "Do this and this." No one knows what that is. So, every person doing it is learning on the job. Your parents are literally just winging it all the time.'

Sam (21)

We've been rumbled. They're onto us. They know we're making it up as we go along, and it perhaps never feels more so than during those teenage years. That beautiful, biddable, adoring child is undergoing a dramatic transformation before your very eyes, and every day – sometimes every moment – can feel like a process of trying to work out all over again how to be the parent that emerging young adult-to-be in your home most needs. There's so much going on, inside and out, in these days of drama. There are hormones raging, a brain that's rewiring and a body that's doing all sorts of very new things. Friendships gain new intensity. Hearts can be given, lost and broken. Important schoolwork piles on pressure, mental health issues can start to appear and very big decisions have to be made about very big things for a future that's looming ever closer. And throughout it all the inevitable, totally natural, normal and healthy goal of independent adulthood is drawing them out of their old childhood relationship with their parents, and into something completely new to everyone involved – a pull that is rarely pain free.

As they grow up, so our parenting of them needs to grow up too, and all of this changes the way we communicate with each other. This chapter is all about making sense of what on earth is going on, and how we can talk our way through it, because that can make an enormous difference when the tough stuff comes along. And be reassured. The fact you're reading this book means you're committed to being the best you can be, and that in itself can make all the difference in the world, even when it all seems to be going horribly wrong. Perhaps especially then.

TEENS (AND TWENTIES) TALK

'I think for me personally, the best thing about being a teenager was the friendships. Being in a group with loads of different people who are just sort of trying to find who they are, who they want to be. Finding the people who have similar interests to you. And also, when you're in school you see your friends every day. Yeah, that was the best thing about being a teenager – having your friends around you pretty much all the time.' **Flo (20)**

'The best thing about being a teenager is getting more freedom than being a child. Getting the responsibility to make your own mistakes.' **Danielle (18)**

'My teens are coming to an end, but I'd say the best thing about it was the freedom and flexibility. I was constantly (unconsciously) on the search to find who I was as a person. Being socially malleable enough to mould yourself around the people you encounter everyday while knowing that one day you'll have to get serious about life, but it's not coming soon.' **Adam (19)**

TALKING STUFF

- What did you enjoy most about being a teenager yourself?
- What are you finding most fun/interesting/intriguing about having a teenager in your family right now?
- Share all this with your teenager (if you can, and if you haven't already).
- Ask what your teenager thinks is best about being a teenager themselves.

PARENTS TALK

What I enjoy most about being the parent of a teenager is ...

'Sharing a joke together.'

'That you can start treating them as adults, and do more grown-up things with them.'

'Seeing them learning from their mistakes and moving on.'

'So interesting observing them becoming real people with their own opinions.'

'The friendship that develops through increased levels of maturity and communication.'

'Watching the unique person form, with an increasingly equal relationship.'

'Celebrating their successes.'

The journey from child to adult

Adolescence is an adventure that lasts about 15 years. It takes them from childhood to becoming an adult, starting at around the age of ten, and lasting until their mid-twenties. Along the way, all those enormous physical, intellectual, emotional and social developments fall into place, and have an impact on everyone around them, especially those in the front line, which is you as their parent. All of this can be exciting, intriguing, bewildering and, at times, frankly terrifying for you, but it will also be for them, too. It's new to you both. It can definitely help to have older children who've been through all this before, and broken you in to a certain extent, but each new emerging teen is going to get through it differently, and you will be doing your best, but doing it differently, alongside them.

PARENTS TALK

'I don't know if there's any one big thing that I'm worried about, but I think it's just every stage that they go through is going to present challenges, because they've never done it before, and I've never parented that before. I think every step, "Oh, I'm going to worry about them doing that. I'm going to worry about their first boyfriend – or girlfriend. I'm going to worry about them moving out of home. I'm going to worry about – oh, just everything." I just do, I worry about them all the time. With everything! And hoping I've got it right, and hoping that they get it right. But you don't know, do you, until they're older?' **Meera**

What I find hardest about parenting a teenager is ...

'When you try to listen but can't begin to empathize, or when you try you "get it wrong".'

'That they don't listen to anything you say. (Or at least pretend not to, but actually they do, in some instances, eventually.)'

'Learning that their opinions matter, even if you think they're wrong.'

'That they think they know it best, don't listen, and then realize they were wrong – but don't apologize!'

'When your children are younger, parents all seem to know and support each other. With teenagers, parents seem to start believing if your child does something wrong they should be labelled, rather than being supportive of each other as parents, but teenagers are risk takers and make mistakes.'

'As a parent I struggled asking for help, or even telling friends of my struggles, because everyone seemed to portray perfect lives.'

'Keeping them safe, avoiding dangerous choices, keeping them alive (we've had suicide attempts in the last few months).'

Adolescent ages and stages

There are roughly three stages of adolescence, and you'll have seen these first-hand if you have young adults as well as teens.

Personality, personal circumstances and so many other factors can affect how all this manifests, but the physiological, neurological and sociological changes will just go ahead and happen, in the normal run of things, whatever else is going on.

Early adolescence: 10(-ish) to 14(-ish) years

> **TWENTIES TALK**
>
> 'I think when you're really young, the only people you want to be accepted by is your parents, and then at some point that shifts to your friends, and I think that's a difficult thing for parents to accept a lot of the time, because their child has suddenly gone from almost worshipping them to, "No, I want to be accepted by *them* now." It's not a decision or anything, it's just a sort of change of mindset. Sometimes you kind of lose that connection, and I think that can be difficult to deal with – on both sides, but I think more for the parents.' **Sam (21)**

This is when puberty begins to be evident, so there's a lot going on physically, some of which shows in the changes to their bodies, and some of which you'll experience in the changes to their behaviour and moods, which can swing quite dramatically thanks in part to the hormones behind the whole process. Risk-taking can start to pick up, as can pushing at boundaries and challenging family rules, and conversations can become less straightforward as they move through these years. Their friends begin to become all-important, their social lives all-absorbing, and you as their parent are no longer idealized (though you may already have picked that up).

TALKING STUFF

Do you remember ...

- your first celebrity crush?
- the boundary you first battled?
- what was most embarrassing about your parents?

Can you see these things happening for your early adolescent child? Could you talk to them about your own experiences? There'll be more on what you can do to maintain connectedness during this period of change, but sharing stories, and finding common ground, can be good and simple starting points.

Middle adolescence: 15(-ish) – 17(-ish) years

TEENS TALK

'The "coming home late" thing drives me mad. Like, obviously I'm getting older, so I need to have the coming home late extended, but it just ends up causing arguments every time for no reason.' **Connor (16)**

PARENTS TALK

'One of the things I find hardest about parenting teenagers is letting go, and getting the right balance between enforcing discipline and giving them the support they need, with giving them freedom to learn and develop and gain independence.' **Bruno**

The dramatic changes of puberty settle during this time, though may be ongoing for boys. Physical growth will usually stop for girls, though boys will keep growing (and eating their way through the refrigerator). This is the age of acute self-consciousness, as their concern about their appearance is joined by deep sensitivity to how they think (and fear) their peers perceive (and judge) them, and it's their peers who are their primary focus.

The drive for independence intensifies, but they can still struggle to manage risks safely, especially when they're with their friends, so letting them go is a difficult judgement call for parents. Conversations can come to feel like a bit of a battleground, though it's good to know it can also begin to get better during this time. And with independence comes concern about the future, that time soon to come when they really will be out there on their own.

TALKING STUFF

We'll talk some more about negotiating boundaries later on, but for now perhaps you could sit with your mid-teen – if Connor's frustration resonates – and note down together which boundaries are causing most chafing at the bit. Then read further on for some insights and practical tips for you both.

Late adolescence: 18(-ish) – 24(-ish) years

They're all grown up now physically, they're much more stable emotionally and they may be moving on from their family base, but alongside that you'll (hopefully) find them reconnecting with parents within an adult relationship. Their brains still have a few more years of connecting up to do before they can fully and quickly access the useful bit that helps them rationalize and think through consequences, delay gratification and manage pressures from peers, but it's getting better all the time.

Chatting with Jacob

Me: So, Jacob, what did we have most arguments about when you were younger?

Jacob: Um, I think vegetables.

Me: That's definitely what I'd have said! So, whose fault was it, yours or mine?

Jacob: I don't think it's about fault. You were doing what you had to do; I was doing what I had to do.

Me: What was it that you had to do?

Jacob: I had to not eat them, because they were disgusting.

Me: Genuinely disgusting?

Jacob: Genuinely disgusting to me. I wasn't doing it just to be annoying, so I don't think 'fault' is the word for it …

Me: Ha-ha! Even though I was right?

Jacob: Well, you were right to say they were good for me, but I was right not to eat something disgusting.

Me: Hmmm. So, was there anything that could have made those conversations go better?

Jacob: Well, I was listening to this podcast, and they were saying the best thing is not to force children to eat anything they don't want to, or make them finish things.

Me: OK. So, tell my readers how much you love vegetables now.

Jacob: I really love vegetables now. My favourite vegetable is roast Tenderstem broccoli.

Me: Hah! And how much was that to do with the fact I nagged you to eat vegetables when you were younger?

Jacob: I really don't think it bore any relation to it. It was just getting older, and not wanting to be the one in a group of friends not eating something. And finding they weren't disgusting any more.

Me: So really, your advice would be to give up on the vegetables, and wait for it to pass?

Jacob: Yes, pretty much …

Note: Jacob will still send me photographs of meals he's prepared that include a particular abundance of vegetables, and it always brings me joy, and reminds me that arguments don't always by themselves bear fruit (or veg).

So, there are lots of changes that come thick and fast, with very few aspects of family life left untouched, and all of this changing the way, the where and the how we talk about stuff. We'll start with a little more detail on some of the social, emotional, biological and physical transformations, before we move on to the intricacies of what's going on inside those incredible teenage heads.

Friendships

TEENS TALK

'I think what's most fun about being a teenager is all the socializing and hanging out with friends. 'Cos when you're a child, obviously, it's all organized things, like when you go round a friend's house it's all organized by parents. And then when you're an adult, when you meet up with friends, it's generally less random than when you're a teenager. When you're a teenager you can, like, just go and do anything. You can go to town, or the park, or the shops. You just go and have a wild time together.' **Megan (15)**

Friendships are a great big deal for teenagers; all part of the shift from their family base to the life to come as independent adults. Friendships matter with an intensity and level of loyalty never before experienced, and require the investment of vast tracts of time – online and in person. Friendships generally modulate during these adolescent years. You can expect some fairly decisive realignments between 13 and 14 years, when childhood friends can be displaced by new ones, often those whose values and attitudes fit with theirs more closely. For many, a similar process will happen again around 16 to 17 years, sometimes coinciding with changes in their educational setting.

TEENS TALK

'I think maturing is a hard part of friendships and relationships because as you grow you realize certain people aren't growing with you, especially when you're around 16. I think that as you get older as well you're experiencing things for the first time. You're getting into things you weren't into before; you're sort of experimenting with your own personality and seeing the things that you like. And sometimes other people don't mesh well with the path you're going down, I suppose. Sometimes you just have to let go and move on from it. I don't think that's a bad thing: it's just a part of growing up and evolving as a person, and some people don't fit into that space with you. I don't think it's only for teenagers, I think it's just every stage of life. It just feels more intense now 'cos this is the first time it usually happens and it's, like, "Oh wow, this is really intense!" – feeling like saying goodbye to someone I was really close to. But then you sort of just … I don't think it necessarily gets easier, but you realize that it's just the way it is. I dunno …'
Aleesha (18)

Belonging is incredibly important, even if it's only to one very best friend, but being part of a group is a sought-after ideal for most. It's all part of that process of self-discovery, but it's often fraught with disorientation, questioning and self-doubt. Finding their place can be one of the biggest sources of worry, pain and turmoil for teenagers, and it doesn't always bring out the best in them.

TEENS TALK

'There's so much social pressure on teens in school. There's an unspoken social hierarchy which is incredibly apparent in school years, and it takes loads of confidence for a teenager to truly be themselves in school because of this. If they have unpopular traits or interests they lose popularity, which can have a really bad effect on the mental health of some teens. Unfortunately, not everyone has the kind of confidence in school they need.' **Adam (19)**

Teenagers can also find themselves burdened by the weight of responsibility for the problems of their friends, as well as their own – desperately wanting to help, not always knowing how to, and feeling all that with a keenness they might not at another stage of life.

TEENS TALK

'I think that sometimes you wanna be that friend where you allow them to be comfortable talking to you about their issues – you know, you're just going to listen to what they have to say without any judgement, kinda thing. But then there's that weight that you have to have carrying their issues around with you along with all the ones that you might have yourself.' **Tianna (17)**

TALKING STUFF

You remain your teenager's role model in so many aspects of their lives, and that includes how to have healthy friendships. Nurturing your own friendships during these years is important for them, but it's also important for you, as your own life moves from being the parent of a child, to that of a teenager, and then a grown-up who'll need so much less of you. The life of a parent can be far too busy for spending much time with your friends, and you can feel guilty if you do sneak away for a catch-up, but now is the moment to start to reinvest in these relationships if you need to, perhaps finding ways to do them differently at this different stage of your own life.

Hormones

PARENTS TALK

'I find all the hormones the hardest thing about having teenagers at the moment. Some days are fab, others are a minefield, but for the same reasons!' **Jo**

TEENS TALK

'Usually it's, you know, being a teenager, like, everyone's hormones are rife, and that can cause an argument and boil over really easily.' **Ashleigh (17)**

The hormones responsible for so many of the changes adolescence brings – oestrogen and progesterone in girls, and testosterone in boys – are nothing new. They've always been around, even before they were born. What's new is the levels they need to be at to make sure all those big, important physical and sexual developments happen as they need to during these years, and that's what can take everyone by surprise – including their brains, already going through so much. The teenage brain has a lot going on, and a long way to go, and one of these things is to learn to manage the often dramatic effects of this inconsistent influx.

These three hormones are particularly busy in the limbic system – the emotional centre of the brain – which is one of the reasons why teenagers can find very powerful feelings running the show at times. In girls the concentrations of oestrogen and progesterone fluctuate with the menstrual cycle, and as both of these hormones are linked to chemicals in the brain that control mood, emotions can lurch between extremes in the blink of an eye. Oestrogen stimulates the release of serotonin and endorphins, those happy feel-good hormones. A sudden spike of oestrogen is what stimulates the release of an egg, and then it generally fluctuates more gently during the rest of the menstrual cycle. Progesterone has more of a depressive effect, and acts on the amygdala, the brain's chief alert system, triggering a fight-or-flight response – an angry outburst or floods of tears. And it's the amygdala that's most responsive to testosterone in boys, which is what can sometimes lead to a show of aggression, a wall of defensiveness or a total shut down. As with so much of what's going on, all this will settle, stabilize, and generally calm down, and there's an extent to which parents just need to ride it out, and be there consistently, withstanding the storm and waiting for it to pass, as it will.

TALKING STUFF

For many parents these hormonal teenage years often naturally coincide with the changing hormonal levels menopause brings, with its challenging physical and emotional effects. The ebbs and flows of all these hormones within one household can easily destabilize a conversation between parents and teens.

Most women will begin to experience the effects of perimenopause in their mid-forties, although, of course, this varies, and it will be years before they emerge the other side of the menopause itself. It's worth getting advice from your doctor if this resonates, because there are various options for managing anything that's making life more difficult than it needs to be, either for you, or your teens or anyone else around.

Puberty

Every parent has been there, done it and lived to tell the tale (though it may not be one for the squeamish). However, many of us will have got out the other side without really understanding exactly what was going on, and many of us will have been parented through it by people who felt ill-equipped to talk to us about it.

PARENTS TALK

Clare: I had nothing when it came to important conversations. Not even periods. She left a book on my bed and said, 'You need to read this,' and then scuttled out of the room. That was it. That was the sum total.

Me: And that was it for everything – that covered everything?

Clare: That really was everything. That was as much as we got. No boyfriends, no kissing, no …

Erin: I didn't even get a book.

Clare: You didn't even get a book?

Erin: No. It's funny, because the discussion of periods came up at school when we were probably, maybe, nine or ten? And I was, like, 'WHAT?' My friend Zoe told me *everything*, and I was, like, 'I'm pretty sure that can't happen. If you bleed from there, you're going to die.' And she was, like, 'Actually you don't, and it happens every month.' It completely blew my mind, and I went home and said to my mum, 'Zoe told me this today. Is it true?' And she said, 'No. It's not.' It was, like, '*Move on* …'

Clare: She actually denied it?

Erin: She *actually* denied it! She's not a bad person – my mum's amazing – but she was dealing with my dad. My dad was an alcoholic, a really serious alcoholic, so I think it was just 'Keep everyone alive' day to day. So those sorts of things just didn't come up. I think she probably thought, 'You'll work it out,' and I did, I was fine, so, yeah …

The point of puberty, in physiological terms, is the transformation of our children into sexually mature adults. This very concept is something that can cause not a little discomfort to parents. It starts a lot earlier than its physical manifestations, and sooner than many parents realize. The hormones that get it all going begin to be released by the brain soon after most girls' eighth birthdays, and when boys are around nine or ten. Its physical effects then just go ahead and happen, all being well, like it or not, and some of these are plain for all to see. But whether visible to those around them or not, all of this can be the cause of great embarrassment and self-consciousness, and often anxiety. Hair growing in lots of new places, a deepening voice, a different body odour, an altering body shape, menstruation, masturbation and so much more.

The often wide disparity in the rates of physical development between young people within one year group, especially in those earlier stages of adolescence, can have a big impact on self-esteem, confidence and social allegiances. One who appears much older than they actually are can be sitting alongside a classmate who's just the same age but who might still look like the little boy or girl they won't be much longer. It can be a worrying time for teens, and although some may be comfortable talking about it, others won't, especially if they're worried they're not 'normal' or they're lagging behind. The more they feel free to talk, the less their anxiety will build up.

TWENTIES TALK

'The biggest barrier to me talking to my parents around puberty was the perception of being judged. Your body starts changing, and you're like, "Is that normal?" And you start worrying about being judged or being made to feel embarrassed. It wasn't a huge one, but it was always the fear, not necessarily that I thought it would happen, but it was one of the things that stopped me talking to my parents. "Is this really abnormal about me? Because I'm different does that mean that I'm worse?"' **Sam (21)**

TALKING STUFF

- *Start talking early.* This is a conversation to start around the ages of eight or nine, when all of this process is beginning, but if you've missed this moment, it's never too late while it's still going on.

- *Do your research.* Find out what to expect and in roughly what order, so you can anticipate all the developments coming to your child, and prepare for the practical things they'll be needing, and the conversations around these. If you were a late developer, you might be surprised by things happening earlier than you expected for your child. There are books and websites aplenty to help parents know how to talk about puberty to children at different ages, and for children to refer to themselves. And make sure you talk to girls about boys and boys about girls as well.

- *Be brave but sensitive.* Sometimes something needs to be said, whether it's welcome or not, but all this can also be the cause of acute embarrassment. Reflect on how individual children might find your support most comfortable. Some are much more self-conscious than others and need privacy and space, while knowing the option is there to reach out and ask for help or advice if they think they need it. They may want to talk about everything and in great detail, or they may prefer to have reading material left around. You could offer various options, but let them know you know they need to know stuff, and you're there to help.

Relationships and sex

TEENS TALK

'I tend to have no idea about how girls' brains work, so it's helpful for me to get a very slight insight when I need some advice about something, because I'm like, "What in the world do I do here?!" And my mum's quite helpful with that. My dad would have no clue, whereas if I needed to set up IKEA furniture we could do that together. Like, he'd tell me how to change a light bulb or set up a shelf, but he couldn't tell me how to deal with a girl problem, not a chance, because he'd have no idea himself.' **Jamal (16)**

> 'I would maybe talk to my mum about relationships, but I'd never speak to my dad. He's very much like, sweet little girl, and if anything's outside that he's like, what's going on?' **Talia (17)**

> 'I'd just refuse to talk to anyone, like any family members about stuff like that. It's just never, like, on the table.' **Connor (16)**

All these hormones bring sexual awakening, and it's during these adolescent years most young people will have their first crushes, first romantic relationships and first sexual experiences. They'll be exploring their sexual identity, and perhaps their gender identity. It can be a source of huge distraction, preoccupation and sleepless nights, for reasons of excitement, anticipation, anxiety – a jumble of tumbling thoughts and emotions. It's one of the items that's top of the list when it comes to the tough stuff, for parents and teens. I asked a large group of 14 to 15-year-old girls what they find most uncomfortable to talk about with parents, and the immediate and unanimous response was 'Sex!' Relationships are safer, although also scary for parents because sex is always there, lurking on the horizon. Many parents feel embarrassed at the thought of talking about sex to anyone, let alone their own children. However, it's an enormous part of teenagers' lives, and enormously important. There'll be more on all of this in Part 2 of this book.

TWENTIES TALK

'I think that's another thing parents really need to talk about with their kids, and help boys understand girls. I understand why that can be a taboo subject, but it's really needed. Boys need to understand what's going on for girls, and girls about boys. I think if boys are brought up not really understanding what's going on for girls, they can struggle to form meaningful relationships, and they're also more likely to be sort of using them, because they don't know what's going on – there's an emotional disconnect, and, in some instances, they can be abusive, and there's no empathy, there's no sense of "I just hurt that person because of what I wanted". I saw that quite a lot in my peers, and it really, really, really frustrated me.' **Sam (21)**

Fears for the future

TEENS TALK

'I think it's like a certain sense that you're running out of time with deadlines. I mean, like, people our age are planning for university, and that'll impact the rest of our lives and what we can go and do when we're adults, and, like, we're making such big decisions already.' **Ashleigh (17)**

'There's the pressure of what you want to do in the future, and if you don't want to do what's already sort of cut out for certain people then it feels like you've failed in a way – so, like, if you don't go down that specific route, you haven't succeeded in educational terms, or people's expectations. There's that pressure of what people kinda expect of you, on teens in particular.' **Tianna (17)**

'It's also trying to figure out what you wanna do, 'cos I know quite a lot of my mates, like, don't know what they want to do when they're older, but there's this pressure to make all these really big decisions that are going to affect the whole rest of your life. And it's your future on the line, if that makes any sense? It's not your parents' future, not your grandparents' future; it's your future. They don't always understand that it's incredibly important to you already, 'cos this is your life.' **Dylan (17)**

One of the weights many older teens carry around with them, on top of everything else, is a fear for their future, which they feel is imminent. Just around the corner lies independent adulthood, and much as they may have been striving towards this seemingly unattainable goal for the last few years, and straining against all that they felt held them back, now it's in sight it's a bit scary. They are burdened by the pressure of feeling that what they do now, and how well they do it, and what they decide to do next, will dictate the direction the rest of their lives will take. Added to this is a sense of the possible bleakness of what lies ahead. If they don't get good enough grades, will they get to go to university? If they go to university, will they ever pay off their student loan? If they don't go to university, will they ever get a decent job? If they don't get a decent job, will they ever be able to afford somewhere to live?

And will there be anything left of the planet by then in any case? There's the weight of the world, on top of all this, and all the frustration that those with the power actually to do something don't seem to be taking it seriously, or listening to those who do, and definitely aren't using this power to rescue the world for this generation, and all those to come.

Meanwhile, school adds to the pressure, and however much the schools themselves might try not to, they share the weight of responsibility for these young people's futures. Teenagers (and schools) also feel the additional burden of their parents' expectations, whether these are spoken, implied or just assumed.

TWENTIES TALK

'Parents can make it worse by adding onto the pressure. I definitely saw some people who had more pressure from their parents than others. You could see it was adding onto the stress, especially if their parents wanted them to specialize in a certain field, they'd feel the pressure of that, and especially if it was something they didn't want to do. You could just tell they were more stressed overall. If you've got that pressure of what your parents want you to do, you're sort of backed into a corner. So, you either do something you don't want to do, or you disappoint them. You're left with those two negative scenarios.' **Sam (21)**

TALKING STUFF

Much as we want our children to do and be the very best they can, at this stage of their teenage years, try to gauge the level of pressure they already feel in themselves before you're tempted to add any more. Ask them how it feels, what makes it better or worse, how you can help, or who else could if you can't. Talk to their school or college together if you're concerned their struggles are stretching their capacity to cope.

Worry, stress and strain

TEENS TALK

'Adults often don't validate the stress of teenagers – I mean they don't understand how much it affects them. I feel they don't see it as the same stress they experience, and so it's just seen as less than it is, and especially stress with school and stuff. It's not usually seen as stress the same as, like, work is, and their stress. And obviously we don't understand their stress; I mean some people work but not to their extent and having to pay bills and stuff like that. But yeah, I think that validation in the sense that they don't understand that the stress teenagers have is just as important as their form of stress. They think it's not important, when it is.' **Tianna (17)**

These are the years when mental ill health may start to appear, in addition to all the stress and anxiety of simply being a teenager. We'll be looking at mental ill health in more detail in Part 2, but for now, it's useful to remember as a parent – and also for your teen – that a certain amount of stress and anxiety is a normal and natural response to what life will inevitably bring along from time to time.

TEENS TALK

'I think one of the things that's difficult growing up in this society is because we've been made to think that the way we feel are problems or issues when really they are just natural responses to everything that we deal with, if that makes sense? Like, it just makes us feel like something is wrong with us and that we need to be fixed.' **Aleesha (18)**

We've just been exploring some of the everyday stresses of adolescence, which are all on top of any additional strains caused by challenges going on in the lives of families, schools and communities. A certain amount of stress and anxiety can help us respond appropriately to the situations that give rise to them, but can also easily tip from productive to paralysing. Learning to spot the signs, knowing how to respond and finding ways to try to prevent it tipping over another time, is the stuff of a useful and important conversation. Developing the skills and resilience to manage the difficult stuff of life, which we won't be able to avoid, is a key part of becoming a healthy, happy adult.

When our children were smaller their problems were often easier to fix, and our instinct as parents is to do just this – to fix their problems and protect them from pain. Strong arms to lift them up when they fall. Plasters to stick on a grazed knee. But there have always been problems that couldn't be fixed, and these can get more prevalent and prolific during their teenage years. Sometimes there's something practical that can be done, a plan that can be developed together or a strategy they're willing to try, and there'll be much more on this in Part 2. But sometimes we just need to sit with them, listen to them, acknowledge their feelings (and acknowledge our own to ourselves) and be as available as they need us to be while they work it out for themselves.

PARENTS TALK

'My eldest does like the solution-based stuff, and to discuss it, but the next one doesn't. Actually, the biggest thing he always wanted from me was for me to go, "OK, that's fine." That was all he needed me to say. I've got really good at saying it now, in all different ways. He didn't need me to go, "OK, let's talk about that," and go on. It'd make him groan, or it'd make him more upset by us pulling it apart. He just wanted reassurance. I'd have been going through this whole encyclopaedia and breaking it all down, and it'd make him more anxious basically. I tried to fix a lot of stuff for him. I didn't want life to be difficult for him. I always tried to make it smooth and easy.' **Erin**

TALKING STUFF

The model of a barometer is often used to gauge whether stress or anxiety is helping or hindering, but you and your teen could decide on your own measure that would help them assess the levels of pressure they're feeling, and questions or pictures you could both use to help them identify these. There are lots of resources online to help teenagers cope with stuff that you can explore together. Try things out, adapt or adopt, and keep on talking about what does and doesn't help.

If you have concerns that the issues and feelings your teen is experiencing may be more serious, please look ahead at this section in Part 2 for more advice, talk to your child's school, or your family doctor.

3

UNDERSTANDING ADOLESCENCE (2) – WHAT ON EARTH WERE THEY THINKING?

'Sometimes I'm with my friends and I find myself doing something I know is stupid – well, I kind of know – but I just do it anyway. I don't know why. Then I'm thinking, "Why are we all doing this thing we know is really dumb?"'

Grace (15)

The amazing adolescent brain

Our brains are amazing, whatever age we are, and more is constantly being discovered about just how amazing they are. The brain has an incredible capacity to change, which neuroscientists refer to as 'plasticity'. As well as a continual process that goes on all the time, there are also critical periods of change, and one of the most critical of these is adolescence. What we need our brain to do for us as a child is very different from what we need it to do as a fully grown, fully functioning, independent adult, and of all the many transformations going on in teens, this one takes the longest. It's basically a major rewiring operation that starts at the very beginning of adolescence and goes on right to the end, in our mid-twenties.

To simplify, the brain is made up of different areas, each of which has different roles and responsibilities. In adolescence these areas are developing, and connecting and reconnecting, all at different rates, and it's the sequence in which this process takes place that gives rise to some of the more characteristic elements of teenage behaviour: impulsivity; risk-taking; social sensitivity; emotional intensity; problems with thinking things through to a seemingly logical conclusion …

There are two key areas of the brain developing at very different rates, one of which is sometimes nicknamed 'the feeling brain', the other 'the thinking brain'. The limbic system, the 'feeling brain', develops first and is hypersensitive in adolescence. Our prefrontal cortex, the 'thinking brain', is the bit of our brain that helps us with useful things like organization, planning, decision-

making and thinking ahead. It takes to our mid-twenties finally to connect, when it starts to help manage our 'feeling brain'/limbic system – but until then it's trailing behind, just when we're most in need of emotional regulation, impulse control and the ability to think things through.

> ## PARENTS TALK
>
> 'I found myself start to feel some frustration when they started to be "teenagery", and then my wife gave me a book to read about the teenage brain [*Blame My Brain*, Nicola Morgan (2012)], and it was phenomenal. My copy is just plastered in highlighter 'cos there was so much in it. It just gave me a perspective and more patience with it, and I feel like I'm probably better speaking to my 13-year-old now than I could have been, having understood all that. It helped me to show and understand a bit more empathy about what's actually going on. And some things are completely and utterly outside of his control. He can't process it or understand it. He doesn't know what's going on there yet. Having the understanding of it massively helps.' **Aaron**

Risk and reward

We all know that teenagers love a risk. It's a reputation that seems well deserved, and we want (and need) our children to be confident to take risks, in certain times and places at least – giving an answer in class, getting involved a new activity, trying a different vegetable. It's only by taking risks that they're going to learn to manage them, and we know they'll have to face risks without us there beside them sooner or later. But we're risk-averse Gen X parents, told that we're wrapping our Gen Z children in cotton wool, not allowing them out to roam the streets like we did, holding their hands far too long and generally holding them back.

Our teenagers accuse us of the same thing. Many tough conversations revolve around risks a parent fears may cause harm to their child, fears that mean that they prevent them doing whatever it is, fears that their child feels are totally unjustified and unreasonable and unfair, and that result in frustration and often fury. This is a hard one to balance, especially as they get older, and we'll look at some tips when we come on to boundaries later on.

TEENS TALK

'Parents stir things up between them. They send something around WhatsApp – you know the parent group chat thing, right? Say something happened five years ago, like a boy got shot in the park, and then before you know it it's like, "I heard this boy got killed in the park just yesterday." and it goes on like that, and then next thing is they won't let you go to the park again.' **Kadeisha (15)**

The changes taking place in their brains mean that managing risk is hard. That well-developed limbic system is the area of our brain that's particularly associated with dopamine, the chemical that gives us that natural buzz of joy and happiness we get when we're doing something that brings us pleasure. In adolescence the release of dopamine is enhanced, as is the brain's response to it, so pleasure can be experienced at levels of intensity that are a distant memory for us adults. It's the part of our brain where we experience reward, and where positive memories are stored – the ones that tell us we really should do that again, and this is where risk comes in. The biggest rewards can be gained in response to taking a risk, surviving a risk and even in anticipation of a risk, and the sensible prefrontal cortex – the part of our brain that's our natural handbrake – isn't fully operational yet.

Risk-taking usually peaks between 13 and 16 years old. After this the limbic system starts to settle and the prefrontal cortex begins to catch up, and life gets gradually safer, but these are the years when your teenager needs most support with understanding and managing risk: helping them grasp the nature of a particular risk (without going overboard, or you'll lose them); helping them develop the judgement to work out which risks might be positive for them, and which might do lasting harm, and repeating and reinforcing those messages to help them to stick in their heads, at this time when there's so much going on in that busy brain of theirs. Sometimes you just have to stand in their way, however, and stop them doing whatever it is, because in your judgement, as their parent, they're not yet ready to manage that risk safely themselves. And sometimes you might feel the need to prise them out of their bedrooms, and try a few low-level risky steps by themselves.

PARENTS TALK

'A lot of it is us almost encouraging them to take a few risks. By the time we were 15 or 16 we were getting the bus into central London on our own with friends and hanging out up there all day or whatever, you know? Our 16-year-old has been up to town with his mates a couple of times on the train, and he'll text us saying, "What platform do I need to get a train from?" Well, you know, it's as quick to check an app as it is to check with us, but I think a lot of it is we're not encouraging them when they get to that age to go out and do more.' **Andy**

TALKING STUFF

- If you have a teen who relishes a risk, are there activities they might enjoy that involve managed, supervized risks? If they're already doing these things, is there something more they could do, if you feel this could help, whether regularly or as one-offs? Could you find something you could perhaps do together?

- If you have a child who's the opposite, and your concern is their caution and wariness, could you find something that might just take them a small step outside their comfort zone – perhaps one that could lead to more small steps and build their confidence? Again, maybe you could do something together, or get a friend involved?

The influence of peers

TWENTIES TALK

'Social acceptance is so important to people – I think it's probably one of the most important things, for someone to feel accepted within a group. I think it's really tribal – it goes right far back, the need and want to be accepted by those around you. If people didn't like you, you were dead, and it can feel just as massive when you're a teenager.' **Flo (20)**

For teenagers, this is a time of acute self-consciousness, intense self-scrutiny and excruciating self-doubt, when the people around us can have a powerful influence over how we behave, and this is always a worry to parents. It's useful to remember, though, that this is something we're all susceptible to. We all follow the crowd. It can save us a whole lot of time to assume a collective wisdom is at work when a majority takes a lead. Back in those ancestral days of primitive survival, there was also literally safety in numbers, as Flo points out above. If you fell out with the people around you, you could find yourself on your own, out in the open and vulnerable to predators.

With teenagers something similar is going on. As a child your survival is dependent on your primary caregiver, and your safety lies in their hands. As an adult you need to know you can survive outside that safe family unit, and that means needing to know you're acceptable to your peers. Add into the mix the acute social sensitivity their well-developed limbic system brings, and sometimes teenagers end up doing things they'd never have done on their own, and sometimes these things bring risk.

TEENS TALK

'I think teenagers go into this unprepared, because they're told when they're younger that they're gonna be influenced by these bad people, and they're gonna be offering them all these bad things, when you don't actually realize that it could actually be nice people, or your friends, and then they could end up being bad influences without you sort of realizing it. 'Cos, like, what teenagers don't realize is that it can be people that they trust and people that they like who can influence them the most, and sometimes they don't influence the right things.' **Megan (15)**

PARENTS TALK

'I worry that my 16-year-old has got in with friends that I don't think are going to be very good, and I can see that I think it may be trouble. But then I had older brothers who did, and so I wonder if I'm placing that on him. The other two are fine, it's just him … But you cannot say, "Don't be friends with those people." It just backfires. They just do it more, and then they tell the friends as well, "My mum says I can't be friends with you," which is just about the worst thing. So I guess it's just trying to instil a moral compass in him, so if they're doing stuff, he might pass. Or it's the difficult part, which is standing back, allowing it to happen, and just having to be there to catch it if it does go wrong. That's hard.' **Dawn**

The 'social risk' factor

TEENS TALK

'You know that popular boy group at school – like, all different year groups have a popular group – and I've known some of them for so many years, and you talk to them on their own and they're really, really nice, but when they're in a crowd, they're erm … I'll say it politely – they're a bit stupid together, and they kind of egg each other on.' **Dean (14)**

However kind, careful and naturally cautious your teenager is, they're likely to behave differently when they're with their friends, including taking more risks. This is useful for both you and them to know, because with awareness can come strategies to manage this. Teens have a need to weigh up the risk of a particular decision or action against the risk of social exclusion. Gaining social approval from peers can also prime the brain's reward system to seeking further reward through taking a risk. All of that dopamine makes us want more.

TEENS TALK

'I notice that with my peers they tend to do more wild things or more things that would be perceived as dangerous when they're in a group or with their friends. They wouldn't do it when they were on their own, but when they're in the moment and with their friends they feel safe and so they'll do things that could in fact be dangerous. I think when they're in the moment, they don't think about all the consequences, they don't think about how this could be bad for you, because they feel like they're invincible when they're with their friends so they feel a lot safer.' **Megan (15)**

'I feel like, yeah, if these people are doing it then, if I don't do it, it makes me look bad – it makes me look boring kinda thing.' Joel (15)

'In my experience it's less about pressure and more about the carelessness of being in a group. You're together so you can get away with more and be noticed less than if it was only you.' Ellie (18)

The frog and the boiling water

Sometimes there's someone setting out a clear challenge, or piling on the pressure, but more often than not there's nothing explicitly spoken at all. Sometimes we all do things we think other people want us to, without anyone saying a word. Sometimes we all do things, too, just because it seems churlish not to, or because it seems fun, or because we don't want to feel left out. But sometimes it's a gradual shift, an invisible drift into something becoming normal, and acceptable, that never was before. The frog and the boiling water is a useful illustration of this. The analogy is well known: if you put a frog in boiling water, it'll jump straight out. But if you put it in cold water, and bring it slowly to the boil, it doesn't realize, and ends up a boiled frog. It's just a picture of how people's personal values and boundaries can change imperceptibly along with the people around them, and why it's important to be ever vigilant, especially where there's a risk involved.

TALKING STUFF

- Has your teenager seen similar things at work among their peers? Have they ever felt that pull themselves? If they won't admit it to you, they may still listen to stories from your own adolescence.

- Can you come up with a list of strategies together to manage negative peer influence? What do they think can help? If you can involve older siblings or cousins who've been through it themselves more recently, they may listen to them differently than to their parents. There are some examples below.

- Can you encourage them to be the positive peer influence in the group? Remind them if they're feeling uncomfortable it's likely at least one of their friends will be, too, and if they have the courage to be the one to speak out, it can release others to do the same. Peer influence is a powerful force that can be used for good.

PEER INFLUENCE – MANAGING THE NEGATIVE STUFF

- *Have a reason (and say it with confidence).* It can help to plan ahead, for specific situations where they may feel pressured (or tempted, or carried away) and end up doing something they don't really want to do. Help them think of a reason they could give that would work for them. We're programmed as human beings to respect a reason, even if it's a bit lame, but if they have a reason, and say it with confidence, and stick to their guns if they need to, this can really help.

- *Take your time.* So they don't act on impulse but have a chance to think through the possible risks and consequences. You could help them develop a toolkit of stalling tactics to buy themselves some time to access their prefrontal cortex, or excuses they could use to get out of different situations.

- *Set up an escape plan.* In case they need an excuse to get away from a situation they feel uncomfortable or unsafe in. Agree a code they can message to you – a letter or an emoji. You can then call and give them an excuse (you can plan these ahead). The hard part for parents is that, in order for this to work, you have to promise not to ask any questions if it gets triggered, or they'll think twice. (See Bert Fulks's X-Plan for more on this – https://bertfulks.com)

- *Avoid situations or groups where there may be pressure (or temptation).* Sometimes it's best just to avoid being somewhere, if they know they might end up doing something they don't really want to do. This is where their excuses can come in, and you can help them with this.

- *Reflect on the pressure.* The more self-aware they can be about those social dynamics the better they can manage them self-assuredly and safely. Remind them how easy it is to assume the people around you want you to do something when really they're not bothered. You could reflect on your own teenage years and experiences, or get older siblings involved.

- *Have faith in your friends.* They may find it hard to hold on to, but their friends – or at least the friends who are worth holding on to – really will respect them more if they're firm and clear about what they do and don't want to do, and what is and isn't right for them. This is a good opportunity to get in some positive stuff, too. Tell them you know they'd never want to put one of their friends under pressure themselves to do something they weren't comfortable doing, and so they should expect the same from their friends.

- *Remember you're surrounded by other teenage brains!* It's useful to keep in mind that the people around them are also going through this critical period of change. They're not thinking things through to their possible consequences, or managing their emotions and impulses as well as they could, and they're also acutely self-conscious and concerned about how they're perceived by their peers. They're not the best role models to follow, and especially if there's a risk involved.

Learning a lesson

One of the things the prefrontal cortex does is store our negative memories – all those things that didn't work out as well as we hoped or that went disastrously wrong, or anything in between. This means it's harder for adolescents to learn from their mistakes than it is for adults, because they're stored in the part of their brain they don't yet have ready access to. The limbic system that holds on to all the things they enjoyed, that gave them that dopamine rush, is firing away, and consequently your teenage child is likely to remember what went well but forget the things that went wrong. Teenagers might fully intend never to do something again, or to do something differently, but when it comes to it they're just not accessing those negative memories quickly enough. This is one of the reasons that sanctions and punishments need to be handled carefully with teens. Carrot really is more effective than stick, if we want to influence their behaviour, and sometimes they need a (gentle) reminder that it didn't work out so well last time from those who remember it only too well.

The changing nature of risk

Each generation of teenagers will have taken risks, but the landscape of risk is constantly changing. Even where the general areas of risk and potential harm may be the same – sex, drink, drugs, fights, taking a physical risk and having an accident, taking a legal risk and getting a criminal record – the nature of these will have shifted. And all those risks online that we looked at in Chapter 1, risks they encounter in the safety of your home, and the sanctuary of their bedroom, need just the same skills and confidence to navigate safely as the physical risks of the outside world. With the risks and opportunities for our teenagers changing all the time, it's normal to feel overwhelmed, and powerless, and panic, but this is an excuse for a curious conversation, and a chance to build connection as well as understanding, and consider the risks together.

TALKING STUFF
Build on the questions and conversations suggested in Chapter 1 around life online, go through the practical tips that are relevant and read on to find out how to build their resilience, online and off.

Protective factors

Much as we want to, we can never entirely protect our children from taking the sorts of risk that could cause them harm, but there are things we can do that can build their skills and resilience to navigate decisions more safely, and they're all things that will help them in so many other ways. Mental health issues and mental ill health can make this more complicated, but tailoring how you do this to your child is still likely to help, alongside the sorts of specific advice and support we'll be looking at in Part 2 of this book.

Positive physical development

This doesn't have to be organized sports, although it can be, but just general physical wellbeing and self-care. Exercising and staying active, eating healthily, getting enough sleep, and knowing why all these are important, helps them value themselves as a person, in the process of looking after their physical selves.

And what about you? Are you getting enough exercise, healthy food and quality sleep yourself? You are their role model, as always, as well as needing to look after yourself.

These are all things you could talk about together and put plans in place to improve as a family. Could you set each other goals – which will probably need to be very small steps – and check in with each other regularly on progress, and be accountable to each other for how well (or not so well) you're doing? You could set a time limit and then honestly review whether you feel better or not.

If you and your teen aren't in a place to do something like this together right now, you can model this to them in your own life, and even if they may not appear to care or take any notice at all, remember they're always watching and listening, and what you do and say matters.

Strong self-esteem

This is a time of life when it's very hard for your teens to feel good about themselves, or secure in who they are, as they go through this process of becoming and needing to know they're going to survive out in the world. But you are their number-one fan, and even if that might not appear to be something they value these days, hold on to the fact that it is.

It's easy to overlook the importance of praise in the busyness of family life, and it might take a conscious effort to remember to vocalize some of the positive things you'll doubtless be thinking and feeling, but it's an effort that will bear fruit, even if not immediately. And it can help you, too, if you're in a place where you're only seeing the stuff you're not so keen on in your teen, and finding it harder to spot the good that will also be there.

Whatever you say, it must be sincere, specific and honest, because they can see straight through general adulation around how amazing they are (which of course, in your eyes, generally speaking, they are). Praise a particular act you've witnessed, a specific personal quality or something they've said or done that shows what a good friend they are: 'I was so proud when I saw you …' or 'It was really kind of you to …'

Giving them plenty of opportunities to play to their strengths is also important (as it is for us all), and will help build their confidence and self-esteem. And make sure they get all the praise they deserve for doing whatever it is so well.

PARENTS TALK

'I would say if you can try and ensure that for every one piece of negative feedback you give to a teenager, there are five pieces of positive reinforcement, that would definitely be a very important element of building children up – so they have the self-image that allows them to accept that they're not bad people because they've done something wrong. And help them explore their gifts. Be a capability hunter, not a disability hunter.' **Aidan**

'I remember a couple of days with my 13-year-old. I was saying to my wife, "We need to find something to say 'Well done' or 'Yes' to him because it's been a disastrous day! Everything he's tried is not working. But you need to find that bit where you can say, "Well done!" You actively have to go looking for it and say, "Well done for that." I feel that's quite important so they can feel positive about themselves rather than got at the whole time. But it can be a trail of disasters that you follow, I mean a total trail of disasters. So, that can be quite fun!' **Kofi**

TWENTIES TALK

'I think the kids whose home life maybe wasn't so good were acting up more, to take those huge risks. You could see they desperately wanted to maintain their part in that group, because they didn't have that acceptance at home. If your parents make you feel good about yourself, then it's not so much of a risk if you lose those friends, because you've got that support at home. Whereas if you've got no support structure, no safety net at home, that school life and those friends there become so much more vital, because if you lose them, you have nothing – or you have a perception of having nothing.' **Sam (21)**

Emotional self-regulation

Depending on their age and stage of development, emotional self-regulation could be something they're really struggling with, but helping them develop strategies to take a breath, take a step back and take a moment before they respond, will help them do the same in that moment of decision with their friends, when emotions may be running high all around them. It can also help them manage stress, and cope with life's challenges better.

Emotional fluency is something that can be learned, just like any other language. Sometimes teenagers can't tell you how they're feeling because they don't know themselves, or don't have the language they need to describe it. Being able to recognize and name an emotion is hard enough, and working out what might lie behind it, and then articulate that, is something that can take time, especially when it's often not just one thing but a mix of powerful emotions.

Focusing on the feelings that might have given rise to what they've said or done, rather than the words or actions themselves, can help you be more understanding, help your teenager learn how to describe what's going on, help you both manage that heated moment and help you both find ways to work through whatever it was that set it off.

The time to step in with some sensible advice isn't while the emotions are raging. In that heightened state of arousal, they're not going to be able to process your rational insights. If you can catch the moment before it's let loose, or, even better, help them do this themselves, by identifying signs something may be building up, you can help them develop strategies to avoid an outburst, even if it's something as simple as walking away.

Your teenager will face strong emotions because of the physiological, emotional and neurological changes going on, and then there are all the external pressures they may be shouldering. Think through together things they could do to channel, process or calm overwhelming feelings. It could be listening to loud music, going for a run or gaming with friends and taking it out on a virtual enemy. Or it could be colouring, or mindfulness. Or playing with the dog. And sometimes they just need to sit with those feelings for a while.

And if they're too furious with you to talk about any of this, observe their behaviour for what the triggers are, what can help them calm down and think of ways you could help reduce the former and enable the latter.

How good are you at this yourself? Teenage emotions can trigger the inner teenager in us all – especially if we're on the receiving end, but you can model how you manage your own responses in moments of pressure. We all lose our grip and fly off the handle from time to time, but if you do, how you respond to that is what matters, as we'll go on to see later on, along with more of all the above.

PARENTS TALK

Have you been able to find ways to repair and come back to a conversation that's gone haywire, and if so, how?

'Accept sometimes you handle things badly as a parent and apologize for your part. Explain you handled something clumsily, but you'd like to listen and understand and talk without falling out. Validating your teen's feelings is important, too.' **John**

'We let things calm down and revisit the conversation when everyone has had time to sort themselves out. We explain the importance of having to have the conversation – despite how difficult it might be – and make sure that we are all calm and all have a chance to speak.' **Bushra**

TWENTIES TALK

'I think if your parents have dealt with pain well – if you fall over, they'll pay attention to it and make sure you're actually OK – then I think then that really helps. You can have parents who massively overreact – "Oh no! What's happened to my child? They're really hurt!" – and then you've got the completely opposite side of that where they just ignore you, or tell you to "man up" or something. And I think both extremes mean you're more likely to seek that external need from other people.

'That's the same with all the emotional stuff, too. I think if you've got emotionally unavailable parents then you've got no idea how to communicate emotionally, whereas if you've got overemotional parents then you sort of develop in yourself the idea emotions are a big deal, when that's not always the case, and you live in extremes of happy–sad–happy–sad, and you don't have that little grain of normal content. I could see some of my peers who definitely would fit that. Everything's either amazing or rubbish. There was never any real middle ground. And I felt that was quite difficult for them, but it also made it difficult for the people around them. You just want to chill, and just, like, do nothing, and not have any particular hyper-ness, and they'd either be up here, and trying to bring everyone else up, or down here, and dragging everyone else down with them.

'And I think that's massively to do with how their parents dealt with emotion, and I think that makes it so much more difficult for kids to then deal with their own emotions, because they're not taught what to do if you feel a certain way. They're also not taught how to communicate it properly, which means you're also not able to communicate emotionally with yourself. Teenage years are the years when you find yourself, and if you can't communicate emotionally with yourself, that becomes so much more difficult. And then you don't know how to deal with external stimuli that cause those emotions, and then you act rashly, or act badly, or in any kind of negative way, and I think that holds you back massively.'
Sam (21)

Good problem-solving skills

Developing skills to work through problems can help build teenagers' strength, stamina and confidence to face any problems that come along, with a mindset that believes they can turn things around and learn from mistakes. It can help them work out possible strategies, and try out solutions, and all this can equip them to deal with problems they might encounter involving risk. It can also help parents to work through this process for themselves, too, especially if there's an issue that's causing contention, and it's so much the better, if there is, to do it together.

These are some steps you can talk through together, either next time a problem comes along, or reflecting on something that's happened. And if you've run into an argument, or a conversation has turned a bit toxic, this is a valuable and important exercise (once everyone's calmed down).

1. *Identify the problem.* This may not be as obvious as it seems. The presenting problem may be they're in trouble yet again for being late to school, but really the problem is they keep getting up too late and missing the bus, and behind that is going to bed too late, and behind that is chatting online too late, behind which is a friendship group in which they're feeling insecure.

2. *Consider possible solutions.* There are various things that could help with the immediate issue in this scenario – getting your help to rouse them, making sure they've got everything they need for the next day organized the night before – and then talking about setting boundaries on their late-night chatting (which might need some negotiation), and, importantly, working out how to manage their friendship group.

3. *Choose a solution.* Which solution do they think might work best? What do you think? Having a few solutions to fall back on can help them have courage to risk one not working, knowing they can have a go with something else. Sometimes small steps are best, or trying something simple to start with.

4. *Give it a try.* And if it doesn't work, reflect together on why that might be, and what might work better, and then try that.

Sometimes there won't be a solution that makes everyone happy, but learning to compromise when that's the case is a valuable and necessary life skill. And sometimes problems just can't be fixed, which is a very hard lesson in life, but helping them learn to find strategies to cope when things can't be mended is incredibly important. And sometimes they can surprise us, in this as in so many things.

PARENTS TALK

Erin: Apparently one of my 13-year-old's fish died last month, and he took it outside and buried it and didn't tell me, and I found that really hard. I tried to kind of, like, break it down a bit, and work out what was going on for him, and I was going, 'Can we just talk about it?' and he said, 'Look, in the end, it just didn't really matter. It just didn't really bother me, and so I think that's why I didn't want to make a big deal about it.

Meera: Maybe he was worried you would worry, and have a big funeral or something.

Erin: Yes, exactly! That's exactly what I'd have done! I found another one today – another one had died, and I flushed it down the loo, and I had to do the whole 'I'm really sorry but one of your fish has died.' And he was, like, 'Oh yes, I'd seen that.' And I went, 'How long had you known about it for?' And he said, 'Probably a couple of days.' And then he said, 'Oh, yeah, another one died as well.' And I was, like, 'WHAT??!' I felt, like, 'Oh gosh! We're not connected! His fish died, he buried it in the garden, and he didn't tell me!'

Meera: But actually he coped, all by himself, which is really good. He worked out what to do and just got on with it, and it was OK, and he was OK.

Erin: Yes, that's true. I said to him, 'Did you know you could just flush it down the toilet?' And he was like, 'Really? Oh. That's a bit weird.' Which it is, really, when you think about it. It's just what we always used to do when I was little. You're right, Meera. I should be really proud of him because he just sorted it out by himself and he didn't need me. It wasn't what I'd have done – but it's probably better for the sewage system actually not to be full of his dead fish! There I was, worried because I felt like we weren't connected about this dead fish, but actually it was a good thing.'

Meera: But maybe you ought to check what's going on with those fish, because that's a lot of fatalities ...

Engagement and connection with school, sports, employment, religion or culture

Being part of something bigger than themselves, where they have a role and an identity and others do, too, where there's structure, and order, and something they need to get on with, can help build all sorts of skills, personal qualities and confidence. Is there anything you can do to encourage, enable or nurture any of these connections? Ask them what would help, if help is needed?

Of course, each of these can also do just the opposite, and load pressures they feel unable to bear, and expectations they feel unable to meet – in which case, if you see them seeming reluctant to go along, or downright refusing, encourage them to be honest about the ones that are hard (and perhaps doing some problem-solving if you can, as above), and see if there's something else that might work better.

Where possible, positive engagement with one or more of these has potential to do a lot that can stand them in good stead when they're managing risks.

TEENS TALK

'When you become a teenager, that's when you start seeing how you can sort of access the world around you, and how you can make an impact.' **Megan (15)**

'Best thing about being a teenager I think is the opportunities you get. I know as adults, you know, you do get a lot of opportunities, but it's, like, our time of getting opportunities, if you get what I mean? Like, as a child we weren't allowed to do some of the stuff we can get to do now, like setting things up and getting involved in things that are making a difference in the world.' **Dean (14)**

4
TALKING ABOUT TALKING

Me and my dad are always chatting. He doesn't
know about a lot of practical things, but he knows
lots of other stuff. He doesn't know how to tie a tie,
he's not the most well-prepared in the world, but
it's great, because when I learn things I can teach
him, and when he learns things he can teach me.
So, like, he's useless with technology, but he runs a
business, so I help him with stuff ... It's nice he'll
come to me when he needs some help with things.

Jamal (16)

I've got quite a small room, and my chair at my desk has wheels, so I like to be able to wheel back and forward down my room, but then my room gets messy so I can't do it. So I was about to clear my room, and I'm like, I need to clear my room because I can't move my chair, and my mum will come into my room and go, 'You need to clean your room, you can't even move your chair!', and it's like, I don't want to do it now. I think it's just one of those things – I was going to do it, but now you've told me to do it I don't want to do it.

George (16)

Talking with teenagers can be a fascinating, rich, entertaining, educational, heart-warming experience. It can also be confusing, frustrating, hurtful, heart-breaking and really tough. Sometimes it's the subject matter that's tough; sometimes it's the response you get when you mention it; sometimes it's working out how to mention it in the first place. Sometimes it's working out how to respond to something tough that comes your way; out of the blue and without warning. Sometimes it's putting your parental radars on full beam to search deep down behind something that's said – or unsaid – to uncover the issue that's lurking. Sometimes it can get so even the everyday, ordinary, humdrum stuff of a teenage conversation becomes an immediate battlefield or stand-off.

When we find ourselves talking the tough stuff with our teens, it's useful to go back to the bare bones of what communication actually involves – how it works, and how and why it works well, or why it breaks down. Most of us spend much of our time immersed in communication of one sort or other, but often only think about what's going on when something goes wrong. Having a set of tools on hand can help when it gets tough, and sometimes stop it getting tough at all.

When we talk about talking, we also mean listening, which for parents is often the harder part of the transaction, although equally often the most important, and never more so than with teenagers.

Nurturing, building or rebuilding those day-to-day conversations, however tiny and trivial, is not only important for its own sake – and for the sakes of both us and our teens – but it also prepares us for when we need to tackle the big and significant stuff, and tackle it well.

PARENTS TALK

What do you love best about being the parent of a teenager?

'They keep you on your toes, introduce you to all kinds of new things – songs, new words, different ways of seeing familiar things. Their energy, fun and laughter! It is amazing to see them become who they are and can be, to see the gap between their skills and their confidence (in both directions) and to see them become more and more independent.'

'I would say kind of grown-up conversations. Just being able to talk about kind of, you know, films that aren't involving toy trains. They definitely make it feel like you're chatting to teenagers. It's kind of easier in a way than talking to small children. They haven't got the same experiences as you but, you know, a 16-year-old knows what's going on in the world. So, I think just kind of normal conversations about normal everyday stuff.'

What do you feel is hardest about being the parent of a teenager?

'Them not wanting to talk about big stuff because they think they know it all.'

'Not being the person they talk things through with any more, despite working so hard with compassionate parenting and developing that relationship.'

'Providing answers to direct requests for advice that then gets chewed up and thrown back.'

'Dealing well with mood changes, silence, etc.'

The gift of communication

We're naturally hardwired to learn language, and we learn it best through interaction. From that very first reassuring wail as your new-born arrives in the world, and your very first reassuring response, life begins with a conversation between parent and child.

Studies have shown us that babies are born already finely attuned to their mother tongue, and their mother's voice, having spent all those months in the womb, listening. Finally, here they are, getting their chance to join in. So many things can complicate that, of course, in the fragile process that childbirth can be – and the start of life rarely follows a tidy and predictable pattern – but the principle remains. We were born to chat.

How does it work?

So, what's going on in the conversational adventure you embark on with your child, that takes you from that tiny baby to your great big teenager and beyond? The sender–recipient dynamic of parent and child in the earliest days is sometimes referred to as 'serve and return', because the instinctive responsiveness between them leads to a natural to and fro. Often, the parent returns the serving of non-verbal eye-contact, preverbal gurgles, incomprehensible babbling and deafening yells with a volley of sing-song sounds and simple words. Over the years language skills grow, and that conversational serve and return modulates with their expanding comprehension, widening experiences and broadening expectations.

But many of us feel by the time adolescence gets going that our early instinct has abandoned us. How do we communicate with this rapidly changing child-cum-adult? And our adolescent can get stuck, too.

TEENS TALK

'I think I can speak easily to my parents and my parents are quite good at understanding and accepting, but I know, with my friends, some of their parents don't fully understand some of the things they want to talk about, like mental health and all of that, so they don't understand where they're coming from, or understand how they could know this sort of stuff at this age and so there's a barrier of communication. I think because they're unaware of completely everything that's going on the teenager might not talk about everything 'cos they think that the parent won't understand. It kinda forms a barrier and lets the parents see less of what's going on in the teenager's mind.' **Megan (15)**

PARENTS TALK

'Sometimes I know my teen feels my understanding is so outdated I could never understand, and I feel that, too, and I know that sets up a barrier for both of us.' **Brianna**

TALKING STUFF

It might be useful to take a moment to reflect on ways in which communication with your child has evolved over the years, from those early preverbal days to talking with a teenager. If conversations have become tough, there may be things you can take from back when they flowed more comfortably that could perhaps help now, or in the future.

- What has their natural mode of communication been in the past? Are they someone who's generally processed new information or ideas by talking them out, or someone who's preferred to take their time to reflect and digest, and share a more formulated response? What's your own preferred style? How might this affect how conversations work now? What other dynamics are worth considering?

- Have there been particular times or places when conversations have happened most comfortably in the past? In the present?

- Is there an identifiable stage of their lives when communication changed significantly? Does that link in with any of the developmental changes we looked at in Chapters 2 and 3?

- Are there ways in which you've been able to modulate your own conversational approaches to accommodate these changes that have worked well, even if only once or twice? Are there things you could take from these that might work again?

Getting their attention

PARENTS TALK

'I definitely feel you have to pick your moments. That makes a huge difference because there are certain times they're just so preoccupied with something else, it's not going to work.' **Sue**

'I think it's difficult just to get their attention 'cos, you know, they've always got their phone next to them and it's hard to grab a minute of their attention, when their attention is everywhere else 'cos the phone is beeping 'cos a friend is sending a Snapchat or a girl is sending a picture, or selfies, or whatever they do. I think that is a barrier – it's more interesting to them than us. It's distracting, isn't it? It's a distraction even if they were listening to us.' **Giovanna**

It can be hard to capture the attention of our teens, and if we don't have it there's limited point in trying to talk, especially about anything of any significance. Screens are an easy and obvious target to blame. There's so much to look at, and listen to, with notifications constantly pinging, and that compulsive need to know they're not missing out on seeing something coming through they might never see again, or being part of something of vital social importance. But there's so much more. Even without the phone, or tablet, or laptop, even without social media, or YouTube, or headphones blocking out incidental chatter, they have so much going on in their lives, as we've seen. Simply the everyday preoccupations, stresses and strains of adolescence – which aren't simple at all – can be enough to take their attention away from a parent with something to say.

PARENTS TALK

What can help get your teenager's attention in a conversation?

'At mealtimes, leave the conversation for a few minutes so their energy is boosted and they become more amenable. Never talk when they're hungry or tired!'

'Chat in the car – never turn down a request for a lift. With my son, it's sports. With my daughter, conversations tend to be deeper. She loves our car journey conversations. 'Talk to them over a meal out. At home they might get angry and just walk out, but in public they have to behave better, and it can help them listen to what you have to say, even when they don't like it.'

'Avoid intensity. Chat when you're walking or driving. Never waste a car journey. Let them choose the music.'

TALKING STUFF

- When might be times and places with fewer external distractions around for your teen? A car journey? A dog walk? Cooking?

- When are the times they're most likely to have their mind less busy with pressures or plans? And more likely to be awake and alert?

- Try to be alert yourself for unexpected, unplanned opportunities, too. Be ever vigilant and ready to seize the moment.

Sending a message

One part of this two-way transaction is what gets said. That could be either spoken or written. If it's written, it could be in physical form, such as a card or a letter, or more likely in one of the many messaging options. Whether it's nurturing the everyday chat, or managing the more momentous conversation, what you say does benefit from a bit (or a lot) of thought as they grow and become the evolving teenage version of themselves. One of the wonderful things about teenagers is that they tend to let you know loud and clear if you're getting something wrong, whether in words or in rolled eyes or hostile grunts. It could be a matter of a hormonal moment, or a stressful day, but if the everyday chat is becoming more fraught, take a moment to reflect on what you're saying, and how you're saying it, and whether that needs to change.

If you have tough stuff to tackle, it's even more important to get the message framed in such a way that it says what it is you want to be saying, and says this in such a way your teen will hear what you intend, and then, ideally, respond in the way you hope. This is a tricky business and very much easier said in theory than actually said and done, but working out what it is you want to say is a good place to start, and if it's big, important stuff then taking your time over this, if you've got that luxury, can really help.

TALKING STUFF

- Why do you want to raise this particular issue? Are there things that have worried you in your child, or in what might be going on around them, in the community or in the news? Reflecting on your motivation can be valuable and could be a good place to start as a route into the conversation.

- What do you want to achieve as an outcome of this conversation? To open the conversation up or prepare the way for another? Address a specific concern directly? Remind them of a boundary? Reinforce something you've talked about before? Find something out?

- What is the best way to frame this message? Can you keep it short, simple, direct – covering as few different points as possible? Or would it be better approached more indirectly and delicately?

- What do you think their response is likely to be? Where might there be scope for misunderstanding or misinterpretation? What can you do to pre-empt or avert that by changing something about the way (or time or place) in which you communicate this?

- Why now? Is it the best time? Does it matter if it's not now?

PARENTS TALK

'With my son, my 19-year-old, I find with him it's like a bit of a drip-feed of different things to him. When you're trying to talk to him about something, it's like different bits at a time. He can't cope with it all in one go, and it just takes him a while to come round to our way of thinking sometimes. Initially it will be, like, "Nope, I'm not listening to that, I'm not going to hear what you're saying" almost. But, I don't know, if you give him little bits, eventually over time, he sort of absorbs it and starts to agree almost.' **Sue**

What about what's *not* spoken?

In addition to what is said, there's communication above and beyond our words, and even without a word being spoken. Our body language and non-verbal communication can make sense of what's said, but equally it can confuse or distort its message, or undermine its meaning. It's powerful, and generally totally unconsciously done. Those messages and cues we send (and receive) through our posture, gesturing, facial expression, intonation and so on, can speak very much louder than whatever is said. If the words of your mouth communicate something different from what the language of your body is saying, it's likely the latter will drown out the sound of the former, because we all have an instinct that this mostly unconscious form of communication is the more sincere of the two. And remember, it's harder to interpret all of this accurately in adolescence.

TEENS TALK

'I know it seems very generic, but my advice to parents is just, like, be open-minded with what you're thinking in your own head, not just what you're saying. Try to be more understanding, and reasonable, because you can tell if your parents don't really mean what they're saying. It just comes across.' **Connor (16)**

TALKING STUFF

Be very aware of the message your non-verbal communication might be sending to your teenager. Even though you may have taken your emotions in hand, taken a deep breath, and taken great care to construct what you want to say to ensure it comes across just how you intended – your folded arms, frown or rigid stance might betray you.

Being mindful of what your body is communicating can work both ways. Saying something you know will be unwelcome, along with all you can non-verbally muster in demonstration of your love and concern, can also potentially send a powerful message, and help it go down better.

Also remember your teenager's behaviour is a form of non-verbal communication to you. Interpreting it may need some careful and sensitive observation, and gentle probing for guidance from them, preferably in verbal form. This can help us as parents focus less on the behaviour (though that may need its own attention at some stage) and more on what it might be trying to tell us.

The dreaded Mum/Dad lecture

TEENS TALK

'When I try to talk to my mum about stuff it always becomes a bit of a lecture, so I have to be selective about what I say and the words I use.' **Connor (16)**

'They just go on and on about something! You know, you might ask a question and you'll end up with some ten-mile rant about something completely off topic, and like you're in trouble.' **Daisy (16)**

'I feel like if you say something to your mum she kinda, like, twists what you're saying, and she'll give you, like, a whole lecture on what you should and what you shouldn't do, but you know what you did was, like, not relevant to all this. She just goes on at you for little things.' **Tamara (15)**

PARENTS TALK

'One of the things I find hardest about being the parent of a teenager is not turning everything into a lecture. Even when something good happens, I sometimes find myself turning it into a point to drive home ("Be proud of yourself" and so on), and I feel like I'm lecturing them all over again, even though something good just happened.' **Sarah**

It's the easiest thing in the world to launch into a lecture, especially if we're concerned, and want to change our teenager's behaviour in any way. We can see as clear as day that they're going to do themselves no good, or even significant harm, if they carry on as they are, and we want to do all that we can to protect them. Tempting though it is to do it, a lecture rarely achieves the desired outcome. Even the most intelligent and motivated university student will absorb, retain and actually learn far less from a lecture than any of the other ways teaching can be delivered. It also risks doing more harm than good if it shuts this conversation down for the future, and other ones, too. Most of us, if we're honest, would try to avoid being on the receiving end of Daisy's parent's 'ten-mile rant'. If you find yourself launching off, stop. Take a breath, apologize and take a different tack (read on for ideas).

When one-way does work best

Lectures might not work, but sometimes there are things that need saying for which no response is needed. Reinforcing that message to our children that they're loved unconditionally, that there's nothing they can do or say that could possibly make us love them less, that we're always there for them, that we'll always be on their side no matter what – these are a few of the things that need to be said, over and over again.

TEENS TALK

'My mum's always said I'd rather you talk to me and tell me what's happened, than be in a place where you have no one to help you out of a situation. She's like, it doesn't matter what it is, I'd rather you just say. My friend – she'd lied to her mum and gone out to the park, and stuff had happened and she didn't feel she could go back to her house so she came back to mine, and my mum was, like, "If you were in that situation and you were out in the middle of the night, I'd rather you came home and you could say, 'I did this,' and you'd be safe, rather than in a situation where you're not safe because you're too scared I'll get mad at you." Obviously, there'd still be things I'd be nervous about telling her, but I'd definitely still tell her. I'd feel guilty if I didn't.' **Sara (16)**

These are the most important things we can ever say to our children, however much we may be struggling with how little we like how they are at this stage of their lives. As a parent this love is totally immovable. It's far too vast and too deep for anything to budge it. You know this, but your teenager may need reminding. And these things can be said in so many ways. Find a way that works for you, and for them, and explore different ways, and even if you have to set yourself a regular reminder, make sure you keep on doing it.

PARENTS TALK

'I write our kids letters every few months. I can't remember where I got the idea from. I started it when they were babies and non-verbal. I'll write down something like, "You're six months old, and this is how I feel," and I'll put that in an envelope and shove it in the loft in a box. And then write another one a few months later, then another one and another one. Even as they got older, I still write them, especially when big things are happening. They're in a box for each of them in the loft. My daughter got hers when she turned 18, and I'll give the boys theirs when they do.

'The letters thing helps me. They can be really short, but they always end with, "I'm doing the best I can" – basically a caveat saying it's not my fault I'm rubbish at this! And then a declaration of love. They're full of love. I find it easier to express this stuff on paper.' **Jim**

Listening matters

TEENS TALK

'My advice to parents is actually listen to your child before you make your own conclusions in your head, because a lot of parents take out little bits of what they want to hear, and they put it into one big thing, and they don't actually listen to what the child is saying to them. If they actually listen to them, and listen to what the actual story is, they might understand more, and understand why they did it.' **Keisha (15)**

'My advice to parents is probably to say, "Listen," because whenever I talk to my mum about anything she always just listens to everything I have to say. Because my brother was in a bad place at some point, my mum really knows how to listen to people now, and she'll just listen to me, and then say something afterwards, instead of trying to interrupt and stuff. So I'd just probably say, "Listen." I think she feels guilty about the whole thing, because it was tough for my brother, and I think she feels guilty that no one knew, because he didn't talk to her.' **Josh (17)**

We all know how we feel when somebody really listens to what we're saying (affirmed, valued, cared for, important) and how it feels when they don't (rubbish). We also all know what it feels like to listen to someone else with our full focus tuned in to them, and when we only spare a little attention to what someone is saying. Sometimes that someone is one of our children, and there are all sorts of perfectly understandable reasons why we do this, but the better we can listen to them, the better it will be for all our communication. Apart from the importance of giving their words the time, attention and respect they deserve, and picking up not just the detail of what they're saying but what might lie behind it, it also models good listening to them, which will come in handy when we have something we want them to hear.

PARENTS TALK

'My second one is very different from my eldest – very much more open, very social, always chatting. If I ask, "How are you?" after a while, I'm starting to get bored 'cos he's there for 45 minutes talking! All I asked was what did you do at school today, and I know what he's done for the first hour, the second hour, who he had lunch with. So, he'll talk, but the other one, I don't know, he's just so different, and I find that really difficult sometimes.' **Giovanna**

There are definite ends of a conversational spectrum with teenagers, from the silent and inscrutable at one end, to the never-ending late-night chatter at the other, and both can present their challenges to tired, busy, stressed parents with lots going on in their lives when it comes to listening. Our minds may be full of the general buzz of planning what to do for dinner, or they might be totally stuck in a worry back at work. Or we might be composing an appropriate response in our heads instead of listening to the rest of what's being said. Or maybe we've already jumped ahead to the inevitable catastrophic conclusion of whatever it is our teenager is still in the middle of telling us. But being present and listening well is one of the greatest gifts we can give to our teens.

TEENS TALK

'My advice to my mum would be let me finish first. Let me finish. That's what I'd say.' **Connor (16)**

'I guess my advice to parents would be keeping that dialogue open maybe, but also not pushing yourself too much into their life, 'cos obviously they're experiencing all these things – you can't force yourself to be too involved. But, like, keeping that conversation going, asking questions – I dunno, it might not be for everyone. I'm quite chatty, so I dunno – but not inserting yourself so much as a parent so it's like, "Hey, go away! You're getting too involved now!"' **Amy (17)**

TALKING STUFF

Here are some tips for good listening:

- *Focus.* Give them your full attention, even if you're doing something that also needs your concentration, such as driving, cooking or walking somewhere. Try not to let your phone distract you, or your thoughts. Try to be present, with them, in this moment, if you can.

- *Show your interest.* It's important not just to focus, but to let your teens know you are focusing. This could be through your body language, eye contact (though sometimes teens might consciously or unconsciously choose a context when eye contact isn't possible), facial expressions, encouraging responses, nods of the head and so on. Switching your phone off or putting it away is a clear message your attention is on them, as is simply saying 'I'm all yours, go ahead,' or whatever might fit the moment best.

- *Don't interrupt.* Hard though it can be to hold back, letting them get to the end of what they're saying lets them know it has value to you, and shows them respect. It also stops you inadvertently cutting them off before they get to the most important bit. They might never get back there.

- *Empathize.* Acknowledge their feelings – which is hard if you think their feelings are misplaced, or their response is inappropriate or ill-judged, or you want to make them feel better, or you don't agree with what they're saying – but how they feel is how they feel, and they need this to be validated. Simply saying, 'That must be really hard,' or something similar, can be enough.

- *Check in with them.* Repeating back to them what you think they've said in your own words gives you time to begin to digest it, makes sure you've understood it properly and allows them to clarify or expand. It also gives them the opportunity to hear it themselves from the 'outside'. They may have got lost along the way, and stuck in a tangle of complex thoughts and emotions, but hearing it all articulated by someone else can give them a different insight and perspective, and in some situations may enable them to begin to build their own solutions.

- *Ask thoughtful questions.* Open questions – ones that can't have a yes/no answer – are good for prompting and encouraging them to go on, as well as eliciting more information. What did they say next? How did that make you feel? Closed questions are useful for checking a detail or clarifying understanding. It can help to guide them towards their own ways through. If the subject in hand is sensitive, it's especially important that questions are thoughtful and compassionate and stick to whatever it is our teen has been saying. Take your time: don't feel you have to come up with a response straight away, and don't expect them to, either. Take your time to register and process what they've said, and how you want to respond. Checking in with yourself is important, because our parental emotional balance can tip very quickly if our teenager is telling us something that's tough. Deep breaths really can help. If you need to take time out and come back to it, let them know, make sure you do, and don't leave it too long.

Wondering and wandering

PARENTS TALK

'For years we've "wondered out loud" to try to get to the problem.' **Ian**

Sometimes a bit of indirect, calm curiosity can, if you're lucky, lead to a conversation that may never have happened had a more blatant approach been taken. And most parents would genuinely love to know more about their teenagers' lives (at the same time as there being parts that even the nosiest among us would really rather not know). Our teenage children are already likely to be of the view that we're ill-informed and generally hopeless – and we know we are too when it comes to many aspects of the teenage worldview, so adopting the persona of someone who knows nothing comes quite naturally. The curious conversation could be prompted by something you saw in a film or drama, heard in the news or saw going round social media. Or something you heard from another parent. Or it could be 'wondering out loud' about what's going on in the hunt for virtual zombies, or a complicated new dance move, if you can get to sit (or dance) alongside them.

TEENS TALK

'Yeah, I think because they've always wanted me to be open and honest with them, my parents have sort of learned over the years what I've been explaining to them, and sometimes they still don't understand everything but they try to. They try to let me educate them on how the teenage life is these days so that they can understand me, and we can have open communication.'
Megan (15)

Time, space and silence

TEENS TALK

'Teenagers can sometimes feel forced to share an opinion or conversation they're not ready for. Like, they just need a bit of time to process it or to think about it or to work out what they want to say. Sometimes it's nice to have a bit of time to think about what a parent's said or how you want to respond. So, just not having it done in a time that's suitable only for the one side like the parent is nice, and just not expecting an answer right away.' **Jasmin (18)**

PARENTS TALK

'I've learned from being a foster carer as well as a dad that all this quality time stuff is rubbish. You have to spend hours and hours to get to the gold bits. So, you might, you know, go to the park for three or four hours and in that time you'll get ten seconds of coherent, cogent conversation, and that was worth it. But you can't get straight to 'Let's go to the deep and meaningful'. You have to put the time – the hours – in, you know, doing whatever activity it is, so that then you get to that moment of depth, shall we say.' **Jim**

'I think the hardest thing for me about having teenagers would probably be not having enough time with them, because the more time you have, the more chance you can tease out what's going on in their heads and get them to relax and open up. So, trying to maintain relationships in less time than you'd ideally like is really hard. And perhaps they need more time than when they were little, because things are getting more complicated, and they're having interactions outside of your sphere of influence – then it takes more time to understand their perspectives, their pressures, their daily lives.' **Eoin**

Taking your time, giving them space, sitting with silence – these are important, and sound sensible, but can be hard to put into practice. Time is pressured, sometimes impossibly so, but teenagers need this, and we do need to try to carve out what we can, so conversations can happen when they're ready, in their time, and be revisited and continued. And we need to let them take their time to respond to something we've said, or they've said, either in that moment, or sometime later. This is hard when your worry radar is on high alert.

It's also good, but difficult, to let there be silence – ours, theirs or both. There are different sorts of silence, of course – some comfortable and some awkward, but the silence that lets people take a while to sit with what's been said, and absorb, and process, and think about how they feel, what this might mean, what they might say, or do, is one that might need to happen. It may be in that moment together, but it may need to be the silence of not revisiting the conversation too soon. And try to learn the language of your teenager's silence. What is it saying to you? Observe their body language, take in the context and check for distractions, because it might be their mind has just moved onto something completely different.

TALKING STUFF

- How do you feel about silence generally? Does it make you uncomfortable? Do you feel the need to fill it? Or do you need spells of silence and space yourself to process, or just to be?

- Do you feel you have to respond immediately, or are you comfortable taking your time to reflect, and to process your own emotions and reactions? If you tend to rush in, try letting yourself take a little while, and see how it feels. Does it help?

- If there's a silence that feels uncomfortable, check if it's just your own discomfort, rather than there actually being anything wrong. Could you try sitting with it a while, and see if it still feels that way?

PARENTS TALK

Meera: We have something we call Circle of Truth, so that if my 13-year-old has something to tell me, that he thinks I'll get angry about, or upset about, or overreact, he needs to start the conversation by saying, 'Can we have Circle of Truth?' And then within Circle of Truth he can say anything, and I can't react, I can't tell him off, I just have to listen to it, and we can talk about it. And it just means he knows if he's done something he shouldn't have, or whatever, he's not going to get in trouble. It doesn't mean he won't ever! But it means in that moment he can talk about things and he doesn't have to worry about getting a reaction.

And it goes both ways in that if I think he's holding something back, I can go up to him and say, 'Can we just have Circle of Truth?' And then I can say, 'Did this happen? Did that happen? Sometimes it works, sometimes it doesn't, but the idea is that if he says, 'Can I have Circle of Truth?' I have to think, 'OK, take a breath, don't react.'

It's usually stuff that he thinks I'll be angry about. Something he might not have told me, or he might have had to eventually, but he was scared of the reaction, so this way he could do it sooner, because he knew the reaction wouldn't happen there. And he's quite good at stopping me if I'm having trouble holding on to my reaction. He's, like, 'No, come on, you said ...' And to be fair, he's still young, so there's not been anything too enormous yet, so it might get harder.

Dawn: I think it's such a brilliant idea – but I have to say I think if I tried to do that now with my 16-year-old, he'd just run screaming!

Where and when?

What are the times and places where talking happens best with your teenager? They may be few and far between, but keep an eye out for any opportunity, and manufacture some if you need to. Parents often wryly report the inconvenient times their children will pick to launch into an important conversation, but we can do the same to them, especially if time is tight, the need is pressing and now is all there is. But try, if you can, to find the times and places where they're less likely to be distracted, more likely to feel relaxed, safe and where you can both walk away, take some time or change the subject comfortably if you need to. And try, if you possibly can, to be present for them in the moments they choose – however awkward. As they get older these times can be harder to find, as their lives quite rightly move more and more outside the family unit, but in the midst of the quest for independence they're still important, for you and for them.

PARENTS TALK

Erin: I have to say bed's our big one. It's when we're saying goodnight we get, 'Can I just tell you …?' That's when our 13-year-old told us his friend had texted him and said he wasn't going to be in for a week or so because his mum had died that night of a heart attack – it was awful – so he'd held on to that all day. And I'd been alone with him that afternoon when the others had still been at school and he'd got home early, but it wasn't until he was in bed he went, 'I've got something really awful to tell you.' I think a busy household is definitely a thing that can hold them back. I said to him, 'Why didn't you say something earlier?' and he said, 'I just didn't want to be interrupted, or anyone else to hear.' And he was really serious. He said this friend had said, 'Don't tell anyone!' and he'd said, 'Can I tell my mum, my parents?' And his friend said yes, but it was anyone else at school they didn't want to know, and so I think he thought that if his little brother or sister overheard then he'd be betraying his friend, because it was only to be his parents, so that was another thing. So yeah, bedtime is the important time. That's always when he spills, for sure.

Dawn: In a way my 14-year-old does that – not when she's going to bed, but when she knows she's meant to be going to bed, so it's sort of a delaying tactic but she also knows there's going to be an end to that conversation because at some point I'm going to go, 'Look at the time! You really need to go to sleep now.' So we do tend to have quite a lot of conversations when she should be going to bed. When I say, 'It's bedtime,' she'll go, 'Well, actually, I thought we could just talk about this huge thing …!'

Meera: We get car journeys sometimes. They're always the very short car journeys, and it always leaves the 'Aah!' because now she's getting out and we hadn't finished! But it'll always be one on one. I think it's because there's no eye contact because I'm driving and she's just there. I think if you're side by side and focusing on something else … And I think it needs to start from them – as long as it's on their terms. And it's just a short journey – she knows it's time-limited. She can escape if she needs to.

Sue: My daughter's off at university and she's not the greatest communicator, especially now she's left home, and I feel like I haven't connected with her properly for weeks, so we're going to spend the day together. I find with all of my kids if you do something with them on their own they're just, I don't know, more open to talking, really. I think it's because they've got your undivided attention – there are no distractions, like the others bursting in. I've always found I have more fun with them when I'm with them one to one.'

Giovanna: I do something similar, for example when one of them wants a haircut. I tell them I need to pop to the supermarket which is just nearby so I can walk with them. Then while they're there I'm like, 'Call me when you're done,' and I'll walk back with them. It's like finding an excuse or something to walk with them. And then I start talking because while they're walking, they're not on their phones, so it makes it easier to have a conversation. And then I say, 'Oh, you walk so fast! Can we slow down?' We need to go slowly just so I have more time to chat with them. If I'm in the house, it's just impossible 'cos it just gets busy, or I'm doing work or they're doing homework.

Chances to connect

Connectedness and communication go hand in hand, and sometimes when communication isn't coming easily, the best we can do is to be there, around and available. The stronger our connectedness with our children, the stronger our communication will be, and vice versa. Each strengthens the other. However, in the push and pull of the adolescent adventure, taking them off and away into adulthood, those times together can be harder to find, so they're more precious and important than ever.

PARENTS TALK

What do you find can help build connectedness/togetherness?

- 'Eating together in the evening where possible. Watching a TV programme together. Watching them in their hobby. Welcoming their friends into your home – and being kind and generous to them!'

- 'Doing things outside the house together. Inside we revert to our old parent/child roles. Outside the home, ask them for their advice, views and help. Go shopping for your things as well as theirs. Try a new place together. Go where they want to eat and try their meal. That sort of thing.'

- 'Shared experiences – listening to something together in the car, or watching something funny.'

- 'Doing things together. Doing things they particularly enjoy. Picking up on things they've said (sometime later) and showing that you took it in and "saw" them. Allowing them to have different views and opinions. Moving away from the parent role into one that is less hierarchical and more relational.'

- 'My son has suddenly gone from not wanting me to watch him play sport to asking if I'll take a day off and drive halfway across England to watch a game – and bring his grandfather, too! It seems I'm no longer an embarrassing dad and may even be someone to be proud of!'

- 'Enjoy every routine, even the school run. One day it will end.'

Why parents matter

Let's (almost) end with the wisdom of someone just out of their teens. You may not feel as though you still matter but you do, and so does the talking. In fact, as their own stuff gets more tough, they need to know they can talk to you more than ever.

TWENTIES TALK

'It can be so damaging and difficult for people to deal with some of these things as teenagers if they don't feel they can communicate about stuff to their parents, who are the mature people who should really know what's going on, and should be able to give proper, legitimate advice, as opposed to your peers who don't know anything more than you do.

'I think if you're just bouncing off your peers at that age, you're not going to get any mature decision. You're also just going to get those people's lack of experience of knowing what the best thing to do is.

'I always felt I could talk to my mum, but some of my friends found it harder to talk to their parents, so they'd load onto their friends more. And I could see a lot of people making mistakes they wouldn't necessarily have made, had they been able to communicate the issues they had with their parents. Not thinking things through, being aggressive, or rude, or spreading rumours. Whereas if they'd been able to say to their parents, "This person was an idiot today, and they really upset me. They did this," they'd have been able to say, "OK, that's not your fault, you've not done anything wrong. This is that person's issue."' **Sam (21)**

And finally ...

Chatting with Jacob

Me: So, were there times that you felt that I didn't listen to you – that you wanted to tell me something and I just wasn't really listening?

Jacob: Definitely the food thing.

Me: We can't be having all our chats in my book about food!

Jacob: Hmm, well, I'd say, 'I don't like this, I don't want to eat it,' and you'd say, 'You have to eat it,' and I'd be like, 'Why?'

Me: So it's not to do with not listening; it's to do with not agreeing?

Jacob: I dunno. I'd be saying it's genuinely unpleasant for me to eat this, and I'd have thought if you'd actually heard that, and made me eat it anyway, then that would be very callous of you ...

Me: Ha-ha! I wasn't being mean; I just didn't believe you.

Jacob: That's because you weren't listening to me.

Me: I was listening! I just thought you were just being fussy. How bad can a carrot really be?

5

WHAT COULD POSSIBLY GO WRONG? (AND WHAT TO DO IF IT DOES) – THE TEENAGER

'There are so many things going on. Stress with exams, changing friendships, uncertainty about the future, lack of sleep, getting told off or criticized for something you shouldn't be ...'

Emma (18)

Where to begin? And where to end? When we're talking the tough stuff with teens, it feels like the scope for something going wrong is interminable, and it's far from all one-sided. There are plenty of ways that both teens and their parents can knock a simple, straightforward conversation off balance, or send it plummeting headlong into the abyss, but there's also plenty you can do to avert this – and to repair the damage when you don't. We're only human, and sometimes we mess things up.

So let's have a look at what can go wrong, and what can be done, and we'll start with our teens.

1. (Not) getting a different perspective

Let's go back to their incredible brain and all the changes it's going through. One of the things we can blame on teens' brains relates to the ability to understand each other; essential for effective communication, whether speaking or listening. This isn't fully developed until early adulthood, and adolescence is a time when it's just that bit harder to step into someone else's shoes. It's not just that it's hard; as a teenager you don't necessarily feel the curiosity you'd need to try, or to understand how it might help. Of course, it can also be hard as a parent to see through their teenage eyes and hear what we said with their ears.

TEENS TALK

'I've got this uncle that I talk to, and he gives me advice, and one of the things he says is that sometimes you have to understand your parents' perspective. Like, they might have other things going on in their life, and they might be really stressed out. And also, they're your parents, and obviously they want to protect you as much as they can, so if they do hear something bad, then their initial reaction is going to be, like, oh, go crazy, but then when they've calmed down, they're sort of going to understand.' **Matt (17)**

> **TALKING STUFF**
>
> Being honest with your teens about your own side of things can help them understand what's behind your words, decisions and actions. Asking open questions about what's going on for them, too, can help you in turn grasp their own perspective on things, which might influence your own insights in a helpful way another time.

2. (Mis)reading the signs

Essential to decoding what someone says is the ability to interpret facial expressions accurately. As adults, we use our prefrontal cortex to read the emotions in someone's face, which enables us to exercise judgement and regulate our response, and hopefully avoid jumping to a (possibly inaccurate) conclusion. In childhood and adolescence, it's the amygdala that does this – the bit of our brain linked to gut reaction and raw emotion. A parental face full of concern could be misinterpreted as showing anger, and prompt a defensive response, for example. This is worth remembering if your child's reaction surprises you; perhaps you might try a (calm and) honest conversation about what you'd intended to communicate, and what they thought you'd really meant.

3. (Not) getting organized

Some of your frustration with your teenager (and theirs with you) might focus on how absolutely impossible they seem to find it to organize themselves – to remember all their kit for school (again), not to lose their keys (again) or to get their homework done before the deadline (again). They also may well just not register the chaotic mess in their bedroom for some considerable time, if at all, and if they do it may well not bother them.

This is because being organized is really difficult for young people at this stage of life, and it's down to that prefrontal cortex again. One of the many things it's responsible for is all our executive functions, and higher-level cognitive skills, like planning, organizing and acting with consequences in mind. Understanding why it's difficult doesn't mean these things don't matter (though sometimes they don't), but it helps us appreciate why as parents we do need to do our best to cut them some slack, draw on our deepest stores of patience and help them as much as they'll allow. And turn a blind eye to the mess – or just close the bedroom door. Otherwise, the arguments may just keep going on.

TALKING STUFF

If you find yourself getting into disagreements about disorganization or mess, there are two key questions to ask (though, as always, it's rarely quite that simple). The strategies that follow them build on what we looked at before. These can all be applied to a lot of the mutual problem-solving that can help deal with various issues in both of your lives, that will hopefully help them develop the skills to go through a similar process themselves another time, with or without you.

1. **How much does this really matter, compared to other issues in your lives?**

If it doesn't matter enough to get in an argument about – if it isn't bothering them, only you, and it isn't affecting their lives – how can you avoid an argument happening next time? How can you manage and change your own response? Could you take some time to reflect on where this response is coming from in you?

- It can sometimes help literally to compose different words to use – out loud or in your head – for the next time this happens. Some parents have a mantra they repeat silently to themselves in response to particular situations, to help them resist the urge to launch in.

- Or you could commit – out loud to your teenagers, or again just in your head – to the decision to say nothing at all about the mess/forgetfulness, and next time take a deep breath, back away and close the door behind you.

- Or even better, if you can, think of something positive to say instead of the critical comment that hits you first. Sometimes this can be a challenge, but there's always something good to find if you look for it.

2. If it does matter, can you fix it together?

If rotting food on their bedroom floor is becoming a health hazard, or the neighbour's getting fed up with them knocking for your spare keys, or they're getting into even bigger trouble at school for not having their homework/gym kit/violin, then how can you help them to help themselves? Here are a few further questions to consider:

- *How does it make them feel?*
  - It can help to help them to identify and own their feelings, and to recognize this as a situation they're not happy about either. How do they feel when they realize they haven't finished their homework/remembered necessary kit for school, and/or when they get in trouble for it?
  - If it's affecting someone else, trying to help them see how they might be feeling about it, too, can also help, especially if it's someone they care about. The teenage conscience is a powerful force.
- *What do they think might help them?*
  - Trying to help them work through possible causes and solutions themselves is the best approach. Ask lots of prompting questions, encouraging them to work through possible 'what if' scenarios in response to suggested solutions.
  - Try to avoid leading questions, tempting though it is – they're likely to spot these a mile away, and even if they don't,

it generally won't help in the long term as much as them working it out for themselves. (That said, sometimes a good leading question is the only way to help them find a realistic way out.)

- What do they think is the reason they end up leaving their homework too late? Is what they think it is what's really going on, or is there sometimes something else? If their answer is to get on with their homework as soon as they get in from school, for example, would that solution always work? What if they feel too tired when they get home? What about when they have football training after school and get home late? Prompt them to work through solutions to each of these scenarios.

- *How do they think you can help them?*
  - As part of their problem-solving, offer your services. Again, their ideas might need some prompting and pruning to get them into realistic shape, but helping them in the way they suggest – if they've pinned it down into something realistic and manageable – is better than jumping in direct yourself.

- *What will they do if it doesn't work?*
  - Help them to recognize they may need to reflect and assess whether their plan is working, and agree you'll both go through the process again if it needs it.

4. Coding errors

The encoding and decoding of one simple message has enormous scope for going astray – miscommunication in the way words are framed, misunderstanding in the way they're interpreted – and that's before you even consider the role non-verbal communication plays. In adolescence there's more scope for misunderstanding than at any other time of life. But the more you are both aware of this, the better chance conversations stand of staying on track.

As we've seen, the relationship between parent and child is altering as adulthood beckons, and that includes the way communication takes place. Your message may be the same, but it might now sound like a threat to their vital steps into independence. A straightforward question might now be heard as an interrogation. What seems to a parent like a simple bit of information, or a useful piece of advice, can be received as yet another interminable lecture, going on and on, and having a go at them, again. Or just another load of 'blah, blah, blah' they filter out. So, the message may need to be rethought.

PARENTS TALK

'I'd say to him sometimes after a party, the day after, "Oh you look really tired today," and I'd say it out of general concern, but he'd take it as an accusation. I dunno, it's probably because he already felt guilty and took it like an accusation from me that he'd been drinking the night before, and he'd know that I wouldn't particularly like that, so he'd feel very defensive, when really all I wanted was to know if he was feeling OK.' **Giovanna**

TALKING STUFF

- Is there a pattern in any misunderstandings? Are there particular things you say, or particular times or places or contexts in which they're said, that seem to trigger an angry or defensive response?
- If so, what could you do to reword what you say, or just retime it? Could you ask for your teenager's help with this?

5. Stress

Everyday life for the average teenager can sometimes feel full of stress. There's so much going on – in and around friendships, relationships, school, exams, the future, the planet, as well as all the 'Am I OK?' stuff (without going into the serious stress experienced by teenagers with a mental health disorder, which we'll look at more closely in Part 2). When we're stressed, we're in fight-or-flight mode, and a parent might get one or the other in response to something said – a battle or a closed shop.

TEENS TALK

'It's when I get stressed out from outside things that have nothing to do with the actual argument, or I've just had a bad day and I'm really stressed out, and then I get home, I always take it out when I'm stressed on the people I care about, so it's always my mum that gets the rough bit, and she'll just say something, like, just ask me about my day, and I'll be like, "You don't care – why are you asking me about my day?" And I can hear myself doing it, but then once you've said it you can't go back.' **Kayleigh (16)**

'It's probably school that causes the most arguments in our house. I dunno, I think it's just irritability, because school can be stressful, so I can get annoyed, and then I'll probably say the wrong thing,

> then my parents will get angry with me for saying it and stuff. I don't really argue with them about anything else, pretty much just school. School's just stressful sometimes.' **Kelsey (16)**

Managing our own response to their response is always important. It can be hard, especially if we were already loaded with stress ourselves. But we're the adult, and the parent, and more appropriately placed to bring a more calm and measured approach to the conversation. We'll come back to some strategies for going about this in the following chapter.

6. Big emotions

TEENS TALK

'It's sometimes hard to get your point across about how you're feeling because they don't understand it, and sometimes you can't understand it.' **Hannah (15)**

'It's really hard because sometimes you feel really down but you don't even really have a reason, so it's really hard to talk about it when you haven't really got a reason to give why you're stressed or something.' **Kayleigh (15)**

'Sometimes I feel like I can't talk to my mum about things because I feel like she sometimes invalidates my feelings. Like, I remember once – I think it was on my birthday – and we got into this really big argument. I'd been upset about something else earlier, and obviously the argument we were having wasn't a big deal, and my mum knew that, and she was just not bothered by it all, but I was bothered by it, and I knew it was silly at the time, but the fact that she didn't care that I was bothered by it, and because of what had set me off, and even though my emotions were probably out of whack, it doesn't mean they aren't valid. I might be more upset than I should be, but something still did upset me, and it feels bad that you invalidate that.' **Anna (16)**

There's a lot going on for a teenager, and some of this can cause their side of a conversation to become heated or shut down. As well as hormonal surges creating emotional turbulence, there's their developing brain with its supercharged limbic system, adding extra intensity to all those social and emotional variables. And as we've seen, a lot of this is new to them, and can take them by surprise as much as it can their parents.

Just as they're constantly repositioning themselves somewhere between child and adult, we're continually having to adjust our perceptions of where they are, and it's important to remember that, although they may look to all intents and purposes like their adult selves, they're not there yet. When it comes to managing their emotions, these can be powerful and overwhelming and can take them by stealth, and they may not be able to name what just hit them or what has increasingly been dragging them down. They may need your help, but first they need your validation. We all do, let's be honest. Empathy is what's most important, and that has nothing to do with agreeing with what our teen may have said, or condoning what they may have done, or even knowing what is going on. It just means sitting with them in it, for a while at least. We do need to try to understand, but even if we don't, we need at the very least to accept that how they feel is how they feel, whether they 'should' or not. When it comes to big emotions, 'should' is neither here nor there. It is what it is. And the time for working on solutions and strategies together will almost certainly come, but especially with the stuff of feelings, it's best to assume that's not the place to start.

And if they won't tell you what's wrong, it might be because they're not ready, or because they can't pin it down themselves, but at least if they know what they say will be acknowledged for what it is, that won't present a barrier when the time is right for them.

PARENTS TALK

'I've found it's best just to validate what's being said and resist the urge to take action, which is what I naturally want to do. It's generally when I say too much that conversations in our house can get heated or just shut down.' **Jim**

TALKING STUFF

There are various ways we can find ourselves trying to make our teenagers feel better when they're upset or feel bad about something:

- *Minimizing their feelings.* It can be tempting to say something like 'Well, at least ...' and add something that could have been worse, or, 'It really doesn't matter ...' in an attempt to reduce the magnitude and impact of whatever it is and make them feel better about it. Try to notice if you're doing this – and also reflect on how this makes you feel when it happens to you. Sometimes it can help us to get some perspective, but generally it just makes us feel what we're feeling is out of proportion, and that makes us feel worse. The time might come, and they might get there themselves, but for now it is what it is.

- *Bypassing their feelings.* Say, for example, your teen is upset because they've got into trouble at school for chatting in class one time too many, and now they have to stay back after school on Friday, when their friends were all meeting up to do something long-looked-forward-to. How many of us, honestly, might at this point find ourselves starting by getting cross that they're in trouble? It's not surprising to feel angry/disappointed/ frustrated, but hold back on that for a moment, if you can. They're upset, and that's the best place to begin if you want to help them to avoid this happening again.

- *Overriding their feelings with logic.* Suppose your child is fuming with you because they've not been allowed to do something they desperately want to and feel they should be able to. It's really important to explain the rationale behind your decision, but it's also important to recognize their feelings in the face of a barrier and acknowledge their response.

- *Giving in to something to make them feel better.* Sometimes we can find ourselves compromising under the pressure of their emotions, especially if we're someone who basically likes peace and harmony and everyone around us to be happy. In the scenario above we might give in and agree to something we're not really sure is going to be safe, wise or appropriate for them. There are times it's right to bend boundaries, of course, but judging their capacity for keeping themselves safe is the bottom line if we're letting them go. Try to stay in the moment with their feelings of frustration and fury and empathize with them, and hold on to your judgement about your decision as their parent.

7. Sleep (and lack of it)

For parents of babies and toddlers the question of sleep looms enormous, but by the time they reach their teens the worry is no longer getting them to stay asleep and in bed, but getting them out of it at all. How do you get them to wake up, drag themselves out from under their duvet, through the shower, into some clothes, find their homework and gym kit, ideally grab some breakfast en route, and all in time for the bus to school? Or, at the weekend, before it gets dark?

Sleep is a gift whose wide-ranging benefits have come under much closer scrutiny in recent years. Getting enough, and good enough sleep, can help us in so many ways, and the converse is also true. Plenty of struggles – and arguments – could be avoided, or reduced, if only we'd had sufficient sleep. Anyone who's faced insomnia knows how elusive sleep can be at times, however, and we know how much of our lives can be affected. As well as all sorts of physical things, lack of sleep can affect our mood, our mental health, our concentration, cognition and ability not to fly off the handle or dissolve into tears at the drop of a hat, or a seemingly misplaced word from a parent. If your teenager is more than usually snappy or grumpy or generally down, it's worth checking in with them on how well they're sleeping.

Teenagers need between eight and ten hours of sleep a night, but that becomes hard to fit into the usual weekday routine because in adolescence their circadian rhythm alters, shifting the natural falling-asleep and waking-up times till later on in a 24-hour cycle. This is largely to do with the hormone melatonin. When this gets released, it makes us feel sleepy, telling us to go to bed, but in adolescence this happens later on in the evening (or night or early hours of the morning), so teenagers are naturally programmed both to fall asleep and wake up later. However, the average school day doesn't allow for a lie-in, and by the time they reach high school many teenagers also have a bus or train to catch, and an even earlier start than they may have had when they were younger. Catching up at weekends may seem the only way to cope, and a lie-in can help, but the more we can all do to stick to a regular pattern the better. If you can work together to develop better sleep hygiene that will help not only with sleep but with everything else, including conversations at home.

TALKING STUFF

There are various things you can try with your teen to help them to get more sleep. Some may work, others may not, some may need time, but all will need their commitment. A small-steps approach, as with many things, is often the best way forward:

- *Get into a good routine.* Work out a regular pattern of winding down and switching off – literally when it comes to phones/ gaming devices/screens of any variety. What would make this work for them? A hot chocolate? A warm bath? Shutting their phone away downstairs an hour before?

- *Get exercise during the day.* Teenagers should be getting at least an hour of exercise a day, and this will help them sleep better, as well as their general health and wellbeing. It can be hard to persuade many teens to get moving, but try to find something they'd enjoy. It can also include a walk to and from school (though this should be a vigorous stroll for it really to count, not an amble chatting with friends). If they can do this in daylight, so much the better for regulating that circadian rhythm.

- *Avoid caffeine and eating too much (or too little) towards bedtime.* It's best to cut out caffeine, with its stimulant properties, from early afternoon onwards, and it's also worth keeping an eye on overconsumption of caffeine during the day to cope with lack of sleep. Having too full or too empty a stomach at bedtime can also affect our sleep.

- *Create a sleep-friendly bedroom.* This should ideally have the potential to be dark, calm, quiet and cool when it needs to be. Would blackout blinds help? Are there noises from the rooms below or next to theirs? Some people find a tidy space helps their mind settle (it's worth a try ...).

- *Sharing their worries.* Sleep can be fragile for all of us if we have things on our minds, and we've seen how much these can multiply in adolescence. This book is all about having the conversations that count about the things that matter, and sometimes it's bedtime when these things come out, but sometimes they don't when they need to. Trouble with sleep could indicate worries racing around in their heads that they haven't been able to share. This could be a good opportunity to give them the encouragement and space to do so, if they can, starting with wanting to help them to sleep. Are they worrying about anything?

- If your teenager's problems with sleep are more serious and are concerning you and them, especially if it's part of a bigger picture of negative feelings of any sort, then it's worth getting advice from your family doctor, because it could be a symptom of something else going on, including physical or mental ill health.

8. Trust

PARENTS TALK

'When my eldest was being difficult, when he was around 14/15, it was trust. He kept saying I didn't trust him because I'd want to know who he was going out with, because that's what I'd always done. I didn't know any other way, because he was growing up, and he was my first, so it was the first time we had all this. He'd be going out with people who we didn't know, and we didn't know the parents so I couldn't just text the mums and say, "Is he really at your house? Where is he?" you know. So, he would come back at me all the time really angry and shouting, like proper screaming at me, '"You don't trust me! Who do you think I go out with? These are all my friends!" That was such an issue, the fact he felt I wasn't trusting him.' **Giovanna**

Trust is a big deal. It's incredibly important to teenagers they feel they're trusted by their parents, and it's equally important we feel we can trust them as we gradually let them go off into the world. It's also important to know when they can't be trusted, especially if it means they may not be safe, and it's important that they know this. Parental trust has to be earned, but equally it has to be learned by parents for whom it won't seem very long ago they were holding a little hand tight to cross the road. Both can often best be progressed with small-stake, low-risk responsibilities.

If trust that's been granted is broken, it's appropriate to feel disappointed. The depth of this disappointment will depend on the breach of trust involved. It's also appropriate to feel concerned if as a result they've put themselves at risk of harm, and to explain to them why. It's also appropriate to ask them if there are reasons behind it. There may be some genuine – if not necessarily very good – ones. Equally, you may be told some plausibly genuine and good-sounding reasons to avoid any trouble or future trust-related consequences (see the section on lying below). The judgement call is then yours as to whether you step up or step down the trust, but another chance to prove themselves will need to follow, at some point. It has to be done – we have to let them learn to fly off safely by themselves.

TALKING STUFF

- What might some of the small-stake, low-risk responsibilities look like for your teen (and for you), depending on their age? Can you agree these between you?

- What safeguards could you put in place together, to reduce any risks? Try to involve your teens in thinking these up, too, as well as going through 'what would you do if' scenarios. All this will help them to problem-solve in real situations as well as hypothetical ones.

- What will the consequences be if they break your trust? How will you respond? It's good to make the former explicit, and again agree it between you if you can. It's also useful to think through the latter, so you can be prepared ahead to manage your own feelings.

Chatting with Jacob

Me: What are some of the things you know you didn't tell me about? What was the sort of order of things you wouldn't mention? Like, for example, maybe, having a party on New Year's Eve when we'd left you on your own at home, thinking we could trust you to be responsible?

Jacob: That's an oddly specific example …

Me: Hmm. So, why was it that you didn't tell us about that?

Jacob: I think it's one of those 'ask for forgiveness not for permission' things.

Me: If you'd told us, we would have said no, of course.

Jacob: Yeah.

Me: So, obviously, that's why you didn't tell us, but tell my readers what happened at the party.

Jacob: Oh, well ... Too many people came, so I had to call a neighbour to close it down.

Me: Yes indeed, I remember it well, and so does Sam [the neighbour] I'm sure! But actually, on reflection, I guess you did act responsibly in the end. And nothing was damaged ...

Jacob: Nothing was damaged, nothing was broken, no harm was done.

Me: But thank goodness Sam came round and sorted it out.

Jacob: And nothing bad was happening either; I just thought it was too crowded, so ...

Me: So you weren't enjoying it anymore? It wasn't that anything was getting out of hand, it was just getting stressful?

Jacob: No, nothing was getting out of hand. I just thought, this is too many people, so I'm going to ask someone else to come and sort it out. Yeah.

Me: So you problem-solved in the situation and got it fixed, so actually I guess you were kind of OK to trust, in a way, looking back, though I have to say I didn't see it like that at the time. And I can't help thinking it could have very easily all have gone horribly wrong if it hadn't been for Sam ...

---

9. Truth and lies

TWENTIES TALK

'I would definitely lie to my parents about the content of video games that I wanted to play. So, if my mum said, "You can't play this game, it's an 18." I'd say, "But that's just because of this one thing," and I'd go into some complicated detail that made it seem like it was OK really and it was kind of a glitch in the grading. That was the case with *Call of Duty: Modern Warfare*. All my friends were playing it, so I wanted to be able to play it with them. And it wasn't like I was twelve or something – I was 16/17 – but my mum just had this thing about 18s. She'd always say, "It's 18 for a reason!" You just have to ask yourself, though, is it a good reason?' Josh (23)

Be honest. Did you ever lie to your parents when you were a teenager? And could you truthfully, hand on heart, say that you never, ever tell a lie now, however much you value the truth? That includes, by the way, the full spectrum of telling an untruth, telling a half-truth and withholding a truth, even if it's for the best of all possible reasons.

Closely connected to trust is truth and lies, and unfortunately, like it or not, all the above are totally normal for teenagers. Although it's infuriating for parents, and it's scary to know we won't know absolutely everything they're up to, we have to be realistic and expect it to happen, without letting feelings of betrayal and violation of trust take over a rational response. This doesn't mean it's OK; nor that it doesn't matter (though sometimes it doesn't in the grand scheme of things), but it comes back to trust, which is important when it comes to allowing them independence, and it's important they know that. So, call out a lie when it matters, especially when we feel they're putting themselves at risk, but try to keep the focus on keeping the lines of communication open using the full range of strategies we're looking at in this book, and on trying to uncover and understand what gave rise to the lie. Remember, the issue is primarily trust, not morality – though that's important, too, because honesty is a virtue of value, and they need to be someone that people can trust as they become independent adults.

PARENTS TALK

'I probably have said to my kids I don't care what you've done, just tell me the truth, and when they have told me the truth, I've then been really angry. So, they're like, "Stuff that, I'm not telling you the truth. I'm not playing that game anymore." So, I think there's something really important about parenting when they're younger, to make sure they understand that, as long as they tell the truth, it will be OK. Just tell me the truth. And I think that's something which, yeah, when they are in the teenage years, is far more difficult. I would say, if they aren't telling the truth, then spending time getting them to understand that, if they tell the truth, it will be all right, is going to take a lot more energy, a lot more time, but it's vital. It's absolutely vital.' **Aidan**

'Never punish honesty, which I see some parents often do, when kids tell the truth about something that had caused upset. It just trains kids to keep secrets. The dialogue and openness is much more important than the subject matter.' **Matt**

There are all sorts of reasons why teenagers lie. They might fear causing disappointment (see below), or the truth giving rise to misunderstanding, judgement, anger, repercussions or being prevented from doing whatever it is. They also need to begin to have an existence apart from their parents, and not telling them absolutely everything is part of this. What's important is trying to do all we can to establish an environment where big important truths can be told safely, and talked about sensibly, and alongside that to strengthen our teenager's sense of what's safe and what isn't, when they're deciding to decide things without their parents' direct jurisdiction and sage advice.

Sometimes the tables are turned and it's us withholding a truth or telling a lie to our teens. This is often to protect them from worry, but it has potential to generate more. Our teenagers are finely attuned to our feelings, as we are to theirs, and they'll often know when something's up. Of course, we don't want to load them with concerns too big for them to understand or to shoulder, but giving them something can sometimes be better than brushing it off. This is a judgement call for you, I'm afraid, based on knowing your worries, and knowing your child.

TWENTIES TALK

'Kids can tell if you're upset, stressed and tired, but if you don't communicate to them what's going on for you, they'll make up reasons, and they go into their own fantasy world. If you're not telling them anything, they're going to fill in the gaps themselves. If you see people around you struggling and they don't tell you why, you think, maybe, "They obviously don't trust me, they obviously don't feel like they can tell me this. There's something wrong with me. It's my fault." You load it onto yourself hugely. Your imagination can go all over the place, and all you've got to go on is your own experiences.' **Sam (21)**

10. Rebellion

TWENTIES TALK

'As a teenager you have that natural desire to sort of be a bit rebellious, to push the boundaries, and if when you push the boundaries you get the almightiest reaction, I think that's hugely damaging, especially when the parent's desperately trying to maintain control, and the kids see that, they then lose that personal relationship with their parents and they don't really care anymore. They're like, "Screw you, I'm going to do what I want; you're going to have to suffer the consequences."' **Flo (20)**

PARENTS TALK

'It's very tempting to say "No, under no circumstances; you're not going out dressed like that, young woman!' and actually to be able to say, "Look, we just need to have a chat about this," is kind of awkward if you've got the type of child that won't listen at all. How do you stop them doing something kind of risky? Or maybe not risky, but not appropriate. It's very difficult in those circumstances.' **Aidan**

We'll go on to look at boundaries – and control – in our examination of all that can go wrong from the parents' side. We tend to think of boundaries as being something for parents to set, monitor and manage, but we all have our personal boundaries, and teenagers are working out where theirs lie now, as part of the business of working out who they are, and what their place is in the world, and in their family. Part of that is testing out where these lie in relation to those their parents have set. Having boundaries is important in families, but it's also important to know where the interface lies between those of our teen, and those that matter.

PARENTS TALK

'I would say, you know, give them the opportunity to say no to things, and respect their no when it's not important. Almost I'd say try to find opportunities – I'm busking here a bit – but I'd probably be encouraging parents to try and find opportunities to respect their teenager's no, so they build up a sense that this isn't universal opposition to me as a person; this is because this isn't a good idea, and it's serious enough that Mum or Dad think it's a good idea not to do this.' **Aidan**

11. Not wanting to disappoint, upset, worry, burden ...

Hard though it may be to believe at times, your teenager really does care about you, and your good opinion really does matter.

A disappointed parent is so much harder to cope with than a furious one for most teens. Anger tends to beget anger, and of course sometimes our teenagers may not be telling us something because they know we'll be cross – and they may well know we'd be justified in being so. If we do live up to their expectations and fly off the handle, it's easy just to get cross with us in return, whereas how do you deal with a parent you've disappointed, worried, burdened or upset? The teenage conscience is a powerful force, at its most sensitive when it comes to their parents. They may at times hide how much they care, but they do.

TEENS TALK

'I wouldn't be scared so much that they'd be cross, but more like that their expectations of me would go down, like – I don't know how to explain it – like, they'd think worse of me. They wouldn't – but I'd worry they would.' **Kyle (15)**

'I'd be too scared I'd upset them. My parents are really lovely, and I've spoken to them about loads of things, and they've never shown getting upset, but it's still a thing for me, that I'm going to upset them. Because they do so much for me, so I'd just feel like I was letting them down. But I'd probably still end up telling them.' **Maria (15)**

'I think it is really, really quite difficult to talk to your parents; it's actually very, very hard to do that, 'cos you want to always be on their good sides, you see. You never really wanna be on their bad side, and I know that, you know, like, parents care, they do care, but … ' **Dean (14)**

'I'd find it really hard to talk to my parents about mental health because I wouldn't want my parents to think they're the reason, or they can't help me, or it's all their fault. I wouldn't want my mum to think, "Oh you're anxious and because of me." I think it's really hard to talk about when you don't want them to think it's all their fault, and you don't want them to feel guilty.' **Kayleigh (16)**

'My mum's always said, "If you're not happy, I'm not happy," so I don't want to put that on her.' **Maeve (16)**

'Sometimes you don't want to worry your parents. You don't want to put more things on them. My mum has a lot herself – my grandad died three or four years ago, and my grandma now has leukaemia, and that's both of her parents, and so I don't want to put more on that plate for her when she's already got so much on there, so I feel like I'd rather just do it myself to save her the problem.' **Ben (17)**

It's worth bearing this in mind when we're working with our teens to build up and bolster that conversational space. Sometimes they're holding things back to protect us, and part of our work is to reassure them that we're big and old and strong enough to bear whatever they bring us.

12. Not listening

We know, and they know, they don't always listen to what their parents say. But then neither do we always listen to them. It could be simply to do with getting their attention, but it could be they heard but didn't remember, or didn't quite get it, or chose to ignore it when it came to whatever 'it' was, or didn't agree in the first place. Not listening to what your parents have said can take many forms. If you know your teenager hasn't taken on board what you've said – and you may have said it in various ways and on multiple occasions – take some time to tease out what might lie behind this. This gives you the chance to tackle something bigger, if there's something more substantial there, and to try to get their buy-in, find another way forward or renegotiate or reinforce boundaries if you can't agree and it matters. There's always a reason. They may not know what it is, of course, but they may work it out with your help. And this will help you.

Chatting with Jacob

Jacob: Were there times I didn't listen to you?

Me: Well ... I don't know ... It's hard to think back ...

Jacob: It is hard to think back. I think I did listen to most of what you said.

Me: Ah, well, apart from – but maybe it's not so much to do with not listening, but not taking any notice of what I told you? For example, leaving your bike locked up at the front of the station, where it got stolen, and I said, 'Don't leave it there again, leave it in the safe bike racks round the back with the CCTV, or it'll just get stolen again,' or words to that effect. And what did you do?

Jacob: I did leave it at the front of the station again.

Me: And did it get stolen?

Jacob: It did get stolen. Not the next time though, to be fair. I left it there a few times.

Me: But not very many – it wasn't long after that it got stolen again. That's because you didn't listen! Or you didn't believe me ...

Jacob: Ah yes, well, maybe. I was naive in my youth.

6

WHAT COULD POSSIBLY GO WRONG? (AND WHAT TO DO IF IT DOES) – THE PARENT

'I cannot be bothered. I come out of most arguments feeling drained, like a lot of energy's been used up I could have used for something else. That's why I don't really come out and have those conversations, because, well, in case they do get blown out of proportion. It's a lose-lose-lose situation. My relationship with my parents has gone back to square one, I'm in the open now, you know, everything's revealed, the repercussions might be negative – my phone might be taken away – so, like, what's the point …

Zain (16)

If you thought there was a lot on the side of the teen that could make a conversation go off track, this is the point where we take a deep breath and a long hard look at ourselves. There are, thank goodness, so many things we can do to try to prevent things going wrong on our side, however, and to repair them if they do go awry, which they will because we are, as we've already said, only human. It never hurts to remind ourselves of this. We're humans doing our best, with the very best we can bring to the role of being a parent, wanting the very best for our children, and loving them through it all with that enormous, intractable parent-love that even the most maddening, saddening teenage behaviour can't budge a fraction of an inch – something we've also already said, and which it also doesn't hurt to remind ourselves of. To start with, though, we must grow up a bit.

1. Growing up our parenting

TEENS TALK

'Sometimes I personally feel, it's … well, it's not a lack of trust but it's more of a lack of them thinking that we're as mature as we are. Like sometimes I'll be left at home on my own and my parents will go out for the night, and they'll tell me over and over again, "Oh don't leave that on, don't light a candle," and I know these things! I am 16; it's not like I'm 12 or 13, and I understand that they're being protective of me, trying to make me safe, but sometimes I don't think parents understand that we know these type of things already. Parents do find it difficult to accept that we're older.' **Jamal (16)**

PARENTS TALK

'I love seeing their confidence grow and their orbit increasing, but it's sad, too – it's lovely when they're little. Knowing that they'll fly the nest is hard, but I know it's wrong to, even subtly, try to hold them back.' **Matt**

Our mission as parents is to grow up good grown-ups, but in the process we have to grow up our parenting, too, and these last years of childhood, and transition to adulthood, can really push our capacity for change to its limits. There's an enormous transformation going on in them and their lives, and that means a massive amount of adjustment for us, too. The modulation from one to the other is generally neither smooth nor seamless, and this complicates things for their parents. You can see the little child still there in that not yet big grown-up, sometimes quite plainly, other times invisibly and sometimes simply imagined. There's also the fact that we're both beginners, (parent and teen) when it comes to them leaving their childhood behind. We're learning all over again every day, every moment, how to do this as well as we can. It's a process of finding ways to embrace, and to celebrate, all they're becoming, but it's a process that's far from pain free, and there's plenty of loss, and letting go to get through, which is harder for some than for others.

The child they once were is still there, though, embedded in today's teenage version of themselves, and tomorrow's, and to be embodied in who they'll become as adults some tomorrow to come. Loss isn't all it seems, and with loss comes gain. Honestly.

TEENS TALK

'There's one thing that helped me really communicate with my mum. It was, like, maybe one or two years ago, I had a pretty deep conversation with her. I just basically told her, look, right, I'm getting older, I'm starting to make my own decisions. We'd sort of had an argument, and I was pretty frustrated. I felt like I was being really restricted, that I wasn't able to make a choice if I wanted to go somewhere or didn't. It was about half an hour later when I'd got a bit calmer: she was in the lounge, and I basically went in there and we talked about it for an hour or so. Once I sort of opened up, she understood. I told her to stop treating me like an 11-year-old, that I can do stuff independently now, and she just became a lot more level-headed when it came to decisions. I'm assuming she told my dad about it, and then they both just became, like, more relaxed about what I'd do.' **Jake (16)**

TALKING STUFF

Take some time to reflect on the positive ways your child has changed as they've moved into and through their teens. What would you celebrate? What are you enjoying? What are you proud of? These may be tiny things, but that doesn't matter; there'll be something there, and almost certainly lots of good things, even if you have to look hard. Tell your teenager about these things and why they mean so much to you.

Are there things you find hard to let go? Is this affecting your relationship now? Maybe you could take some time to reflect on whether you need to do something with any sense of loss – share this with someone, or write something down? Could you talk to your teen about what you find hard?

2. Not listening

> ### TEENS TALK
>
> *What would your advice to a parent be if their teenager wanted to talk about something difficult?*
>
> 'Listen without judgement.' **Esther (18)**
>
> 'You have to be prepared to work with them. Give them the time they need to articulate themselves and always wait for them to finish what they're saying.' **Adam (19)**
>
> 'Listen and take in all the points, and don't see the problem as being the same as your child, if that make sense? See your child as a whole instead of blaming them.' **Keira (18)**

We've already spent some time thinking about listening, but it needs to be here, too, on this list of what we can get wrong as parents, and towards the top of it. It's a big deal for teenagers, and it's a big deal for their parents, too. Listening well was the primary piece of advice teenagers issued for parents to heed – listening with concentration, with patience and an open, non-judgemental mind. Listening around and beyond the issue itself, rather than letting it deafen our ears to the bigger picture, and blind our eyes to the child we love who's bringing it to us. Not doing any and all of these things is the cause of collapse of many a tricky conversation. If you feel this is something you could work on, flick back to Chapter 4 and take another look at the advice given there – focus, show your interest, don't interrupt, empathize, check in with them, ask thoughtful questions. Ask your teen for forgiveness when you get it wrong, and for help to get it right. These last two stand for all of what is to follow, and much of what has gone before.

3. Trying to fix stuff

PARENTS TALK

'As soon as he mentions a test, he doesn't even have to be worried before I'm thinking, "Right, we need to revise!" And I'm wanting to know what it is, and making a plan, and he's saying, "Well, I'm not going to tell you when I've got the next test, because then you'll make my life hell," and you think, gosh, I've just got to try to measure it, because you want them to tell you. And I know he needs to work it out himself, too. And that's just a test! He's only 13, and there hasn't been anything major coming along yet, but what about when it's something bigger? I can't keep trying to take everything in hand for him – and he doesn't even want me to anyway!' **Clare**

We're programmed as parents to leap into the raging torrents of life and rescue our children from harm, and their survival as infants depends on this, though thankfully not many of us actually have to put ourselves in harm's way. But this is one of the things on the 'parenting differently' list when our children become teenagers. What was once a lifesaving intervention when they were small can become an inhibiting hindrance to their growing skills and confidence. It can drag out their dependence or drive them mad, or both. That powerful instinct to fix their problems has to be scrutinized and, more often than not, squashed, as we take a deep breath, and a step back, and stand on the riverbank, watching them find a way to climb out of the torrent themselves.

Hard though it is, especially when their stuff gets more tough as they go through their teens, taking that moment and stepping aside is one of the ways we must grow up our parenting. Try to focus instead on all the listening, validation, empathy and support you can muster, asking the occasional question to help them along if they need it. You may be surprised at what you see them come up with themselves. You may not, of course, and you do need to be ready to jump in and get them, but try to leave it as long as you safely can.

Often, they actually don't want it fixing anyway, or not there and then. They just want to unburden themselves of whatever it might be, pouring it out to a parent. All they want in that moment is someone who cares to listen.

PARENTS TALK

'My advice would be: try not to chip in too quickly, just let them talk, because sometimes they don't want your advice, they just want to talk at someone and if that's me, I can just be talked at for a bit and then not instantly suggest what they should do, and that might be just enough. It's really hard not to jump in and fix it though – even not to fix stuff, just to have an opinion about what they're talking about when they probably don't want your opinion, they just want to vent at someone for a bit. I think probably in the past I tried to maybe get more involved than I needed to when they were just talking about stuff that had happened or having a moan about something, and it didn't necessarily need fixing or advice. It was more them wanting to talk about stuff rather than have me do anything about it.' **Andy**

'One way of getting conversations going with both of mine (11 and 13) is to watch them trying to organize something with their friends, and it's like watching an impending doom of disaster happening. At that point you can gently step in, and you can ask the questions: "How's this going to work? Where are you going to be?" Just gently talk it through with them. And it feels like it's quite non-confrontational, because you're not saying, "No"; you're saying, "How's this going to work?" And that model, I can imagine it working for other things as well, about being prepared to not say no. So, when they want to go out when they're older, working out how will it work, how is it safe, where's the guardrail, you know? But then I haven't had those conversations yet ...' **Kofi**

4. Breach of privacy

PARENTS TALK

'My older son was very insular, and when he became a teenager we went through the stage where he wasn't wanting to talk to me much. I found it extremely difficult. And then when we would talk, it was just me asking questions and then it would become an inquisition, me coming with a list of things like, "What did you do last night? Who did you go with? What did you eat?" I just hated it the way it sounded.' **Giovanna**

Where once we were there all the time, and we had them in plain sight, and had a fair idea of what was going on in their lives, now they're off and out, or lost in an online world, and away from us.

However open and chatty they are, they won't tell their parents everything, and it's important that they don't. They need to have a sense of their own, private lives, and set some boundaries with their parents. In the process of establishing their autonomy and identity, and gaining the ultimate goal of adult independence, teenagers need to have spaces their parents aren't part of, and aren't aware of, and that can be a worry. We know we don't know stuff, but we don't know if it's stuff that matters – stuff that we ought to know.

TEENS TALK

'If you ask for a little bit more privacy, they automatically think you're doing something wrong, and it leads to an argument. They feel like you want more privacy because you're trying to hide something, or you'll try and do something behind their back, and then it just causes a big argument about why you want privacy, and actually you just want a bit of space.' **Talia (15)**

'Sometimes you don't want them to be involved. Sometimes parents can be just too much, like, in your stuff.' **Keisha (15)**

TWENTIES TALK

'I think it can be difficult for teenagers to know where their boundaries are for themselves. I don't know, they might just prefer to spend more time in their room, but they don't know why, they just do, but actually it's like they have a boundary which is "I need to have some personal space that's just my own, and I need to spend some time in it, just to recharge the batteries."' **Josh (23)**

This is one of the aspects of loss and adjustment for parents of teens. In forging a separate life of their own, outside the security of the family tribe, teenagers need to have parts of their lives they have a go at managing themselves. The important thing is to learn, as best we can, to respect their boundaries, and give them space when they need it, while keeping an eye out for risks, doing all we can to embed those protective factors (see Chapter 3), and, most importantly, keeping the channels of communication ever open. One day they'll probably reveal all (although it may take several years before they feel you can cope with the unblemished truth).

For many parents there can be an element of bereavement in the change to the relationship we used to have with our child, and this can affect our relationship with our teenager. Give yourself time to grieve if you need to, talk to others and get help if you need it, as you learn to accept the new (even if, secretly, you much preferred the old) way of things.

PARENTS TALK

'I think the turning point was spending time with friends, computer games and other things rather than with family. For me that was a turning point, when I realized that it was not going to be how it was anymore. This happened when he was, like, 14 or 15. It was a shock, it really was, and I had to go to a counsellor at the time because I was feeling really awful. On a Saturday he would go to a party, and now I look back and I'm, like, "Giovanna, why were you so upset? That's normal!" But the communication just stopped. It was obviously him growing up and him finding out who he was; he's a different personality to me – and my world and my culture and everything.' **Giovanna**

5. Forcing the issue

TEENS TALK

'I personally find it quite difficult when parents overanalyse everything you do and don't really listen when you say everything is fine even if it's not. Sometimes we just need space to figure things out.' **Ashleigh (16)**

'My mum has this horrid habit of, whenever she wants to find out something, always asking me about it in the car, and I don't like it because I feel like I'm trapped there, and I feel like I'm forced into the conversation, and it might be a conversation that I'm, like, not ready to have yet. I might be wanting to tell her, but I've not had a chance to think about what I want to say or how I want to bring the conversation up, and instead she'll just use it when we're in the car, and you have to be forced into the conversation there. Side by side is nice, but sometimes, if emotions rise, taking that little break and coming back and you're more relaxed, it's easier, whereas if you don't know what to say, and you're just kind of stuck in the car, and it just sort of builds the emotions more, and you don't have time to calm down.' **Daisy (16)**

Teenagers talk with frustration about parents who, they feel, try to force them to open up before they're ready. It's a difficult balance. We need them to feel they can share anything with us without judgement, and all the other negative things we're trying to avoid. We need to create the spaces in which this can happen. Sometimes we may need a carefully composed question or comment to prompt them. But it does need to be in their own time, and on their own terms, or they can feel pressured and that can shut conversations down. It also needs to allow them an escape route, in the event it all gets too much, and we may need this, too. Either one of us may need to be able to take a step back, literally or metaphorically, and return to the conversation when we've had chance to process our thoughts and emotions.

TEENS TALK

'I think not forcing a conversation if they feel very uncomfortable is so important. It should be a two-way conversation, and not having them being spoken to, not forcing the parent–child dynamic. Yeah, just not being condescending. Just talking to them casually and, like, if there's something they want to talk about bring it up in a natural sense – instead of it being something quite intimidating, and not so forced, so they feel they can escape it or if they're uncomfortable with it that they can feel like they can tell them.' **Leela (18)**

'Don't force them to open up, just let them know they have a safe space to go to; otherwise it can be overbearing. It might be they're not ready, so just give them a place they know they can go to.' **Adam (19)**

PARENTS TALK

'Mine are just 11 and 13, and I've noticed that when they come in from school, if I have to ask the question, "How was school?" it doesn't go so well, but sometimes they just start and there's no stopping them. So, one thing I've learned is to play the long game and go with the flow, so I don't really worry … well, that's not true, I do worry day to day. I shouldn't; I should just see if they want to chat, and see what happens, see what comes out really and go with it.' **Kofi**

There's a well-known African saying, 'It takes a village to raise a child', and although not so many of us live in villages these days, the principle of involving the wider community of family and friends in conversations with children can be especially valuable in their teenage years. They can provide a safer, less emotionally entangled sounding board; they can filter out what might panic a parent, and get to the nub of an issue, and broker two-way communication when this might otherwise be tricky.

TEENS TALK

'I've got an uncle who's actually much closer to my brother's age than my mum's age, so he's still kind of like an adult, and he knows, yeah, quite a bit, but it's not like speaking to your parents where they'd probably get mad or something.' **Daisy (16)**

PARENTS TALK

'I think there's something massively important about creating a network of relationships around the family where you know you trust their values and you know they'll give good advice. A parent shouldn't be parenting on their own if at all possible. My brother's children have come to me on several occasions, and their parents have said, "Talk to Uncle Aidan about that." I can say things that their parents can't, and likewise my children on a number of occasions have had uncles and aunts they've talked to instead of me.' **Aidan**

TALKING STUFF

- Do you have a network already within your extended family or community, or could you begin to rebuild or create one if not? Who are the family or friends you trust, who share your values, and who your teenager may trust? Can you find opportunities for them to spend time together if they're not already?
- Is your child involved with a youth organization – with sport, music, drama – where there are people to talk to?
- Could you ask your child if there's an adult they feel they could talk to if there was something they felt they couldn't talk to you about? They may not have consciously identified someone yet, and it can help to have an individual in mind if they need them.

Although it's easier to get this established when children are younger, it's never too late. And with all the communication options available to us thanks to technology, the person doesn't even have to live in our neighbourhood.

It can also be useful to remind yourself (and your teen) that you don't actually have to talk – as in sitting down and having a conversation. There are multiple means of communication open to us all now, and some may feel more comfortable than others for some of the difficult stuff. Writing things down, whether in a letter, email, text or message, can give your teenager time to think, to process, and to word it how they want, and it won't get the sort of immediate, perhaps unfiltered response that they might worry about getting in a spoken conversation. There's time to compose a reply, and a reply to that, and so on. Again, this needs to be in their time, when they're ready – prompted and encouraged by you perhaps, with safe non-judgemental spaces provided, but no pressure applied, however desperate you are to find out what's going on, whether they're OK, how you can help.

PARENTS TALK

'My daughter will send me these massive long texts about all sorts of things, and I'll go to her room and say, "Do you want to talk about it?" and she'll go, "No, I just wanted to tell you." Maybe she knew I'd get all involved in it all and go on for ages. So I think I'd say to a teen they can communicate in a way that they want to. If they feel that they want to speak that's great, but if they want to do it in a text, or a letter – however they want to, but the key thing is they should always be able to communicate.' **Kari**

6. Escalation and catastrophizing

TEENS TALK

'Sometimes it builds up, like, something really small happens, and tons of small things, and then it bursts out on each other. Like not taking out the rubbish.' **Kayleigh (15)**

'I feel like parents can get way too aggressive about the conversation, or too strict, and things can get out of hand. Like cleaning your room. My mum has this whole conversation and ends up screaming at me, and then I'm like, now I don't want to clean my room, she's just screamed at me. If she would have asked nicely, and all calmly, I feel like I would have had more motivation to clean my room. If my mum's angry with me, it kind of like makes me want to do the thing she's angry at me about more.' **Kadisha (15)**

'My dad is just, like, you just can't change his mind, so if he believes something he believes it. So if he says it's Wednesday, and I'm, like, "No, it's Tuesday," even if it's Tuesday, he's got it that it's Wednesday, and he'll go to any lengths to prove that it's Wednesday when it's not. And we argue constantly about stupid things. Everything's an argument in my house. He just gets so mad about everything. Very little things. And then I'm really moody, and I don't want to talk to anyone, and I go upstairs and I don't want to come back down.' **Megan (16)**

We've all done it. It started so well. We were calm, rational, reasonable and kind, but somewhere along the lines a simple, straightforward conversation morphed into an infuriating, dramatic and ugly encounter. Was it panic? Or frustration? Or hunger, or tiredness, or the last thread of sanity snapping? Often, the argument that develops isn't about the initial issue at all. It may have tapped into a lurking anxiety about something else altogether. It may have come from the frustration of yet another uncooperative response. It may have been mirroring back their mood. It's not unusual for personalities to clash for a time between a particular parent and a particular child.

PARENTS TALK

'I think it's sometimes difficult not to mirror their side of the argument. If they're starting to get annoyed and shouting, you need to almost step back and refuse it a bit. And that's hard quite often if tempers are raised or everybody's tired about an issue. It's almost our role to not keep adding to it. Sometimes you do just need to stop and step back and calm it down, which can be hard. It's not easy.' **Andy**

There can be so many factors at work on both sides, and we've looked at some for our teens, but as parents we need to try to take the lead on a measured perspective, and regulate our own emotions as much as we can. We have the advantage of age, experience and ready access to our fully developed prefrontal cortex to help us moderate our response. We also need to cut ourselves some slack (we're only human, remember), and apologise, if we need, for our part in it, and try better next time. They may also have crossed a line in what they said or how they said it, and that might need addressing too, but the derailing of a conversation in the present can leave debris on the track that might get in the way of future communication, and this one probably wasn't worth it.

PARENTS TALK

Clare: Sometimes it just pushes your buttons, whatever they might be – and they vary, don't they? – then it's hard to …

Erin: But we are just humans. Sometimes we're hungry, or really tired …

Nisha: And sometimes they just mention something that you've already been worried about. So, I've this underlying worry about my daughter and her schooling, so every time she mentions something I go into a flap, and then that's not helped at all! But it's because it's kind of there, all the time, just below the surface. It sort of triggers you to have that reaction.

TALKING STUFF

If this happens with you, think back to an example and try to replay it in your head:

- What was the issue at the start? If you were to choose the battles you have with your teen, would this have been close to the top of the list?

- What route did you take from the harmless skirmish into a full-blown battle? Was there something else going on for you? For your teen? Was there a bigger issue it ended up being about? If so, was this the best time or place for this to come into play? It may have been, but bringing an important issue into place full of heated emotions and conflict rarely does that important issue any favours for the future. You can always come back to it.

- What was the trigger (if there was one)? What are your buttons (you may know this already) and how and when are they most easily pushed? What can you do to manage them next time?

- Were there practical considerations? Were either of you hungry, tired or stressed about something else?

- What could you do another time to keep the calm?

Something you could try – and if you can do it with your teen, so much the better – is to write down everything that you can end up having an argument about, and everything that drives you mad, and put it all in order of what matters most. Then try as hard as you can going forward to stick to what's near the top, when there's an issue you feel needs addressing, and let go of the ones further down. Perhaps you can work out how to do this together. And remember to be kind to yourself. You're trying.

Catastrophizing is a close relative of escalation. It can have similar consequences, causing the conversational equilibrium to be knocked off balance and the doors of important conversations to slam shut.

PARENTS TALK

Dawn: I get cross when they don't respond appropriately. My 14-year-old keeps getting lots of negative behaviour points at school at the moment, and he's not even vaguely contrite in any way, shape or form, and actually he's acting like it's a badge of honour, and going, 'Yeah, but I'm still overall in credit.' It's, like, that's not the point! So I'm getting more and more irate and I'm, like, 'When are you going to start caring about this?' It's when they don't, well, not necessarily see the error of their ways, but they don't see that actually something might be a bit of a bigger problem than they're making it to be. But then, I had his big brother homeless the other day because he wasn't doing any work for this test, and I was going on and on – he won't pass his exams, he won't get to university, he won't get a job. We just had the most ridiculous argument where literally he was going to end up with no job and sleeping on a park bench, so ...'

Clare: And could you hear yourself doing it?

Dawn: Yes, we both could! And I know it's unfair for me to expect them to think about consequences when they can't in the same way as we can as adults, but I couldn't seem to stop myself. So, it's catastrophizing.

Kari: I overreact as well. I'll drive round areas that aren't great, and I'll be going, 'You know what'll happen if you don't study ...' I try not to, but I'll be like, 'You'll be lucky if you live here!'

Catastrophizing can often happen when something that's said touches an issue that taps into all that powerful parental instinct to jump in and protect our children from harm. This might be big and tough stuff, and for this reason it's all the more important to keep our responses in check, because we really need to keep those conversational channels open. Many of us can find ourselves tumbling down a tunnel of catastrophe at the merest whiff of something potentially treacherous, and before we know it they're right in the worst-case scenario in our heads. However understandable our reaction might be, if a teenager knows they'll get a panicked response from a parent when they broach a sensitive subject, they're much less likely to do so when it really matters, and they need us on side. Read on for more on emotional regulation.

TEENS TALK

'I think parents should be reasonable and practical, where if you tell them about a thing, they shouldn't catastrophize and say the worst that'll happen but give you solutions instead, so then you feel more prepared for that situation.' **Kayleigh (16)**

7. Conflict avoidance

TEENS TALK

'I think the minute a parent shows they want to shy away from a conversation, the teenager will pick up on it and that's when they'll suddenly close off and won't wanna talk about it anymore. They'll have a lot of emotions towards difficult conversations and so it'll take a lot of build up for them to actually speak up. And if it seems that the parents don't want to fully cooperate, or shy away even in the slightest, that's when the teenager is kind of like, "Oh no, I don't feel safe to talk about it anymore." Yeah, I think the response that the parents have towards the conversations is very important.' **Megan (15)**

Very few of us relish a serious clash with anyone, least of all with someone we love more than life itself, but some of us will travel many miles out of our way to avoid a difficult conversation of any sort. We assume the outcome will be negative, the response of the other person even more so, any damage done will be irreparable, and for this reason many parents will tiptoe around a topic that may be tough. For the sake of our teens, though, who do need to talk, we have to find ways to grit our teeth, face our fears and lay ourselves open to getting it wrong, getting that backlash, defensiveness or whatever it is we fear most. We also need to do it for the sake of our relationship with our teen's other parent, if we're co-parenting, because it can load extra pressure on them if we always leave them all the messy stuff to deal with. Talking the tough stuff is harder for anyone who knows they're at the far end of the avoidance spectrum, but the work you put in will pay off. Be brave and just do it, to quote a wise teenager (see below).

TEENS TALK

'My advice for parents would be, I think, I'd just say go for it, no matter how difficult the situation might be for the parent. It's better to talk about it than let it linger. No matter how hard it might be to start the conversation, once the conversation is started it's good to know that it's happened and it's out there, so just be brave and just do it.'
Danielle (17)

PARENTS TALK

'I've found it helps sometimes to be blunt and succinct: "I'm sorry, I have to say/ask this as your dad ..." Keep it short and sweet.'
Matt

TALKING STUFF

If you're someone who goes to some lengths to avoid possible conflict in other contexts – at work, with friends or wider family – it's good to recognize that as a fact, so you can work out the best way to cope with the tough conversations when they come along. Was this the family dynamic when you were growing up? Have there been negative experiences that have put up protective barriers? Is it just how you are?

Can you replay a conversation you've had with your teenager – or one you wanted to have – where you know you skirted around an issue or positively shut it down? What was your biggest fear? How could you have played it differently? What could some other scenarios have looked like if you'd responded in a different way? Can you mentally re-enact it with a happier ending than you feared?

Are there some more comfortable contexts in which a similar conversation could be begun – not necessarily about anything specific, but just to build confidence in stepping into a possible conflict zone, for example something that comes up in a film you're sitting and watching together?

What are the parts of this book you've found most challenging? Is this anything to do with a natural tendency to find this stuff tougher than some? If so, these are the ones to go back to, reread and work on most. Get the people around you to help, if you can. And be kind to yourself. You're trying.

8. Control, lines and limits

TEENS TALK

'My mum likes to have a lot of control, and she has to realize that I'm on a different continent entirely – I'm a full boarder – but every time I'm back she micro-manages everything I do. I just go back at Christmas and summer, and I think when I go back it's still like I'm 13 when I left, so it's very frustrating. My dad not so much, but my mum wants control, and she's very inhibiting of me. In England my life's very different.' **Zain (16)**

'The more controlling and strict your parent is the more secretive you get, and even the smallest things, like, even things that don't even matter, you're just trying not to risk it at all. So then, if you're hiding the small things, you're definitely hiding the big things. And if you hide that, then you're not going to get any education about it; you're just hiding everything. The less open they are about it, the more dangerous it is and the more risks there are by it. You find more ways to hide, you end up basically getting smarter, you get more creative.' **Zahida (15)**

'Parents need to be facilitating their teenagers becoming in control of their own choices rather than pulling that away from them, which is what a lot of parents seem to want to do – trying to maintain that control rather than trying to pass that control over in a meaningful way.' **Flo (20)**

As our children become adolescents and graduate into their separate adult identities, they naturally push at the boundaries we've carefully put in place for their benefit. It's only right that the coercion we had to use when they were young and more vulnerable modulates into consent, and on into gradually taking over the reins of their lives for themselves, but the loss of control we once had over these most precious beings can be hard to let go of. It was how we kept them safe, after all.

PARENTS TALK

'I think for me what I find hardest about having teenagers is the worry about the outside influences. They're exposed to so many more outside influences because they become more self-sufficient, because they're at the age where they're spreading their wings. There's the extra risk of what they're exposed to when they're not five feet away from you, as they had been for most of their life up until that particular point. That's probably the biggest worry, what they're exposed to, now that they're experiencing things outside our control.' **Kofi**

Your role as a parent in keeping them safe and helping them grow into good grown-ups is still vital, but how you go about it must be different to get them through their teens and into adulthood. It's just as important for teenagers as it is for toddlers to know that lines exist for them, to know where they lie, and what will happen if they're crossed. It's also important they know there are ways of behaving and speaking to others that are and are not acceptable in your family and your home. Your values are an essential part of who you are, and how you interact with and inhabit the world. They may (and probably will) kick against any limits you set, it may (and probably will) cause conflict, and sometimes you may (and probably will) be wrong and need to dismantle some of the limits that don't matter as much as others. But the lines do need to be there. Expect resistance, keep calm, be open to discussion (but keep it simple – lengthy negotiations with a teenager that rely on logic and reasoning don't always work so well), but remember they need you to be in charge. They may just not show it. In the instability of existence as a teenager, without someone reliable and who loves them still in charge (even if increasingly less so), the world would become very scary.

This is all yet another thing to consider in the shifting sands of parenting teenagers, requiring your constant vigilance, openness and patience. Where that balance lies between being too strict or being too lenient, when you need to hold on or hold off, when you need to begin to trust them, is down to you and your child, but you are still the parent. Some good advice is to keep the boundaries focused on their safety, and their development of skills and confidence, throwing in a bit of fun and friendship, too. It should definitely not be about keeping a grip on your control, understandable though that can be. How good are they at judging risk, problem-solving and coping under pressure? How reliable are their friends? What would the benefits be to them doing/ having/going to whatever/wherever it is? What safeguards can you put in place? What would your reasons be for saying yes – or no? Is this more about you than them? (Sometimes it can be.) What will the consequences be if they don't stay within the lines and limits?

TEENS TALK

Connor, Jake, Daisy and Zain are all 16–17-year-olds.

Connor: I get really fed up with useless punishments. My parents used to do that a lot. Take away something valuable to – what's it? – scold the behaviour. Maybe it works at a young age but once you get older it's just …

Jake: It just makes the child more frustrated …

Zain: Causes resentment …

Me: So what would your advice be, because obviously there have to be some sort of boundaries – lines you can't cross. What are the best consequences for older teens?

Jake: I think it depends on the seriousness of what happens, because, like, if you got suspended from school or something you can't just have a conversation, but if you've just like, I dunno, gone out when you're not supposed to …

Connor: Or got back home a bit late …

Jake: Yeah, you should just have a conversation, because there's always a reason behind it, you know.

Zain: I think that punishment at our age is intrinsic. Maybe when I was younger, like, my dad used to take away my computer when I was naughty, and that was more a, 'Don't do this or this will happen.' But now if I don't get a good enough grade I feel disappointed in myself, you know, I've let my dad down, you know. There's no punishment now; they're just disappointed in you. It's a lot harder than 'I'm taking your computer away for a month.' I think at our age we've matured enough to know that.

Connor: Especially punishment after talks; that just incentivizes you not to talk to them. You've made the effort to try to explain, and then they just punish you anyway.

Daisy: To be honest, my parents don't really punish me anymore. Just more like long, long lectures from my mum, which is punishment in itself.

There do need to be consequences if the agreed boundaries are breached, and these need to be clear, but they'll be different for different families, and different ages of children, and different personalities. What would be realistic to implement and enforce? What would create a battle that wouldn't be close to the top of your list of those worth fighting? Or is this one too important? Whatever it is, try to stay calm, and try to help them understand the impact on others, the importance of trust and why it matters to know they're safe. Here's a bit of advice from Sam.

TWENTIES TALK

'I think the punishment should fit the crime. So, if you've been rude to someone, then they should be communicating why it was rude, how much it's upsetting them, how that would make them feel if someone had said that to them.

'I think going straight to the most drastic response, that's the issue, because they might have made a mistake; it might not have been intentional – they didn't know they were doing anything wrong. There could be a reason behind their behaviour, and you need to probe a bit and find out what might lie behind it, rather than just what you see. I had friends whose parents would take their phone away and they didn't really know why. I think sometimes parents do that to establish dominance. "Hey, look, I still control you. You do what I say." I don't think that's healthy at all. Not for a teenager, not at all.

'I think it's different if they're consistently ignoring you about that situation. Then you should take that further, be a bit more drastic.

'You can flip it on its head. Say if your kid was late back and didn't let you know, you could say how it made you feel – "Imagine if I said I'd be home at this time, and I wasn't, and you didn't hear from me, would you be worried? That's exactly how I feel when you don't come back on time as well, so we both need to." It's not just saying to the kid, "You need to do this." It's saying, "Let's together make a plan about how we're going to deal with this in the future." Because I think the best way to frame it is, "Let's us together solve this, as a team."

'You're then taking the issue out of the person and it's so much easier to deal with. If it's something I've done wrong, and they say, "You're doing this, don't do this," pointing the finger literally or metaphorically, it's a lot more difficult for me then to acknowledge there's an issue and not get really defensive. Whereas if you separate the issue from the person, and you try and say, "Why don't we together deal with this?" then it's so much easier, and the communication is so much easier as well.' **Sam (21)**

9. Emotional regulation

TEENS TALK

'One thing that's quite frustrating is when they tell you "I won't get angry", and then they just always get angry, get ballistic, about whatever it is. It almost encourages you not to tell them stuff.' **Connor (16)**

'I think if parents react on a large scale with a lot of emotion, it can sort of scare off the teenager and make them worry that they've said something wrong or that they've overshared, and that sort of builds that wall. Yeah, I think that if you're worried about how your parent's gonna react then it makes you worry for the next time and the time after that. It means you'll need more courage next time.' **Megan (15)**

'My advice for parents would be to be prepared for anything, because if you act shocked or repulsed or have any kind of negative reaction, then that can make the teen feel unsafe emotionally, or insecure, and that would encourage them not to want to have these kinds of chats with their parents again.' **Adam (19)**

'I think parents need to think: "My child's already in a bad place, and whatever's happening I don't want to make that worse for them. I should be there for my child, because they're my child and I love them and I want them to be happy, and if they need to talk to me about something I shouldn't overreact or make the situation worse, because otherwise it's going to be worse down the road, because if I overreact and get annoyed at them, then they won't talk to me about other stuff, and that might then lead to bad things in the future." So I think parents should just always know they need to be there.' **Hannah (17)**

Sometimes it's the topic that makes keeping our emotions in check a challenge, sometimes it's the attitude, or the words that come flying our way, and the pain this can cause us – something deeply cutting flung in your face by a furious daughter, or a son telling you're the worst parent on the planet and they hate you. Or it may have been the frustration of yet another blank refusal to comply with a boundary they'd agreed very happily just the day before, or to do something you know is in their best interests, or just to come down for dinner.

Just as our teenagers struggle with managing their emotions and responses, so can their parents, but they have hormones, neurological rewiring and life inexperience to blame. We just have our parental instinct to panic, our normal human capacity to feel hurt, and antagonized, and our individual baggage of buttons from our own childhood, sensitive to particular pushes. But we do need to try our very best to find a way to take all this in hand, because we're the adult, and the parent, and everyone involved in this needs us not to lose it. There are so many big, strong and new emotions whirling around for a teenager, they need to know they can rely on their parents, if at all possible, for a bit of emotional stability, consistency and predictability, especially if they want to talk about something heavy.

TEENS TALK

'I think a lot of parents don't realize how unpredictable they are. Because if, say, the child gets into something, like a tough situation, it'll be, like, "If I go back and I tell them, I'll be thinking, 'What are they going to do, how are they going to react?'" So before anything happens like that, I think parents should try and create, like, just reassurance in a way, then people won't think their parents are so unpredictable they won't trust them.' **Rachel (16)**

'Parents are incredibly unpredictable, even sometimes backwards – like, my mum would kick my head in (not literally) if I got a detention one day, but if I were to get arrested for a very bad reason, they'd probably support me. I don't know what it is about parents, but they tend to be so backwards about some of the things sometimes, and I don't think any of us can ever really know why.' **Jamal (16)**

So, here are ten dos and don'ts, but add to these anything you know helps you already:

1. *Don't panic.* When we panic, or have any sort of stress reaction, we let our amygdala take charge, the home of our fight–flight–freeze response, when what we need is our sensible prefrontal cortex to bring a measured and rational perspective. However, panicking is a natural response to a threat we perceive to our child. This is one of the reasons for taking a breath, even walking away for a moment (though promising not to be gone for long), to give yourself time to calm yourself down and shift your thinking from the back to the front of your brain.

2. *Don't jump to conclusions.* Try to stick to the issue at hand and not plummet to the worse-case scenario, or make assumptions about your child or their friends. And try not to judge either. It will help you manage your emotions, and cope with theirs, if you take your time – and their time – to find out the full story. Give it all your best listening.

3. *Don't take it personally.* Teenagers can say some incredibly cutting things and display an attitude that speaks disparaging volumes, but try not to let this get in the way of the matter at hand, or of your relationship with them. It's not that they don't necessarily mean it – in that moment they probably mean every word/grim look – but the next moment they probably won't. Try to remember they're a work in progress. That doesn't, however, mean you have to take being spoken to rudely and disrespectfully. Just try to stick to the boundaries of behaviour in your family in your response, rather than letting the pain you feel that the child you love appears to despise you take charge.

4. *Don't bear a grudge or store up a grievance.* Again, within the boundaries you've laid out, you have to let things go, at some point at least. Remember, again, your teenager is under development.

5. *Don't get distracted by wanting to win.* This isn't about winners or losers – or about control or loss of control – but that can become what drives a discussion, and it'll almost always lead it astray. If it is, rein it in, and remember what it's about.

6. *Acknowledge your feelings.* This is easier said than done in the heated moment of a teenage encounter, but being able to examine what you're feeling, and what you think might lie behind it, can enable you to disentangle your own stuff from theirs, and not let it get in the way of being the best you can be as their parent here and now.

7. *Acknowledge their feelings.* Being able to focus on how they feel about whatever it is – whatever they're saying or doing, or whatever's been going on – can enable your parental empathy to take charge of your own emotions in that moment, and start to uncover anything lying behind the presenting issue.

8. *Stick to the matter at hand.* Try to keep your (and their) focus on whatever the issue in question is, and keep coming back to it if you start to get side-tracked.

9. *Take one issue at a time.* One thing can lead to another very easily, and there may be a whole load of difficult things lined up waiting for you to uncover, but you'll both fare better if you take them one by one and don't let the conversation get swamped, or the initial issue get side-lined.

10. *Try to stick to 'I' statements rather than 'you' statements.* This takes discipline, and can be hard, but not only can it help you manage your own emotions, it can stop a conversation escalating into a heated encounter with a defensive response that shuts things down. It also helps them do a bit of mentalizing and see things from your perspective. An example might be, 'I get really worried when you don't let me know if you're running late,' rather than, 'You never let me know …' And that's another one – try not to make something into an absolute: 'You always/never etc.'

10. Different parents, different families

TEENS TALK

'I'm close to my mum, but I'm close to my dad as well, and I can go and talk to him about things and he's less strict with me than my mum. If I wanted to go out or something, I'd go to my dad instead of my mum, because my mum would stop me, but my dad's like, "Let her go".' **Ellie (17)**

'I tend to go to my mum about more things, because my dad lives in a different place. They're separated. I don't speak to my dad that much – well, I dunno, I only ever go to him when I don't want to speak to my mum about something, because I know how my mum will react is different from how my dad would react. So I choose which parent I'd talk to about what depending on their reaction to it I guess.' **Kyle (16)**

Mums, dads, what's the difference? And if there is any, does it matter? And more importantly, does it matter when we're talking to our teenagers? Whatever your views on gender stereotyping, societal expectations, heteronormative assumptions of parenting, and so on, the fact is that any two people, whatever their gender, parenting any one teenager, will do this differently, and that can be a good thing. It provides a teenager with complementary perspectives and approaches, and it allows them to choose which parent to talk to about what. Unsurprisingly, there were various topics that teenagers said they'd pick either their mum or their dad to talk to about, and these generally fell into two different categories: which one would give them the more relevant and useful information or advice, or which one would give them the more favourable response, especially when it came to getting permission to do things.

Different approaches can also make things more complicated and challenging, however, if they become divisive or inconsistent, and undermine stability for your teenager. And it may be complex when parents are no longer together. But whether you're under the same roof, co-parenting relatively amicably from different homes, or parallel parenting completely separately, it will hugely benefit your teenager if you can reach an agreement, between yourselves as well as with your teen, on some of the bigger issues, boundaries and consequences, and also agree not to worry too much over the lower-stakes stuff. If agreement isn't possible, a reasonable compromise is still good. Trying to keep the welfare and best interests of your teenager firmly at the centre of any discussion is vital, including how and where that discussion takes place, though I realize for some there are enormous odds stacked against this.

PARENTS TALK

'I think, funnily enough, there are more disagreements between the two of us really than with our 14-year-old, on our relative approaches. I think my wife's more of the approach of "I will do everything for her, I will take her everywhere, I will wrap her up in cotton wool" to a certain extent, to make sure that nothing will happen to her, ever. And I don't necessarily agree with that approach. I think she's getting older: she needs to get some independence, you know; at some point she's going to go to uni or whatever. She can't be completely incapable of actually handling life as an independent person. So, I think I would probably like her to be a bit more independent, whereas my wife would like her to be much less independent. And then our daughter is probably sitting somewhere in the middle – there are some things she would like to do, and some things she things she absolutely doesn't want to be able to do and is quite happy to be ferried around left, right and centre. So, it's a difficult one really.' **Dave**

'I don't know how good I was at having conversations with my children before I remarried. To be honest, I tended to feel, you know, as long as they were fed, clothed and going to school on time, and not too miserable, I felt that I was doing the job that was intended. My second wife is an incredible person to my children because she's very sensitive; she's a very skilled parent. She's just born to be a mum, and she's really close to her own children. It was a different dynamic for us, of course, than most step-families, because my wife had died, so there wasn't another mum around. But we came at things very differently sometimes. We had instances where I'd think, you know, they'll be fine, this won't do them any harm, they should wrestle with it and face it themselves, and she'd say, "No, I think this is tough," and she was right.' **Aidan**

TALKING STUFF

If your teenager's other parent is around and involved, have you encountered differences of opinion on any of the tough stuff? How and where has that come out? Were you able to reach an agreement or compromise, or are there still issues that are unresolved? If so, how can you best, between you, address these?

Where there are differences of opinion, try your best to air these off-stage, and not in front of your teenager, and especially not just at the time when something important is on the table. Prepare ahead as much as you can. You could use this book as an initial checklist for some of the topics you may encounter, if you haven't already.

If it's hard to reach an agreement between you, is there someone you both trust you could talk to together who might help you reach an acceptable consensus that will be in the best interests of your teenager, including how this may need to change as they grow older?

11. Rupture, repair and forgiveness

PARENTS TALK

'I think most parents are doing the best they can with the information they have. And you have to sort of go, "Oh yeah, and there's all that stuff in the background as well ..." I think forgiving yourself as a parent is important. Somebody wise once said to me, "Never take all the credit for your kids, but never take all the blame either. You're doing the best you can".' **Jim**

Almost 70 years ago now, paediatrician and psychoanalyst D. W. Winnicott coined that wonderfully reassuring phrase, the 'good enough' parent. His theory was that, as long as an infant felt safe and loved, they could not only cope with but also forgive their parents' inevitable imperfections. The important thing was to rebuild and repair that connection as soon as possible after it got bruised or broken.

What counts for tiny babies is just the same for teenagers, although it rarely feels quite so simple. If you've read this far, be assured (if you need to be) that you're a parent who loves their teenager, who wants them to be safe and who's doing their best, and wanting that best to be better. You won't always get it right, but you also won't always get it wrong, and the balance for the average parent is hugely in favour of the former. The important thing is what you do when the latter does happen, and a difficult conversation doesn't end well.

PARENTS TALK

'I'm not an expert at this – my kids will tell you very quickly how completely useless I am – but I would say if you can maintain the relationship, you've always got a chance. Whatever happens, you know, there's always a way back – but don't fall out more than you can help.' **Jim**

The first thing to note is the end of that particular conversation isn't the end of the story. The second thing is, whatever went wrong, whatever was said, whatever the issue, wherever the fault (and it's often not helpful to frame it in terms of fault anyway), the onus is on the parent to rebuild the bridges, and the bridges are always more important than whatever it was that sent them flying. Your relationship is more precious than anything else going on, and protecting it matters more than any issue, whatever its magnitude. That doesn't mean there won't necessarily be things that need dealing with, but facing these within a restored relationship will be much more effective (and much less exhausting).

Trying to set things right when they've gone wrong also sends some incredibly valuable messages to your child. It shows them that making amends is possible after someone makes a mistake. It throws them a rope to climb out of any mess they created themselves, in the heat of the moment, or equally going back over some time. It shows them that forgiveness is something of value to seek, to give and to receive. More important than anything, it tells them they matter more to you than anything else in the world.

PARENTS TALK

Have you been able to find ways to repair and come back to a conversation that's gone haywire, and if so how?

'We always apologize if we've got it wrong, not necessarily straight away, but soon after. We've got quite good at agreeing to disagree as they've got older.'

'Accept sometimes you handle things badly as a parent and apologize for your part. Explain you may have handled things clumsily, but you'd like to listen and understand without falling out. Validating your teens' feelings helps, too.'

'When there's miscommunication, we try to meet it with forgiveness.'

'Make a drink and apologize first for you reaction, even if you feel they were wrong first. Show that it's the adult way to approach difference.'

'I think that apologizing when you as a grown-up probably do need to apologize makes a massive difference – when they see an adult apologize for shouting or for overstepping the mark or for saying something in a jokier tone of voice than you should have done, it makes them feel like, "Oh right, blimey!"'

'Leave time for them to calm down and then talk as if nothing happened earlier – don't hold a grudge against them. They normally know they were wrong.'

'If it's hard to remain calm, leave the room, take space. And set expectations when you come back to it about respect and listening, which always get lost the first time around for some reason.'

'I apologize for jumping to conclusions, or if they didn't feel heard. Often, I leave the conversation for a time and then find a time with proper space to talk. Sometimes, I allow my husband to take up the conversation in a different way at another time.'

'I do apologize. And expect them to. Reset. Find a compromise – even a bargain. And you have to let some things go.'

'We let things calm down and revisit the conversation when everyone has had time to sort themselves out. We explain the importance of having to have the conversation – despite how difficult it might be – and make sure that we are all calm and all have a chance to speak.'

'We find the time. We don't like things going unresolved and that's a key value we've had since they were little. We know we are going to reconnect the relationship and carry on the conversation later. We will often pause a conversation and affirm love and the reasons behind the pause. With stepparenting that sometimes means a week or two later. Only on the big stuff, and normally it's more about the relationship the second time.'

Make it happen as soon as you can – but also give it the time it needs. It may be too soon. Keep it simple – but also give it the space it needs. It may take more unravelling. Be patient. And be kind to yourself, forgive yourself and let yourself start again. Life is full of endings and new beginnings, and never more so than when you find yourself being the parent of a teenager.

And finally ...

Some wise advice for a teenager from a twenty-something on talking the tough stuff:

'Work out exactly what you want to say and how you want to say it, because if you just launch in, you open yourself up to miscommunication.

'If you don't know already, try to work out what language would work best for your parents, because obviously you can say something to one person and say exactly the same thing to another person and they're going to take it completely differently. You have to speak to your parents in a language that they're going to understand.

'Try to express to them the emotion this problem's making you feel and ask their advice and how you should deal with it, because most parents want to be able to help their kids, but if they don't know how it's making you feel, they just know that there's an issue, then they can't accurately deal with it. So, it's not just communicating the issue; it's how it's making you feel as a result of it.' **Sam (21)**

And a last word from a dad:

'Your parents aren't actually hatching a plan to ruin your life. Probably ... yeah ... [there are a] few exceptions ... but probably your parents don't actually want to ruin your life ...' **Jim**

PART 2
TALKING THE
TOUGH STUFF

A word before we move on

The second part of this book looks at seven more sensitive, complex and risky areas of teenage life. Before we move on to specifics, however, there are some general points that are relevant to some, many or all of these. They also all need extra-big doses of all that Part 1 has imparted.

- *Self-esteem.* Teenagers facing any of these issues will have an extra-hard knock of their self-esteem, self-worth and self-confidence. All of these areas of adolescent life can leave young people feeling incredibly vulnerable, confused and socially isolated, at a time when all this is felt so much more intensely than at any other time of life. They need to know you're on their side now more than ever.

- *Siblings.* Look out for siblings and take time to make space to talk and to listen to them, too. Having a child who needs your support, and vigilance, can inevitably take attention away from other children in the family – and having a sibling who's struggling can take a big toll in itself. They may feel they need to protect them, they may want to make it better and not know how, they may take responsibility on themselves to be the one to support you, or to be the 'good' one who doesn't cause you any bother. Check in with them regularly, take time just to be together and take time out as a family as much as is possible, just to do some of the things you enjoy.

- *Co-parents.* All of these issues have the potential to destabilize the most steady of co-parenting partnerships, whether you're doing this together or separately. You'll both be experiencing powerful, protective emotions, high levels of anxiety and stress, and may well see a different route through and out of whatever it is. Communication between yourselves is just as important as with your teens. You may have to agree to disagree about various things, but if you can do this away from your teen, and come to them standing together on whatever common ground you can find, it will help them cope so much better.

- *Friends.* What if your child is the friend of someone experiencing these things? Teenagers often share tough stuff first with a friend, and as we've seen, those friendships have an intensity in adolescence that can lead to that leaned-on friend feeling an enormous burden of responsibility for the wellbeing – and even the life – of someone they care for deeply. And they may well be sworn to secrecy. All of these topics do need to be opened up within family conversations, as part of all your best Part 1 work to make communication comfortable, so that – hopefully – a teenager troubled about their best friend can feel safe to unburden at home.

TEENS TALK

Me: That must have been really hard, knowing your friend was hurting herself.

Sofia: Yeah, I really didn't know how to deal with it. It was kind of like a very big thing. She was literally cutting names into her stomach of the people who bullied her and stuff, and she used to show me in PE, going, like, 'Sofia, I've done it again,' and I'd say 'Why? Why are you doing names?' kind of thing. 'Why are you doing this?' She goes: ''Cos then they'll never forget what they've done to me.' I felt like I couldn't do anything for her except, like, be there for her.

Me: Did you feel that you could talk to anybody about her? Were you able to talk to your mum?

Sofia: Oh no. No. It would have betrayed her trust. As soon as you tell somebody else, you lose that connection, and I was kind of …

well, I mean, we are talking about very deep things, and to keep it deep, you are probably the only person keeping this person alive.

Me: And you were how old then at that time?

Sofia: She started when we were 12, I think.

- *You.* Looking after yourself is something I keep coming back to, and that's because it's essential, not just for your teen, and your family, but because you matter in all this, too. You're that vital frontline of support in whatever this is, and that can take an enormous toll. Try to make sure you eat, sleep and restore yourself as well as you can. Find your own networks of friends you can trust with this stuff, tap into professional support where you need expertise and always do your best to practise kindness, compassion and forgiveness with yourself.

7

TALKING THE TOUGH STUFF OF SEXUALITY AND GENDER IDENTITY

'For parents, it's really not the end of the world.
There are different paths to success and happiness.
And people don't choose to be gay. Nobody will
choose to be different, d'you know what I mean?
Nobody wants their life to be harder, and no one
wants their child's life to be harder. For me, I don't
think it's affected me, though. It doesn't feel like
this huge big deal to me.'

Grace

WHO'S WHO?

Grace is in her late twenties and lives with her partner, **Rachel**, in the English Midlands.

Lukasz Konieczka is Director of the Mosaic LGBT+ Young Persons' Trust, a youth organization in London www.mosaictrust.org.uk.

Allan Sadac, MBA, LMFT, is a Marriage and Family Therapist practising in California, and author of *Parenting Your LGBTQ+ Teen: A Guide to Supporting, Empowering, and Connecting with Your Child'* (Rockbridge Press, 2021) www.sadacbehavioralhealth.com.

What do we mean by ...?

Sexuality and gender identity can sometimes find themselves confused and conflated in the minds of parents, along with the rest of society, but they're two separate tracks. Sexuality is interpersonal – who we are romantically and sexually attracted to. Gender is personal – how we see ourselves as an individual in relation to notions of female and male. They can sometimes overlap and align, but often not, and in any case binary concepts of male and female, straight and gay, fall very far short of the colourful, rich and – for some – fluid nature of all this encompasses.

Me: How old were you, do you think, when you became aware you were gay?

Grace: I think I'd always known that I was attracted to girls – certainly before the age of ten I'd say. But I never thought then I must be gay.

Me: Is that because you didn't have the language for it, or just that it wasn't an issue?

Grace: I think maybe a bit of both actually. I didn't feel a need to self-identify as such, so it didn't feel like a big issue to me. But also,

I still fancied boys, but not in the same way as I fancied girls. So, I dunno. I sort of recognized that I had those feelings, but I didn't feel a need to say, 'Right, this is who I am.'

Me: Was there a point when you thought, 'Actually this is who I am,' or was it a gradual thing?

Grace: Yeah, it was probably a bit more gradual, because even up to the age of 16 I still liked boys, fancied boys, went out with boys – that kind of thing – but my first serious relationship was with a girl at the age of 16.

Me: So, was that when you knew that was who you were?

Grace: Yeah, I think that was probably when I knew, actually, because that was the point I felt like, 'Oh, I'll probably never be with a boy now. I'm never going to have these feelings that I have towards this girl as I would do for a boy.'

What's in a word?

'I just think what really matters is how I live my life, not talk about my life in terms of a label, if that makes sense? Unless there's a practical difference, and a positive difference that it makes to my life, what's the point of obsessing over labels, you know? It doesn't bother me. I think that, with my parents' generation, they feel they get a better understanding if it's put in a neat category, but I'd say my friends never really put any pressure on me to say one way or another.'
Grace

LGBTQ+ is the most widely used acronym to cover all these possibilities. It stands for Lesbian, Gay, Bisexual, Transgender, Queer (or Questioning). Queer is generally used as an umbrella term for individuals whose orientation and identity is not heterosexual and/or not cisgender (cisgender, or cis, means someone whose gender identity fits with the sex they were assigned at birth – i.e. someone born with female sexual organs who also identifies as female, and the same for male), although the word is sometimes used differently within the LGBTQ+ community. The plus sign encompasses the multitude of variations on these themes.

It's so much more than vocabulary, but a way of understanding all the many possibilities. There's a fluidity and creativity in the language around all things LGBTQ+, and it continues to evolve, without yet gaining universal agreement about the definition of many terms.

'If they use a term you don't know, just feel free to ask them what they understand by it. Don't memorize it and start searching online, because what your child means by it might be different from what the official definition is. And if you get it wrong, trust me, young people have immense levels of patience. We all slip on things on occasion, but they know when you're being genuine, and when you're really making an effort.' **Allan Sadak**

Language has power. It can stigmatize and marginalize. It can, equally, demystify identities and empower individuals with a positive sense of who they are. Accuracy matters more to some than others, and may matter more to a teen at some points than others, especially if they're still discovering their orientation and identity. Parents of LGBTQ+ teens should listen and learn, and keep listening and relearning, asking what their teen would prefer, and asking forgiveness if and when they slip up. It will mean a lot to your teen that you respect who they are, and do what would make them feel most comfortable and accepted.

'I find that teenagers are most hurt when they feel there's a direct insensitivity to how they identify. And so, for parents it may be having an openness in wanting to learn, wanting to be better and understanding that we make mistakes. The reality is for many parents they've spent X number of years with a certain mental construct in how they see their teenager, and so it's going to take some time to adjust, but as long as they're continuing to display efforts of wanting to learn, wanting to be sensitive and apologizing if they get it wrong – "I'm sorry, you're right, I totally forgot, I'm trying to be better, I want to get it right."' **Lukasz Konieczka**

Gender matters

Everyone has a gender identity. While gender identity is our experience and understanding of our gender, gender expression is how we express that identity to the world – our clothes, our name, our preferred pronoun, and so on. For some, these match the gender assigned to them at birth, which will have been based on their biological sex (though this is also not binary, with intersex people presenting a wide variety of biological combinations). For some, however, this label doesn't fit. A tiny baby boy or girl might emerge into their teens with a growing sense that their body just doesn't align with who they are, and who they are just doesn't sit comfortably with society's (or their parents') expectations of them as male or female. For every teenager figuring out who they are, and how to make it all make sense, there are generally parents puzzling their way through it all, too.

'I have my share of parents who are struggling to understand what's happening with their teenager, and trying to figure out how best to support them. It's definitely a very challenging time for many parents. How can they best explore this, and at the same time understand their own sense of how they're reacting, and what it means to them? And for teenagers, it's a very, very challenging time in their life to try to figure this all out, on top of all those other teenage things they're going through.' **Allan Sadac**

The most helpful approach is to remain open to all possibilities, and openly accepting of your child as who they are, and the identity – or identities – they may be exploring, without trying to define, determine or pin anything down, definitely not before they're ready to themselves.

'We need to have conversations that give young people space and mental capacity to explore. Some of them may be experiencing gender fluidity, so for them that might be changing on a weekly basis, or daily basis, which is also important to recognize, and can be confusing for them.' **Lukasz Konieczka**

'Parents – or other family members – will sometimes say things that sound a bit flippant, a bit dismissive, like, "Oh, maybe it's a phase." That's the classic one that isn't super-helpful to hear. I mean, there might be some truth to it, like, sometimes teenagers say things and they mean it at that time but then it changes. But no one wants to feel like they're not being taken seriously at the point that they're feeling something. So, never assume that things are a phase, and never say you're too young to feel how you feel.' **Grace**

What's the difference?

'I think I always had a strong and acute awareness of the fact my parents did grow up in a completely different generation from me, and I always took that as a reason to not expect too much of them too soon.' **Grace**

This is one of the areas of life parents may find themselves out of step with their teens. When most parents were teenagers themselves, to have peers who were openly gay was not the norm, and gay public role models were few, though things were beginning to change. People experiencing a difference between their sexual and gender identities had also existed, but even until recently an outward expression of this has been viewed with suspicion or embarrassment, and cross-dressing characters on big and small screen have been objects of comedy.

Young people now, however, live with an ever-increasing openness to embracing difference and evading binary definitions, with curiosity and an increased confidence to explore who they are and how they express that. Positive portrayals by strong role models are evident across all forms of media. Gay pride has been mainstreamed, trans rights issues headline national news and the agenda has shifted out of all recognition within the lifetime of most parents. However, society is still riven with firmly gripped prejudices and deeply rooted phobias, alongside fears of being shamed for questioning aspects of the new norm. The times they are a-changing, but sadly for LGBTQ+ teens – and their parents – they cannot yet rely on a lifetime of acceptance.

'When it comes to trans young people, we know that rejection of the trans child is far more frequent than rejection of the LGB [lesbian, gay or bisexual] child. There's a study showing that social transitioning alone can cut suicidality in young trans people by half. Social transitioning* is vital in self-determination, which is always an important cornerstone of development for teenagers. But when we look at society, and what's going on in the media, trans young people see and hear a lot of anti-trans narrative, which does have an impact on their ability to formulate a sense of self, and sense

---

*Social transitioning involves a person letting the people around them know what gender they identify as, which can be expressed in various ways, including through changes to names, clothing or pronouns. Medical transitioning involves making physical alterations, including through hormone therapy or surgery.

of self is important in order to be able to develop positive mental health. I think it puts a huge strain on some parents to be constantly defending their child from the world around them, because that's exactly what's going on.' **Lukasz Konieczka**

What's the issue?

Largely as a result of this, statistically across both sides of the Atlantic, LGBTQ+ teens are at higher risk of any and all of the serious issues covered in this second part of the book – bullying, abusive relationships, high-risk sex, depression and anxiety, substance use, eating disorders, self-harm, suicide. For parents with LGBTQ+ teens each of these sections has potential relevance, and though, equally, none may apply to your child, they should all be on your radar as you talk to, listen to, live alongside and love your child through their teens and into adulthood.

Creating a safe conversational space

All that Part 1 stuff really can help with Part 2, but there are some things specific to the LGBTQ+ teen to be mindful of, and these start with you, and others in and around your family. Examine your own views and be ruthlessly honest. You grew up in a different time, and it would be surprising not to have prejudices, however deeply buried, but as much as possible bring these to light, challenge them in yourself and in others and do all you can to communicate openness and acceptance, so your teen will know they can come to you safely, when they're ready. And it's very important to wait till they're ready, and allow them that process, however strong your suspicions, and however much you might want to ease that process for them.

'I think we sometimes forget how the things that we say, the TV shows that we're drawn to, the topics that we talk about with other people, they speak to who we are, and what we value, and what's important to us. And so, when teenagers see their parents talking in a loving and compassionate way about LGBTQ+ rights, talking about the struggles and displaying sensitivity, I think those can be such great ways to convey that message of safety and openness and supportiveness.' **Allan Sadac**

The coming out conversation

Me: When did you first have that conversation with your parents?

Grace: I'd always been really close to my mum and we'd talk about everything, so the first person I told about it was my mum, but it was only when I had that first relationship. I wanted to say to her, 'Look, my life has changed. It's important. I want to tell you about it.'

Me: That must have really helped that you'd got that close grounding in the relationship with your mum.

Grace: Yes. It did help definitely, because I was scared. Don't get me wrong, I was scared to tell her.

Me: What were you scared of?

Grace: I was scared that she wouldn't know what to make of it and she'd ... I dunno, maybe it was a little bit of judgement I was afraid of. But I never had some of the very strong fears that I know many people have, like, 'I know my parents will disown me; they're gonna kick me out.' That never crossed my mind as to something that could happen. But I still had the worry of what's my mum gonna make of this? Am I gonna be judged? Is this gonna change how she thinks of me? I remember the day I told her. I was very, very nervous about it.

Me: So how did you go about it?

Grace: When I told my mum it was very late at night. I didn't deliberately plan it as such, but you know when you want to tell someone something and you feel like you can't contain it? I said, 'Look, I've got something to tell you,' and she said, 'What is it?' and then I kind of bottled it. I thought, 'Oh, actually, I'm not ready to say it out loud!' Then my mum got really upset.

Me: She must have been really worried about what you were going to say.

Grace: She was, and I could see that she was thinking the worst-case scenario. And then she asked me if I was pregnant, and I thought it was hilarious, because it was the last thing she should have been worried about!

Me: Did it make you laugh?

Grace: Yeah, it did. I was, like, 'No!' I was cracking up, and it kind of calmed me down a bit, which was quite nice, because I thought whatever I tell her now is not going to be as bad as that for her. Eventually, after some more of her saying, 'Please tell me what it is,' I said, 'Right, I'm seeing somebody,' and then I didn't have the guts to say, 'This is who it is and it's a girl.' But she actually guessed. She said, 'Oh. Is it this person?'

Me: And what happened next?

Grace: Because it was late at night, we just both went to bed and didn't talk about it. I remember feeling quite anxious, like, what is she making of this? I dropped this bombshell and then nothing. And the next day we didn't really talk about it. I just went to school, and I think for about a week after that conversation the dynamic felt very weird between us.

Me: Like a big elephant in the room?

Grace: Yeah, exactly like that. We were talking but it wasn't in the playful, relaxed, jokey way that we'd normally talk. It felt a bit stilted. And I remember everything came to a head when she was in her room and I walked in. I can't remember how it came up, but it did. My mum burst into tears, and then so did I, you know? So, then we had another conversation, and that was in many ways more important than the initial, 'This is what's going on with me.' The conversation we had the week later was the bit where we both were very honest, and she was able to express how she felt about it.

Me: And how did she feel about it?

Grace: She said to me that she wasn't ashamed – and I didn't really need her to say that because I knew she wasn't – but she was struggling with it. She said to me as a parent you have this vision of what your child's life is going to be like in your head, and you have these goals and these aspirations for them, and you want them to live a life that as stress-free and happy as possible. And her worry was that because of being gay my life was going to be harder.

Me: Because of social acceptance?

Grace: I think so. Social acceptance, having kids – which there are a lot of difficulties with practically, sociologically I suppose. She was worried about, 'Am I going to be a grandparent?' which she doesn't have to worry about now because my brother has two kids, so that's fine. I was like, fair enough, but I did try to persuade her that there's more acceptance of it now than in her generation, and I think that helped a bit. But yeah, we both had to have a cry to get it out, I think.

So, your teenager has gathered up all their courage and confidence, and they've finally opened up. What do you do?

'I think what teenagers want from parents in those initial conversations is to listen – just listen, and be present with them in the moment. Sometimes just subtle things, like holding their hand or giving them a hug, can be so validating to them. I think it's important for parents to remember that coming out is such a personal experience, and it brings out such a tremendous amount of fear and sensitivity – not being accepted, not being loved – and what that may bring in terms of the bigger family, you know?' **Allan Sadac**

'Be accepting would be the ideal. They've told us something that's been brewing for quite some time. Embracing each other, and saying you still love them, and nothing's going to change that, is very important, because they feel very vulnerable at that stage. There's been research that's shown that the sooner you can come out and be accepted, the less likely you are to develop mental health problems, so there's something about that need for unconditional parental love from the start.' **Lukasz Konieczka**

'What I would say is focus on the here and now. Don't think about it long term. Focus on how your child is feeling at that moment, 'cos remember that being a teenager is at times overwhelming on its own without dealing with sexuality. So yeah, my main advice would be asking is your child happy, and is there a way to help them with that? Because there could be all sorts going on for them.' **Grace**

'There'll be a certain amount of emotion that the young person has held on to all this time before they came out and told you what they felt. There'll be a lot of emotion on both sides, but that's OK. I think it allows for that relationship with that parent to be stronger, and build from there.' **Lukasz Konieczka**

'I think whether we're talking about the parents' perspective, or the teenager's perspective, if we can give ourselves a little bit of patience, and compassion, and understanding, around the complexities and the difficulties and the vulnerabilities that can come up in that initial conversation, then we can be more understanding of ourselves. It may not be this hallmark, perfect conversation, where you say all of the right things. Feelings are going to come up. It may be a total shock, and even if it may be something parents have suspected for quite a while, you need to understand that it's probably not going to be an easy conversation.' **Allan Sadac**

What about other people knowing?

'Please don't say things like, "Oh, OK, but don't tell your father," because those are conditions that you're putting on your child, that for them feels like you're ashamed of them.' **Lukasz Konieczka**

'My encouragement to a parent in that initial conversation is to ask, "So, who can I talk about this with?" I think it's so important to get the consent, and understand: "OK, how do you feel about me talking about this with other people?"' **Allan Sadac**

'I didn't know how the rest of the family was going to react, and the problem is, to be honest, nothing is kept a secret in my family. If you say something, especially on my mum's side, you can guarantee it's gone round the whole family within five minutes. So actually, I didn't really come out to the rest of my family; they just found out in dribs and drabs. It means you avoid that awkward, "I need to sit you down and tell you something about me." so that was quite nice not to have to do that. But it felt maybe a little bit too out of my control, like people were finding out not on my terms, which was a bit annoying I suppose. But, in the end, it all turned out to be fine because no one really judged. Or, at least, not within my knowledge anyway.' **Grace**

What happens next?

'Don't expect it to just be one conversation and that's that. For my mum and me the first one was more emotionally charged, but the second was more nerve-racking, I'd say. I also think you need to give yourself time as a parent, because in a way – this might sound really dramatic – but I think my mum, and maybe my dad to a point, had to mourn the loss of the daughter they were expecting to have. There will be an adjustment. They'll have to get used to this new bit of information, and get used to their child bringing home someone of the same sex, or whatever.' **Grace**

The continual cycle of change and adjustment for parents which starts at birth and builds to an intensity in adolescence, involves more change and adjustment for parents of LGBTQ+ teens. For some it can feel as though the last remaining remnants of their parenting handbook are torn into shreds, and they have to start all over again, again. But this is still your child, and they (and you) need you to know this – and you're still their parent, and they (and you) need you to be this.

'My mum actually asked me about what was OK. It was quite funny! She was, like, "Do I stop her sleeping over now, or is it OK?" I was, like, "You're the parent!" And I remember having that realization that parents are human. They're not these omniscient beings who know the ways of the world inside out. She admitted that there was a lot of uncertainty around her understanding of this stuff.' **Grace**

'Parents can feel at a bit of a loss because nothing matches. We live in a heteronormative society, and everything is all of a sudden upside down. But just because your child is LGBT+ and can be a bit more fragile doesn't mean you give up on the parenting boundaries that are really important, because at the end of the day you're still their parent, and they're still a teenager. So do insist on the house rules. "No, being gay doesn't mean you don't have to do the hoovering..."' **Lukasz Konieczka**

For all that's the same, there will be some differences, and one of the roles you'll need to take on is that of being your teen's cheerleader, champion and advocate. They'll come across prejudice in all shapes and forms – negative or stereotypical portrayals in media, 'banter' and jokes, subtly dismissive or blatantly phobic comments from their friends, their community or your wider family. Your teen may not yet know their own boundaries in relation to what is and isn't acceptable, and what might be harmful to them, in words, deeds or attitudes. All you can do to build their self-esteem, self-confidence and self-worth, all you can do to establish a culture of acceptance and openness in your family, all you can do to create opportunities to communicate, to connect and to validate who they are, how they feel and how they experience the world, will help enormously. You are the one who needs to have their back, fight their corner, bang the drum for all they are, and guide them down safe paths.

'I think it comes down to being supportive, being loving, trying to understand your own internal struggles as a parent, and trying to figure out the balance between what is supportive and at what point your child needs you to intervene, for the sake of trying to focus on keeping them safe – emotionally, mentally, physically, relationally.' **Allan Sadac**

'I think just be mindful that what a young person wants isn't always what they need, and be very careful to separate those two things. They might be like, "I want everyone to know, I want to change my name, I want to be out in the open," but we have to be conscious of the risks that might be involved. In terms of the school, is the young person going to be safe in these spaces? Does the school have a good anti-bullying policy? It's not about telling a young person, "Don't do it!" but helping them think through the consequences. They might still want to do it, but they need help to think it through.

'But there are also bonding moments that shouldn't be missed. Going shopping with them and buying them clothes they feel comfortable in. If they want to use make-up, have an exploration of that. If your child is exploring a name, there might be potential for you to have a conversation about it. There's a process here that you can be part of, that's so important and is going to be such a validating experience for the young person.' **Lukasz Konieczka**

Connecting with community

'I think the big thing for so many parents is making sure they have a support system of their own – one that is open, that is supportive, that is understanding. Recognizing they don't have to have all the answers. Giving them the space; that this is as much of a journey of learning for them as well as their teenage child.' **Allan Sadac**

'Engaging with LGBT+ services is critical for young people, and connecting them with the broader community, to help them meet people like them, because LGBT+ young people experience higher levels of isolation and loneliness, and that can damage their mental health.' **Lukasz Konieczka**

You're not alone, and neither is your LGBTQ+ teen, although it may feel that way early on. There are families right round the world in the same colourful boat, more than happy to welcome you all on board, and help you find your own way. Connecting with the LGBTQ+ community, whether locally or nationally, in person or online, can help you all as you grow and learn together. As always, you don't have to know it all, and you don't have to get it all right, but being open to learning, and to getting it right more often, will help. And keep on showering your wonderful LGBTQ+ teen with the big love, affirmation and validation they deserve. That will help you too.

And finally ...

'I think for parents, just be kind to yourself, and be kind to your teenager, and be willing to grow, and to simply recognize how you and they might be feeling. We're not looking for perfection; we're looking for progress, we're looking for connection, we're looking for safety and stability and trust. Continue to have conversations, let them know that you're there, let them know that that you're accepting, and that you love them.' **Allan Sadac**

FINDING OUT MORE
Online resources
FFLAG: A UK-based charity dedicated to supporting parents and families and their LGBT+ members. FFLAG offers support to help parents and families understand, accept and support their LGBT members with love and pride www.fflag.org.uk.

PFLAG: A US organization for LGBTQ+ people, their parents and families, and allies, with nearly 400 chapters across America. PFLAG is committed to creating a world where diversity is celebrated and all people are respected, valued and affirmed https://pflag.org.

Gender Spectrum: A US-based organization that works to create gender-sensitive and inclusive environments for children and teens www.genderspectrum.org.

Mosaic LGBT+ Young Persons' Trust: A youth organization in London providing support to young people, parents and professionals www.mosaictrust.org.uk.

Books

Allan Sadac, *Parenting Your LGBTQ+ Teen: A Guide To Supporting, Empowering, and Connecting with Your Child* (Rockbridge Press, 2021)

Rhyannon Styles, *The New Girl* (Headline Publishing Group, 2017)

8

TALKING THE TOUGH STUFF OF RELATIONSHIPS AND SEX

'Communication, kindness and empathy are central to all good relationships, and as parents we need to help our children develop all of these skills. I think empathy is the one we think least about, though, and yet it's the one that really determines how we treat others. If we can genuinely put ourselves into another person's shoes, then it becomes difficult for us to treat them badly.'

Alicia Drummond

WHO'S WHO?

Alicia Drummond MBACP is an accredited therapist, parenting expert and founder of Teen Tips, an organization which works to prevent mental illness in children and young people. The Teen Tips Wellbeing Hub provides information, advice and resources for parents, educators and professionals. Alicia is also author of *Why Every Teenager Needs a Parrot* (Let's Talk Ltd., 2013) www.teentips.co.uk.

Faith and her husband brought **Beth** (25) and her brother up in east London. Beth now lives with her partner in the north of England.

Kira is 26 and lives in Scotland.

What do we mean by ...?

We probably think we all know what we mean by relationships, and similarly assume the same about sex, but you may find that what you understand by these words is different from that of your teens and their peers. You may also find that, when you start to get thinking – and talking – the understanding you do both have is somewhat hazy. If so, you're in good company. *Collins Dictionary* defines 'sex' as 'the physical activity between people that involves the sexual organs'. But in what way? Doing what, where, how and with whom, or with anyone? And do organs always have to be directly involved, or can they take part remotely, as it were? And reaching consensus on what's meant by a relationship can be even more slippery. Does a hook-up count as a relationship, for example? A series of dates? And, if so, how many? Does it have to be exclusive, and if so, for how long before it 'counts'?

This is a very good place to start in talking the tough stuff of relationships and sex. Beginning with what we mean by these things has the potential not only to educate parents into the sexual assumptions, expectations and experiences of today's teenagers (prepare to be intrigued/surprised/shocked, depending on what they'll share), but also to think about what makes for a healthy relationship, and to bring it all back to the core, personal values that need to underpin all of this, if your teen is to be happy, healthy and safe: self-esteem; self-respect; empathy; kindness and knowing the value of trust. And you need to be talking about all of this early and often, growing your conversations with your maturing, evolving children.

A little bit more defining of terms

'It's really important that we educate young people about consent because too many of them don't seem to know what it is, or how to make sure it's in place, and that it can be retracted at any time. Many of them don't seem to understand what constitutes sexual harassment, or assault – for example, having your head pushed down and being forced to give a boy oral sex is sexual assault. As parents we don't want to think about these things, but they happen.'
Alicia Drummond

Knowing what something is and isn't, and being able to spot it, is an essential first step to stopping it happening, calling it out or getting help. However, many of us aren't entirely clear on exactly what's meant by many terms that are now widely used, so here are some of the most important ones:

• Consent is to do with giving and getting permission for something to happen, which sounds a lot simpler than it can seem in practice. We'll come back to consent, because this underpins pretty much everything else that's right and wrong.

- Abuse can encompass many different behaviours – the more obvious being sexual or physical abuse – but it also includes coercive control, online abuse, stalking and snooping into someone's messages or social media.

- Sexual harassment, broadly speaking, is unwelcome sexual attention and can happen without any physical contact.

- Sexual assault takes place when someone engages in physical sexual activity with another person without their explicit consent. The extreme end of this is rape. You could think of the former as conduct, and the latter as contact, but both count as sexual violence, because sex is the means by which someone imposes their power and control on another person.

Yes means yes, and no means no

'Both boys and girls really need to understand what consent actually means, and that if somebody's doing something you are not happy about, you can say no at any time.' **Alicia Drummond**

Consent is a word – and a concept – that's new to many parents when it comes to sex. It has never been acceptable to force oneself on someone else, but boundaries were very much more blurred back in the day, as we can see from the number of high-profile sexual scandals only now coming to light and to court. For parents, getting our heads round what consent really means, and helping our teens do the same, is vital for them to be safe, and, equally importantly, healthy and happy. This is one of the many aspects of life here and now about which you can invite them to be your educator, and in the process, you can make sure their own understanding is secure. Having a really strong grasp that no always means no whenever, however and wherever it's said, is fundamental to everything here, whether they're the ones saying it, or needing to hear it from someone else.

'Parents need to know what consent means for starters, and also the implications of getting it wrong, so there's an element of educating yourself first. Start when they're young, and talk about touching other people's things, personal space and personal boundaries and all that kind of stuff. And then take it that little bit further as they get older. Do you think you should ask somebody before you kiss them? Do you think you should ask somebody before you touch them? Do you think that if you've got permission to kiss somebody that means you've got permission to take it one step further? We want them to understand that before you initiate any form of intimate contact, you need to be really sure you've got consent.

'And consent has to be freely given. You can't give consent for sexual intercourse under 16 in this country [under 18 in the US]. But you also can't give it if you're bullied, or drugged, or blackmailed, or drunk, or threatened. It needs to be informed – so, do both parties know what they're giving consent for? It's retractable, and this is an important one, because there are girls who'll say, "Oh, you know, he's been my boyfriend for a year and a half, so I didn't think I could say no, or that I could change my mind." They need to know that whether you have been with someone for an hour, a week, a month or married for 30 years, you can still change your mind. That's OK.

'And then there's enthusiasm – what I say to young people is look, watch your partner's body language. If they're not actively enthusiastic, then just assume that they're not interested, that you don't have consent, because that's a much safer way to go.

'And I suppose the last one is about being specific – what are you actually giving consent for? Because they do need to understand if you give someone consent to sleep in your bed, you've only given them consent to sleep in your bed. That's it. There is no permission or consent given for anything else.

'We have also got to start thinking through all of the different implications for getting consent wrong. If you do, you've harmed somebody, which could cause them long-term emotional difficulties. You've got to think about your reputational damage. And then you've got to think about the legal consequences, which can be devastating.' **Alicia Drummond**

What about sexting?

'It's about empowering your kids to be able to say no. "If you're not comfortable with what someone's asking for or doing, it's your body, you have the right to say no." But it's also about recognizing that saying no can be really difficult, so how can they say no without just saying no? And we really need to boost their self-esteem so that they don't feel they need to do that stuff to try and feel OK about themselves.' **Alicia Drummond**

As parents we need to face up to the fact there's a very big culture of sharing explicit images, and it's not unlikely our teen (or even pre-teen) will, at some point, be asked to do it, think about doing it and maybe actually do it. It's also possible they might ask someone else to do it. It's photos and videos of boys and girls, and from younger ages than we'd like to imagine. Most of these will be taken at home, in a bedroom or bathroom, probably with parents downstairs in blissful ignorance. Sometimes these are taken and sent under pressure, other times they're willingly given and sometimes they're sent unsolicited (known as cyberflashing, or often as 'dick pics'). Motivations can be mixed and complex, but whatever lies behind it, those sending them often haven't thought through the implications or the impact. The adolescent brain really isn't on their side here, so you have to be. It's something every family needs to be talking about, because there's a chance that at some point they might find themselves sending, receiving or sharing something explicit. There can be devastating consequences from any and all of these, including legal consequences if they involve images of under-18s.

'Rather than always just giving them the long lecture, get them thinking, you know: "What do you think the dangers of you sending them might be? How would you feel if you sent a 'dick pic' or picture and the next thing you're going to school and half the school have seen it, and then you go to your gym club in the evening and somebody there's seen it?" Start to get them thinking through possible consequences, and talk to them about their reputation: Your reputation is your responsibility, so how are you going to protect that?

'Ask them things like "What would you do if somebody sent you a picture? What would you do if somebody was trying to push you into sending one of those photos? Or you felt coerced? Or you felt that somebody was blackmailing you to send one of those photos?"

'They need to understand the law, and under UK law if you're sharing explicit images under the age of 18, even if they're of your own body, you're sharing child pornography.

'Understanding that it can be difficult for young people to say no to their friends means helping them find the tools to say no, without just saying no, for example if they are feeling pressured to send a sext they could send a gif as a response. I found one yesterday that was a cat chatting away going, "You cannot be serious!"

'When we're having potentially tough conversations, it can help young people to talk if we talk about other people rather than themselves. For example, you might say "If one of your friends was being pressured, what advice do you think you could give them?"

'We're giving them tools, because if you're 13 and you don't know how to say no, that's really difficult.' **Alicia Drummond**

What about porn?

'Porn is ubiquitous. It's everywhere, and it can be difficult to avoid seeing it because it pops up on their social media feeds, although it's also really easy to find if they want to watch it. I think as parents we're being naive if we don't think that they'll be accessing porn at some point.' **Alicia Drummond**

Gone are the days of the grubby, much-thumbed, sneakily circulated *Playboy* magazine someone had got hold of and smuggled into school. This is the era of easy-to-access, free-to-view, fast-paced online porn, and it's altogether a different beast. Many parents have no idea quite how much porn is accessed by quite how many pre-teens and teens, often unintentionally – at least at first. It's safe to assume, if your child doesn't view porn at some point, they'll be in a tiny minority – especially if they're a boy, but girls are seeing this, too. Many parents also have little idea how totally different this is from the images they may have peeked at in their youth. Generally speaking, this is graphic, hardcore, violent, high-risk stuff. Sex is separated from emotions and often non-consensual, the degradation of women is eroticized, male satisfaction is what it's all about, and, unsurprisingly, this is distorting teenagers' expectations and assumptions about what a sexual encounter should look like – and 'look' is the operative word.

'The girls I speak to in schools often say that hearing what the boys are saying about porn is threatening, because it's that laddish banter which makes everybody, the girls in particular, worry that that's what they're going to have to do. Porn is about performance, and I think this puts pressure on both boys and girls.' **Alicia Drummond**

Be aware, too, that online porn can be addictive, pushing an ever-greater dopamine hit. Porn needs to be talked about and definitely not taboo – part of those everyday, non-judgemental conversations, starting from pre-teens (in an age-appropriate way, of course). Do all you can to protect them with filters, use the resources below to learn more and, as always, allow your children to educate you, too.

> 'We don't want to shame them for it, so I think that sort of gentle questioning, "I've been hearing this stuff about porn online and how young some kids are when they're looking at it. Do you think that's true?"
>
> 'If they have watched it, it's the "ask don't tell" principle. What do they think about the way women are treated? What do they think about the violence? And the depersonalization, and dehumanization, and the objectification? And getting them thinking about what's normal, because they mustn't ever think that what they're watching on porn is a reflection of an intimate and loving relationship. It's not. It's about the mechanics, isn't it?' **Alicia Drummond**

What about grooming, exploitation and abuse?

> **Faith:** It started when Beth was 13. I knew that there was an older lad at the church youth group that she doted on and she liked to talk about and she liked to be with. I think I was probably aware that they were texting each other, and she'd sometimes say what he said, if it was funny or whatever, so she wasn't being very secretive about it. She was very excited really to have this, and there didn't seem anything sinister about it.
>
> **Me:** So when did you start to get concerned?
>
> **Faith:** It was when she said they wanted to meet up outside of church, just the two of them. That was when I thought, 'Ah yeah,

I'm not happy about that.' It didn't get me thinking that there was anything sinister, but it got me thinking I need to keep an eye on this. And I did wonder what kind of a young man would want to see a 13-year-old? But, you know, I've been in youth groups – there's a huge age range, it's all very intense, very spiritual – so I just kind of felt I needed to give it a little bit of oversight. So, I said, 'Yes, you can meet up with him in the park, but I'm going to be in the café, and you're going to go for a walk there, and then you have to be back at the café by this time.' That was it. We went home, and I didn't think anything more about it. It didn't happen again that they wanted to meet up outside of church, so that was the culmination of their involvement as far as I was aware.

She didn't tell me this at the time, but she said he'd looked like he was going to kiss her while they were in the park. She said she felt, 'Uh oh, that's not right,' and she got up and walked away, but he texted her later and said he'd wished he had. She started to complain about the fact that he was unreliable, that he just dumped all his emotional baggage on her, and there were other things that happened that made her feel he wasn't the friend she thought she had, and actually it went on for a good few years. We'd talk about it, and I'd just listen, and I mean, I didn't like it, but I didn't see anything … there wasn't anything in that context that I would have been concerned about at that time. I think she got a bit fed up with it, but not before – I found out subsequently – he did quite a bit of damage, actually. There was quite a lot that I didn't know at the time.

Me: But Beth didn't realize herself until quite recently, and that's how these things work, isn't it? You don't realize yourself that there's something unhealthy about it.

Faith: No, no, and I didn't, but I should have done because I was groomed myself when I was about her age by a PE teacher at my school. Nothing disgusting happened, but it wasn't until decades later – I mean literally decades later – I thought 'Hold on, that wasn't right.' So, I know how that feels – I liked it, I felt special. He was a popular teacher, and I felt like I was getting something that other kids weren't getting. I didn't feel threatened, I didn't feel scared; I felt lovely.

Me: It's such a subtle process, isn't it? It's really difficult to spot.

Faith: Yeah, yeah. I have to say I hold the church very much responsible, and there's a real issue about you just taking a lot of things for granted or on trust as a parent, especially in faith communities. Especially when they're the children of friends of yours, or they're people you've known for 15 years or something. You wouldn't question them because that'd be awkward and unpleasant. Now, I mean, I regret that, because he was sanctioned to go off and think that that was OK.

For a teenager new to the world of relationships, there hasn't yet been chance for a mark in the sand to be set to help them distinguish between what's healthy and what's not, nor when unhealthy strays into abusive. They're also encountering this emotional realm with all the unique intensity of adolescence, which makes objectivity equally uniquely challenging. And let's face it, these lines are often far from clear whatever your age, with love having power to disable the judgement of even the most clear-headed, intelligent and sensible of us. Although understanding of abuse has deepened in recent years, and broadened to include the reality of grooming and coercive control, the very nature of this particular sort of abuse is that it's an imperceptible and cumulative process, obscured behind a plausible front of devotion, and especially inscrutable to the person who is its object. Although the extent of peer-on-peer abuse is increasingly recognized, an additional dimension for pre-teens and teens is that they're surrounded by relationships where the power dynamic puts them at an enormous disadvantage, should someone whose age or position of authority choose to abuse this.

'If a parent is concerned that the relationship their child is in isn't good, it's really tricky, because if you criticize their choice of partner, you risk driving them off into their arms, don't you? None of us want to think that we're not a good judge of character, or that we wouldn't be able to spot the signs for ourselves. So, I think it's about expressing concern: "I'm kind of worried that I noticed this happen, and I wonder, what was that like for you?" We are gently, gently sowing the seed that we think something might be wrong.

'We express loving concern, we tentatively question and we reassure them: "Whatever happens, I am always, always, always going to be here for you. If anything ever happens that you feel uncomfortable or upset about, I'll help you if I can."' **Alicia Drummond**

It's important that parents understand what grooming and coercive control look like, because it's parents who are best placed to spot it, and to help guide their child to see it for themselves. It's generally a subtle, gradual process, so look for patterns of behaviour (and think about keeping a record of these) as well as signs. These can include someone:

- controlling what they do, where they go, who they see or talk to, what they wear
- tracking their movements or monitoring their social media or messages
- putting them down and criticizing them
- isolating them from friends and family
- issuing rules, threats and ultimatums.

A child who's being controlled, or abused in any way, really needs to know they have the absolutely unwavering support of their parent, even if they may show every sign of wanting to shut them out. They risk becoming completely isolated otherwise, which can put them at much greater risk. Use the resources below to find support and helpline details, and if you feel they may be at risk of immediate danger call the police. Abuse is a criminal offence.

ADVICE FOR PARENTS FROM FAITH

'One thing is, just because your child is telling you things in an offhand way, it doesn't mean that it's how you should receive it. Beth would say things in sort of a jokey way and make light of it. There was an incident where she told me what happened in such a light-hearted way that I didn't pay any attention at all, and it wasn't until years later she told me what actually happened, and I was horrified and ashamed that I hadn't picked up on that. That will live with me for ever.

'I think you can be laidback in appearance but in your head, you've got to be, you know, asking what's in it for this young man? Beth's had quite a few nasty experiences actually with people whom she's trusted, you know, but they don't come on like the wicked villain with the swirling moustache. They're people you trust, and you like, and other people trust and like. I think maybe as parents we think we'll see them coming.

'I think it's being very sensitive to those things that sound a bit dodgy: "Oh yeah, it was just me and so and so, 'cos everybody else left." You know, just those little details. You just need to interrogate, but without seeming to interrogate.

'I think you've got to trust and believe your child, and you've got to listen, and offer that uncompromising love. That's where it starts, isn't it? You know, you've got to be prepared to go to the wall, and I don't think I was at that time. What I did with Beth in that particular situation seemed to be sufficient, but it wasn't.'

What about sexual assault?

As we've already seen, understanding consent is fundamental to understanding sexual assault. It's now well known that sexual assault is only rarely done by a stereotypical stranger down a dark alley. Most of the time it's someone we know; often it's someone we trust; sometimes it's someone we're already in a relationship with. It doesn't matter who it is, or how it happens – if one person has said no to a sexual encounter, or at any stage during that encounter, or is unable to give their yes legally for all the reasons Alicia outlines above, then this is always assault, it's always harmful and it's a crime.

> 'For parents, it's really important to help their children understand that when it comes to sexual assault, if they're the victim they're not to blame: "It's not your fault. You don't need to feel ashamed. I'm always here to help you and we'll work through it together."'
> **Alicia Drummond**

If your child tells you they've been sexually assaulted, the first and most important thing you must do is to believe them. They also need to know you don't blame them in any way, shape or form. They also need you to listen. All of this will be tough because your own protective parental emotions will be raging and huge, but it's one of those many moments when you need to catch those emotions, hold them tight and have them later. It's hard for you, but it's worse for your child, and they need a calm, clear head to be there for them.

There are choices they can make – and these need to be their choices – and there are practical things they can do, and you can help them find their way through the immediate aftermath. See the resources below for where to go for help for you both.

> 'It's important for parents not to charge in and take over, because their child lost their power when they were assaulted, so we don't want to take their power away again. We need to work at their pace and allow them space.' **Alicia Drummond**

You'll also need to be there for the long recovery, but being believed from the start, by the person whose good opinion they value more than anyone else's on earth, will aid this process more than anything.

Kira: In my second year at university, me and my friends always used to go to this bar on a Tuesday night because that's when they played the best music and we all loved dancing. There was this girl there I really liked, and so, like, that night I was trying to talk to her, but this guy kept trying to get in between us, and get me to flirt with him instead, and he was trying to kiss me and stuff. I kept pushing him away, to the point I ended up actually hitting him just to get him away from me, but he just wouldn't go. And because it's, like, I'd not long come out and, well, to get the courage to actually flirt with a girl I had to be drunk, and I don't know how much I'd drunk, but it was a *lot* – and somehow, I don't know how, I actually ended up going home with this guy.

Me: Can your friends remember how that ended up happening?

Kira: They'd disappeared! We used to keep an eye on each other, but we'd didn't always stick together in the bar. They said after they didn't know where I'd gone.

Me: What do you remember of what happened next?

Kira: Basically, I just have flashes of things. I remember halfway through, and I was saying no, trying to push him away, but he wasn't listening, and I was hitting him because he was ... ummm ... doing a lot of stuff ... you know? I remember trying to climb out the window at one point just to get away ...

Me: Did you go to the police afterwards?

Kira: I was too scared to, because it was like, I knew my memory, but I wasn't confident I hadn't said yes, 'cos I can remember saying no, but I might have said yes, too. I really don't think I ever would've, but I know I was really drunk.

Me: And did you talk to your mum?

Kira: No. Mum still doesn't know about it.

Me: Would you have liked to have talked to somebody then?

Kira: I think for me, I had this overriding feeling of shame that it'd happened, and kind of not knowing how to deal with it, and not knowing who to talk to 'cos I thought I'd have got blamed for it. And I was scared of what had happened, 'cos, like, I don't know how I got from the bar to his, or why I was there in the first place.

Me: What do you think another parent could do to make sure their teenager could go to them if something like this happened?

Kira: It's all in the groundwork when they're a really little kid. You've got to be able to have those conversations and not fear judgement. Because, like, with my family, I didn't know they'd listen, and I thought they'd say it was my fault.

Me: So it's about listening and not judging? And what about conversations about consent?

Kira: That's incredibly important, and for me those conversations just didn't happen. If I'd known about what consent really meant, I'd have been more confident to go to the police, because then I'd have had more of a thing of 'Right, this is wrong, and it's not my fault.' It's because I was blaming myself for it – it was impossible for me to not feel that – and then to be able to go to someone else and go, OK, help …

And finally, what about us?

'As parents it's super important that we're calling out the lower-level stuff, and to a lot of us this was kind of OK when we were younger, so it can be easy to miss it, but if we don't call out the lower-level stuff, we're giving them the green light that that's OK, and if that's OK, why would it not get escalated up a bit? So, it's understanding that spectrum of behaviour.' **Alicia Drummond**

When we, the parents, were growing up, different assumptions and expectations prevailed when it came to sexual interactions. This will inevitably have shaped our own attitudes, and we need to shine a spotlight on these and reflect on any damaging signals they might unintentionally send our children. Don't judge yourself too harshly, but don't let yourself off the hook either, and do make sure your child picks up the message that they can trust you, whatever, with whatever.

'Whatever happens, we need to make sure our teenagers always know we're there for them to turn to: "I promise I won't be angry. That's not my job. My job is to keep you safe. If something goes wrong, I'm not going to be cross about it, but I want to be able to help you."' **Alicia Drummond**

FINDING OUT MORE

Online resources

Childline and IWF Report Remove tool: If your child is worried that an image or video of themselves has been shared: https://www.childline.org.uk/info-advice/bullying-abuse-safety/online-mobile-safety/remove-nude-image-shared-online/.

National Sexual Violence Resource Center: US non-profit providing information and tools to prevent and respond to sexual violence https://www.nsvrc.org/.

Parents Protect: UK-based organization providing information and advice for parents to protect children and young people from sexual abuse and exploitation https://www.parentsprotect.co.uk/.

Thinkuknow Education: Resources for young people, parents and professionals about sexual abuse and sexual exploitation https://www.thinkuknow.co.uk.

Also useful is: *The Things I Wish My Parents Had Known ... Young People's Advice on Talking to Your Child about Online Sexual Harassment* – a guide for parents, including links to other useful online resources https://www.childrenscommissioner.gov.uk/.

Books

Peggy Orenstein, *Girls & Sex* (Oneworld Publications, 2016)

Karen Rayne, *Breaking the Hush Factor* (Impetus Books, 2015)

Shafia Zaloom, *Sex, Teens and Everything in Between* (Sourcebooks, 2019)

9
TALKING THE TOUGH STUFF OF MENTAL ILL HEALTH

'When it first started, I'd feel sad, I'd feel low, I'd feel low energy – all the classic symptoms – and when it got severe it was really severe, and I felt anxiety but it was on another level – my heart was constantly racing, I felt sick all of the time, I couldn't cope with what was going on around me. Angry as well, very angry. It had gone from irritability to pure anger. Confusion as well, like, why did other people not feel like I did? And yeah, an inability to empathize as well, which looking back frightens me a bit because I think that's part of being human, really, to have compassion and feel empathy for others. I'd lost that. It was all about how I felt. I became quite self-absorbed, but I felt like I couldn't survive unless I was like that.'

Tamara

'A teenager with poor mental health is someone who's not feeling safe. And our job as a parent is to really make them feel that this is a safe moment for them, and until they feel like it is a safe moment, no conversation is really going to happen.'

Anita Cleare

WHO'S WHO?

Tamara is 27 and lives just outside London with her partner. Her parents, **Lois** and **Warren**, live nearby.

Anita Cleare MA AdvDip is a parenting expert, writer and coach, and co-founder of the Positive Parenting Project. She is author of *The Work/Parent Switch* (Vermillion, 2020 [UK]), also published as *The Working Parent's Survival Guide* (Rowman & Littlefield, 2021 [US]), a positive parenting guide for working parents https://anitacleare.co.uk/.

What do we mean by ...?

Health, whether physical or mental, is something we all need to take care of, but sometimes things can go wrong, and if they do, life can become painful, difficult and, for some, feel impossible to bear. Experiencing mental ill health can be confusing, scary and isolating, and particularly so in adolescence, when so much else is going on, and your sense of identity, self-esteem and confidence are often at their most fragile.

'I think for me, being able to talk to people is knowing what's going on in yourself, and I think if you don't know what is going on in yourself, it's very difficult to tell anybody. Even if you would want to, it just becomes very confusing. How can I vocalize it when I can't even get it clear in my head? For me it wasn't, "I've got this problem and I can label it," it was just a series of things, and feeling like something's not quite right here ... but then it's so hard to tell when you're a teenager. You're like, is this normal?' **Tamara**

Just as with physical ill health, there are many different conditions mental ill health can encompass, and often these coexist, overlap and interact. Anxiety, depression and behaviour problems are the most commonly diagnosed mental disorders in children and adolescents. Sometimes a diagnosis of a specific disorder is useful, to understand what's going on and find a way forward, and it may be essential in order to access support and appropriate treatment. As a parent, however, it's often best to focus on how this feels for your child.

'I think it's sometimes not helpful to wonder what the actual label is, because often it all comes as a package. I think more if parents approach talking to teenagers with curiosity about what their experience *feels* like, that's when we start to understand it – "Tell me a little more about that. That sounds difficult. What does that feel like?" – then we're much more likely to understand it, regardless of what the label is or isn't.' **Anita Cleare**

There's not enough space for detailed descriptions of symptoms of different disorders here, so do have a look at the websites listed at the end of the chapter.

How can you tell? Signs and symptoms

Lois: I think where I knew there was something not quite right was when you seemed to go off the rails a little bit. Was it when you were 16 or 17? You were coming home from school and you were feeling very angry about things.

Tamara: Yeah. I'd always stay and do my homework after school, and then I'd come back home. But yeah, I'd come back angry a lot of the time.

Lois: You just said you didn't want to be at home, didn't you?

Tamara: Did I say that?

Lois: Yeah, you did, which made us very sad.

Tamara: I wasn't angry with you, though. I think I was more expressing it to you rather than at you. Well, maybe sometimes it was expressed at you, but I think I'd come home and vent my frustrations about whatever had happened at school that was irritating me. It was all a bit disproportionate to what was actually going on, I think. My response was, like, a bit over the top, I think.

Lois: Yeah, and that worried me. That's one of the things I'm thinking, 'That doesn't sound right.' But there was a little bit of, 'Where's this come from?' Because she always got on with her homework, she got on well at school. Just what I call a very easy, affable, lovely child. Just from the time she was born she was easy.

We will all at times feel anxious, stressed, sad or down, and most of the time, for most of us, this is a natural and healthy response to something that's happened, or going to happen, or a situation we're in. A teenager who's gloomy, or panicked, or angry, or feeling they're useless and nobody likes them and what's the point anyway, is not a rare phenomenon. So how does a parent – and a teenager – know when this has tipped into something more serious?

'It can be incredibly hard just for parents to distinguish between what's "normal" teenage behaviour – for example mood swings – and what are things that we should be worried about, that we should be looking to give further support on, and often teenagers can't put that into words. It's very seldom that they'll come to you and say, "Dad, I'm feeling anxious" – you know? That's not often the way it's going to come out. It very often comes out in behaviour. It might come out in very alienating and aggressive ways such as anger, and they may not be able to identify and understand what's going on themselves.' **Anita Cleare**

Starting a conversation

However mystifying adolescence can be, you're still the leading expert when it comes to your child, and if you've noticed something, and if you're concerned, then there's probably something there. It may be nothing to do with their mental health, but if you feel they're not happy, or not coping, then a conversation driven by curiosity is needed.

'One thing you can do if you're worried is what I call taking a tentative guess. It does involve choosing your moment – a moment that feels calm and safe. And then, rather than asking a direct question, which may well lead them to bring their shutters down, to take a bit of a guess and say something like, "I can't see what's going on inside your head, but from the outside, it looks like you're feeling a bit low. Is that what it's feeling like on the inside as well?" That kind of approach can invite them into a conversation where a more direct questioning approach wouldn't.' **Anita Cleare**

As always, the general stuff about conversations in Part 1 will help with the specifics of Part 2, but you may need some of it in much bigger doses. The ongoing work of connecting, listening and reigning in your reactions, may take up much more of your time, effort and energy, but keeping that conversation open, however much hard work it might take, is important for you both.

Why won't they tell us?

'When we ask children and teenagers, "Why didn't you tell your parents or talk to them about this difficult situation that you're in?" the most common response is that they were worried about their parents overreacting, getting upset, getting angry, and perhaps doing things that they didn't want them to do, or making them do things that they didn't want to do. So, I think there is a fear of response, if I actually said this is how I'm feeling.

'There is quite often shame involved in difficult thoughts and feelings. It's very hard to open up and say, "Actually on the inside this is what it looks like," if you feel your inside is perhaps not acceptable in some way because of what's going on.

'And often they might feel that they're letting us down or disappointing us. Teenagers are under a huge amount of pressure to succeed on every level, and feeling that they're not succeeding, and having to admit that to the person they most want to feel proud of them, that's a really difficult thing to do.

'There could be fear of reprisals and repercussions. You know, many teenagers look for answers to their thoughts and feelings in the wrong places, so if mental ill health has led them to drugs, alcohol, gambling, any kind of antisocial behaviour, then there's worry that that's what my parent's going to focus on. They're not going to ask me why I did it.

'And maybe I'm just feeling angry. I can't explain why I'm so angry, because this is coming from quite a deep, instinctual place, and they might not be able to articulate it.

'So there can be lots and lots of reasons.' **Anita Cleare**

All the barriers to teenage unburdening we examined in Part 1 are of much the same order for teens with mental ill health, with some more specific ones thrown in the mix. They can feel more intractable and insurmountable, though, and take a little more parental patience and sensitivity to dismantle. Use all those Part 1 tactics to build connectedness, strengthen relationships and keep the channels of communication open about anything and everything, however you can.

Coping and conversations

> **Me:** Did you talk to your mum when things were really bad at university?
>
> **Tamara:** I did talk to Mum a lot actually.
>
> **Lois:** She talked to me lots – probably too much. I'd get phone calls and I'd be in the middle of a meeting, and my phone would be continuously going. I'd have to come out and go, 'What is it?' And she'd be crying. It was a really, really bad time, wasn't it?
>
> **Tamara:** Yeah, 'cos I didn't feel I was able to cope. I felt like I could talk to you more than I could my friends and stuff, 'cos I don't think my friends understood, and why would they?

If your child has a mental health disorder, then this will take time and many, many conversations. Whatever is going on for them, whatever coping strategies, or self-help, or treatment they find, there are processes that have to happen. They can be helped but can't be hurried. Sometimes these conversations will seem endless, and repetitious, pouring out the same encouraging words over and over. Sometimes they'll be agonizing. Sometimes they'll feel impossible. It will all take lots of listening, bucketloads of empathy and oceans of patience. And that will take its toll (so looking after yourself is vital – see below).

> 'We know that the presence of a trusted adult is a really key factor in helping a teenager recover from poor mental health, and being that safe and trusted adult that your teenager is willing to confide in means building up their trust again and again and again. It's never one conversation.
>
> 'The most important thing is to stay calm and curious. Being prepared to be personally regulated when they're not. Being

prepared to listen. Being prepared just to ask those open questions and to hold that moment in a really calm way – "That sounds really difficult. Do you want to tell me more about that?" – so that they can look at us and go, "OK, so these thoughts and these feelings that for me are overwhelming, they're not overwhelming my mum or dad in this conversation, they're being held and in a safe place."

'What that means on the inside for a parent, though, is that we have to hold on to some very difficult feelings at that moment, and process them later, because in that moment we need to stay calm and regulated. That can be very hard. I don't underestimate that in any way, and it impacts on us as parents. But it's something we have to keep doing because it can take teenagers a long time to recover from mental ill health, and you often will have to prove to them over again that you're able to do that, to convince them that this is a safe place for them to feel their emotions.' **Anita Cleare**

To fix or not to fix?

Tamara: I think my advice for a parent would be just to listen. I think there's a tendency – and we all do this – where there's a problem, you want to rush in and help. Especially if you're a parent, you want to fix everything. But sometimes the best fix is to not try and fix it. The best fix is just to be patient. Patience is probably my key.

Warren: Let it mend itself.

Tamara: Yeah. To an extent I think it's processing the feelings. That's a huge part of it, and letting yourself 'feel it to heal it'. Validating and patience and not seeing it as something to be fixed. Certainly not overnight.

Lois: That's the thing from my background. I want instant. I want it better.

Tamara: Yeah, but it's a process. In the same way you wouldn't rush someone whose leg had broken; it's the same with depression. It's a process, 'cos there are so many emotions you need to feel and to work through in stages. And all of that takes time. And it's very zigzaggy, and there's gonna be good days and bad days, and it's gonna fluctuate.

Lois: So just listening. Just being there and listening.

Tamara: Yeah, and not judging the feelings. How I feel is how I feel. I think what prolonged how bad I felt was that I wasn't allowing myself to be OK to feel certain things. I kept feeling like I shouldn't be sad about stuff. Had I just let myself feel sad, I think maybe I would have been OK, but, people – well-intentioned people – when you say you're sad about something they say, 'Oh you'll get over it.'

Warren: Or what have you got to feel sad about? What have you got to worry about? Stuff like that.

Tamara: Yeah, and they'd negate it, and you start to think, 'Oh, maybe I don't have a right to feel sad about whatever it was, because why would you feel sad about that?' I remember we went out for pizza, and I remember saying to you, Mum, 'I still feel sad about everything that's happened to me in the last year.' And you said, 'It's OK. It's OK to feel sad, like, sometimes you just need to feel sad.' And that's the point I gave myself permission. That was a turning point for me. That's a major lesson I learned from all of this, which is there's no 'should' with feelings. It's more about how you process them, and how you respond to them, than having them in the first place.

That powerful parental instinct to jump in and make it all better is something we keep coming back to. It's the most natural thing in the world, and the most unnatural thing to hold back. It's so distressing for us to see our child in a painful place, but like it or not, we have to accept that with mental ill health there's no quick fix, and in trying to find one we can make things much worse, in all the ways we looked at before. If we approach that conversation with a solution, our teen can feel disempowered, when they already feel they have little control. If we try to take their pain away by minimizing it, they don't feel their feelings are valid, and they don't feel heard. Take a deep breath, hold back your urge to take it away and make it all better, and listen. We can prompt, we can nudge, we can definitely nurture, but the best thing of all is help them find the way forward themselves.

> 'The most important thing is to constantly use that empathetic, reflective listening that says, "I can see ..." And always to keep acknowledging what they're going through, whether or not we agree with it, whether or not we want it to be there. That radical act of acceptance is absolutely vital, particularly for teenagers who are finding it incredibly difficult to accept themselves. For us to accept them and what they've said to us and how they feel is a therapeutic act in itself. And really feeling that it's not our job to fix this. Our job is to help them see that we understand where they are, and perhaps nudge them towards a coping mechanism or solution for themselves. Actually saying, "That's a hard feeling to be having. Have you got a thought about what you're going to do about that?"' **Anita Cleare**

What about our own tough stuff?

Another thing we keep talking about is the ways in which what we bring to the conversation as parents can get in the way of giving and getting the help our child needs. Many of us have our own stories and histories when it comes to mental health, not least because of the complex combinations of genetics and environment that mean there's very often a generational pattern with mental health disorders. Sometimes this can give us an insight and sensitivity to what our child is experiencing, but sometimes the stigma, or pain of the past, can make the present difficult to deal with. It's worth taking time to reflect on your own mental health legacy, and whether this is affecting your response to your teenager, and whether that matters.

Lois: It's fair to say you couldn't talk to Tamara about anything, could you?

Warren: No, not really. I didn't know how to. I couldn't, I just couldn't. I tried sometimes, but we'd talk about superficial things, just general things, not the actual problem that she had, 'cos I couldn't understand it, I don't think. Well, perhaps I didn't want to understand it.

Tamara: Yeah, 'cos that makes it real if you talk about it. I get that.

Lois: Also, I think it's the history with your family, like, both your sisters have had severe mental illnesses.

Warren: And my dad had psychosis. And his family, some of his sisters. Ruth, his sister, she committed suicide.

Lois: Yeah, and I think my worry was always, 'Oh dear, where's this coming from, and what might it become?' And I couldn't talk to Warren, 'cos he just shut off, so that created a lot of resentment between us.

Warren: Yeah.

Lois: So Dad did the running. Dad did the 'I can't cope', so Dad would go up and get her, or we'd go up and see her. Dad helped with the very practical things.

When talking gets tough

While some young people will talk and talk, others will hide away. There are so many reasons why they may feel the need to do this, and while it's good to take time to consider whether there's something you've done, or not, that may have made this feel necessary – it's likely it's nothing to do with you, and yet another thing not to take personally. It may be they need time to process, to try to make sense of what's going on, to regroup. They may need some space after coping with getting through another day of school with a mental health disorder. They may well be exhausted. But it's important to keep that connection, however broken it might feel, and however impossible to mend. Don't give up. It matters too much. And it'll almost certainly get better.

'I think particularly with teenagers who retreat to their bedrooms, or retreat from the family, it's really important for parents to get the message to keep trying, because we can give up. Nothing seems to work so we think, "Oh, there's no point!" but it's really important to keep trying. You could try going in with a nurturing gift, like a hot chocolate. Whatever is going to make your teenager feel loved, cared for, that might open the door. And then just linger a little, and start a chat, and if they're being grumpy and clearly don't want you there, then you leave, but you've still had that moment of connection. Little acts of kindness and love for a teenager in a low mood don't always reap immediate rewards, but they are valued, and occasionally they do work, and it's really important to keep doing that.' **Anita Cleare**

As Tamara says, mental ill health is a 'zigzaggy' thing, and some of the zigs and zags can be desperate, and sometimes lead to ways of coping that introduce significant risks, such as substance use, eating disorders or self-harm. Sometimes they lead to such a low point that that young person feels no longer able to live with this pain. Whether they want it or not they need help, and so do you.

Lois: I think that was the really bad year, when you came back from uni, wasn't it? That was particularly bad, and it was difficult having conversations because I think you'd shut off completely. I think it's very hard, the thing about empathy — I couldn't appeal to her on any level.

Tamara: I couldn't understand how anyone else was feeling. There's a huge misconception that it's just sadness, and it can be, but my problem was I wasn't letting myself feel sad, so I got to a point where I was numb, I think it's fair to say.

Lois: She'd been talking about suicide, and I ended up off work for six weeks 'cos she kept telling me she was going to commit suicide, and I just sat at home and I watched her, and slept in the same room. And I'd say, 'If you do anything to harm yourself, it harms us.'

Tamara: Yeah, I couldn't see that, but also, I couldn't believe it, because I had such a low opinion of myself. My self-esteem got so much worse. It completely tanked by that point. I couldn't accept that my departure would have an impact on anyone. I just couldn't see that that would be the truth. I just thought everyone was lying, or I thought you'd be sad for a bit but then you'd get over it, and I'd have these kind of thoughts to rationalize how I was feeling.

Lois: That's the hardest thing, I think.

When to get help (and what if they don't want it)?

There are so many things you can do at home as that first responder and frontline support, and you can find out more about these on the websites below, but professional help may be needed. Medication may (or may not) help, too. The general advice is the time to seek help is if your teenager's mental health is stopping them living their life as fully as they want to – if, for example, it's preventing them accessing opportunities open to their peers – and, of course, if their safety is at risk. That's a judgement call, and a piece of a bigger picture, and getting the right help, with the right person, when it's needed, can be enormously challenging. And sometime getting them there in the first place can be the first hurdle to jump.

'Many teenagers are very reluctant to seek help, and particularly if that involves self-disclosure, because of the privacy around their thoughts and feelings. They don't necessarily want to talk about it. There will be times where parents have to insist. But in general, a therapeutic intervention will only be successful if a teenager engages with it.

'So the best place to start is the place your teenager is prepared to start. So, if all you can do is persuade them to do a yoga class or to download and try out an app on mindfulness, start there. Those little positive tiny steps are important.

'Be a little bit careful about constantly trying to push them into support, because actually we can make them feel a lot worse. We're basically saying, "There's something wrong with you, you need help." But instead being able to say, "Have you thought about what might help you feel a little bit better, or what might raise your mood?"

'An argument I suggest parents use is that not wanting to seek help is a symptom of the illness, and that getting help is a way of getting control back off the illness, and taking control of your life again.

'Or use parallels with other areas of life, like if you had a bad arm, a bad leg, you'd go and see the doctor. If the car wasn't working, you know, you'd take it to the garage.

'Or if there's a celebrity, somebody that they know, a friend who's actually recovered from mental ill health through using support, that can be very influential. That also shows them the success stories of people getting better, and I think that's really important.' **Anita Cleare**

As before, do your research. What are the options for treatment? What are the pros and cons of medication? What can you access locally? It may take a few attempts to find what's right for your child, so if something isn't, and you have other choices, try them.

Hold on to hope

Most people do get better, even if better means learning to accommodate and manage their mental health disorder sufficiently to live a good enough, free enough, life. Have hope, for you and for them.

'So, we keep saying and showing that we believe that they can do this, they can face this, they can do difficult things, because we have to radically accept and believe that they can. And even if we doubt that on the inside, we have to hold the hope for them – "I know that just around the corner is a really happy you, is a really confident you, is a you that is doing things that she wants to do and is feeling successful. Now, we can't see her right now because she's round the corner, and we're not quite sure how to get there yet, but I know she's there, and I will help you try and find her."'
Anita Cleare

What about you?

'One of the problems is if you're parenting a teenager who has poor mental health, and that's going on for a long time, it's drawing on all of your resources. So, you've got the mental and emotional strain, that roller coaster of up and down, that effort of continually showing up, of continually regulating yourself, managing your emotions, often blaming yourself, and that's exhausting. And parents' own lives often go on hold as well. A teenager's mental health often envelops the whole family and you've got no control, no choices, no predictability and no pleasure because it undermines family activities.

'And then you may have this thing I call double identification. You have your own pain as a parent, you have your identification with your teenager's pain, and if you had a hard time yourself as a teenager, that often brings back up all the problems that you had as a teenager, too. So, almost always, if there is a long period of ill health, then the parent's mental health will be impacted to some degree or another.' **Anita Cleare**

This will take time, and you need to look after yourself. You need your own safe spaces to talk, and you need just that same empathy. How you feel is how you feel. Try to take a break, make time with friends, find little bits of normality, do something totally different, do what nurtures your wellbeing and get professional help for yourself if you need it. All of this models the value of self-care to your teenager, but it also matters because you matter yourself.

And finally ...

Tamara: I want mental illness to be destigmatized, but I wouldn't say it needs to be celebrated. I wouldn't celebrate being ill, you know. I wouldn't be proud. But I'm happy I'm not depressed anymore, and I'm not anxious anymore. I don't feel plagued by it every day. I did not think I was going to get out of it. I thought that it would kill me to be honest, and it didn't.

Warren: I think the experience made you stronger, don't you?

Tamara: Oh yeah, a hundred per cent. I think I learned a lot from it. I feel that I've learned lessons from it which are very valuable and have changed me as a person really. And losing my empathy has in a way given me more. Like, now that I've got it back, I've got more of it. It's not about me anymore. I think I have a new perspective now.

FINDING OUT MORE

Online resources

Active Minds: US non-profit providing support to young adults with mental health, with chapters across the country https://www.activeminds.org/.

Child Mind Institute: US non-profit providing information, advice and care for children and families struggling with mental health and learning disorders https://childmind.org/.

Kooth: UK online mental wellbeing community https://www.koothplc.com/.

Stem4: UK charity supporting positive mental health in teenagers https://stem4.org.uk/.

Young Minds: UK charity providing information and advice to young people and parents www.youngminds.org.uk.

Books

Suzanne Alderson, *Never Let Go: How to Parent Your Child Through Mental Illness* (Vermilion, 2020)

Ann Cox, *Helping Your Child with Worry and Anxiety* (Sheldon Press, 2021)

Roz Shafran, Ursula Saunders and Alice Welham, *How to Cope When Your Child Can't* (Robinson, 2022)

10

TALKING THE TOUGH STUFF OF ALCOHOL AND DRUGS

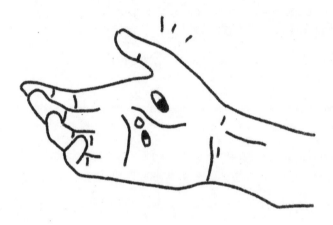

'I guess it's getting to that age where you start
experimenting with stuff, but with drugs, for me
anyway, it's like having that affection and love
from someone, even though it's not a real thing,
but it feels like it kind of loves you back.
It's hard to explain ...'

Ryan

WHO'S WHO?

Luke (20) lives with his mum and dad in the north of England. **Ryan** (20) lives with his girlfriend and their one-year-old baby in the south-west of England. **Raz** (26) lives in east London and works in finance.

I'm stepping in myself as the expert for this section. I'm Director and Founder of the DSM Foundation, a drug education charity that works with young people, parents and professionals across the UK: www.dsmfoundation.org.uk. I'm also author of *I Wish I'd Known – Young People, Drug and Decisions: A Guide for Parents and Carers* (Sheldon Press, 2021).

What do we mean by ...?

Drugs are substances that mess with your head, to simplify a process that's really very complex. Psychoactive substances – and that includes alcohol – make alterations to the messages continually whizzing around the different areas of our brains, and from there around our entire systems – speeding them up or slowing them down, changing what and how they're communicating in so many different ways. All of that has the potential to affect pretty much everything that we feel, think or do, and how we perceive, experience, relate and respond to the reality around us.

'The first time I tried cocaine, I remember the evening, yeah, it was ... I felt ... I felt unstoppable. I know it's a cliché, but I felt on top of the world. I was the most amazing person in that room, right there, and nothing else really mattered. I was sort of hyper alert, and I could do anything I wanted. It felt good, I'm not gonna lie.' **Raz**

What's the issue?

As parents we all know, though, that however amazing they might make you feel, drugs have the potential to mess with your life, as well as your head, and in so many ways. We have to be realistic and acknowledge as parents, however, that drugs are very hard for our children to avoid these days, whoever they are, wherever they live and whatever family they're from. They're around in a way they just never were for most of us as parents. A wider range, at a younger age, easily accessible and, generally speaking, affordable.

'I first started knowing of a lot of people doing drugs when I was 17. I started going to house parties and people were taking drugs along – cocaine, ketamine – and then people started going to raves and there were different things like pills, MDMA, ketamine, cocaine too, and there was a lot of drinks as well. I didn't try anything till then. I had some friends who smoked weed when I was younger, but it was never my thing, and I didn't go out that much then.' **Luke**

Unlike many of the issues addressed in Part 2 of this book, decisions about drugs are something your child will almost certainly have to face before they reach the end of their teens, and that means we have to face conversations about drugs at home. Statistics reassure us that most of the time most will say 'no', but some will say 'yes'. Perhaps only once, but perhaps more often. If they do say yes, most of the time that won't lead to any harm of any lasting sort, but sometimes it will. However, any harm, of any sort, can at best be avoided, and at least be reduced, and knowing how to tackle those tough conversations about drugs at home really will help.

'Drugs weren't something that was talked about when I was younger. As a kid growing up, I was really fit and healthy. I used to be a semi-professional footballer, so I was training every day, playing on the weekends, travelling all over the country for matches. Football was basically my life. But then I got injured, and in the space of a couple of years I went from that to absolutely nothing. By the time I was around 15 I was just going out and meeting mates and hanging around and getting up to no good. It was then that my dad moved out, too. I think that's kind of how it escalated – like, football completely done, Dad leaving, Mum just really stressed and not really knowing what to do with herself as well.' **Ryan**

Different drug conversations

There are many colourful shades of conversation you can and should have with your children about drugs, but they fall into two basic categories: the pre-emptive, preventative ones (and there need to be many of these over the years) and the ones you'll be having if you find out your child has been using drugs (and again, there are likely to be more than a few of these). The more comfortable you can make the first, the less likely you are to need to have the second, and if you do, the less tough it'll be for both of you, and the more likely you are to be able to help, and to find help for your child if they need it.

When should you start to talk about drugs?

The answer to this is: 'Much sooner than many parents think (although it's also never too late).' Children are aware of drugs and drug use from an earlier age than most parents would prefer that they were. Not only do drug-related stories come along in the news, drugs also appear in films, dramas and soaps, in music videos, in gaming and on social media. Seeing drugs being used on our big and small screens has become fairly commonplace, incidental, unremarkable behaviour. And, of course, alcohol use is deeply embedded in Western culture, even if you as a family abstain.

Creating a comfortable drug conversation

'I would say a hundred per cent I wish I would've felt more comfortable talking to my parents before I did. Drugs had always been something that was bad, and I knew that I shouldn't have been doing it. And I never wanted to let them down either, and I felt like I was letting them down. So yeah, I think it would have been a lot better if I could have talked to them earlier, 'cos it only felt that once I reached crisis point, that was when I needed to talk.' **Luke**

Keep in mind all the lessons of Part 1 around strengthening connectedness and communication generally, about listening and not making assumptions, or jumping ahead to the worst possible conclusions, and begin to weave drugs and alcohol into those everyday conversations. Be alert to opportunities and take them as they arise, and create opportunities when you feel it's a conversation that needs to be had. It's also valuable to take a moment to reflect on your own views and values about alcohol and drugs. Sometimes these aren't as clear as we think, and sometimes they're shaped by experiences within our families, friendships or wider networks that may not always be helpful for our children.

'Yeah, drugs weren't particularly an easy conversation at home growing up, and I would say that's due to some of my older relatives drinking quite heavily and being involved with drugs. Also, my grandfather on my mum's side was quite a heavy drinker before he died. So, obviously for my mum who went through that it was a very negative topic, and growing up it was, "You're not going out. You don't go to parties."' **Raz**

- *Early years.* From even when children are at preschool, you can be talking about the risks of medicines and checking the instructions together. You can be talking about how important it is to look after their bodies, take care of their wellbeing and to develop healthy coping strategies.

- *Early adolescence.* From around ten or eleven (or even earlier) conversations can become more focused. Your children may begin to be conscious of – and become curious about – alcohol, cigarettes, vaping, cannabis. It's often around this age that children are moving on to their next school, and they may become increasingly aware of drugs being around.

- *Middle adolescence.* It can often be in the early teens (but sooner for some) that alcohol and drugs will start to appear on their social radars, increasingly so as they move through their teens, both 'in real life' and online. As their independence gains momentum and their social horizons expand, the drug conversation needs to be as embedded as possible within your family narrative around risk and resilience, values and boundaries. These are the years when such conversations can be most prickly, however, so take all the tips from Part 1.

- *Late adolescence.* For most young people, drugs will be around somewhere or other, and in some environments more than others – college and university, festivals and gigs, clubs and house parties. Having honest, open conversations about drugs can become easier with late teens and twenties, but not always. Your good groundwork will help. And remember their brains still won't be helping them out as much as they need when it comes to managing risk, especially with their friends.

'Yeah, so, a lot of people were smoking weed at university and that's where I first tried it, at parties and things. Someone passes it to you and says, "Oh, would you like to try it?" I thought, sure, I'll try it.' **Raz**

Dos and don'ts of the drug conversation

A conversation about drugs at home is akin in many ways to very informal drug education, but don't let that alarm you. It doesn't mean you have to be an expert, or an educator, but it does mean you can take some useful tips from the strong international evidence base of what works and doesn't in drug education. Let's start with what doesn't, because some of this is a little counterintuitive for parents.

The drug conversation – what to avoid

- *Just say no*: This is, of course, always the safest option, and an option your teenager needs to know is always open to them, whether it feels like it is at the time or not. However, as the only piece of advice to call on, and the sole strategy to bring to a decision, it falls short. The high-profile 1980s 'Just Say No' campaign launched by Nancy Reagan became a drug education programme rolled out across the United States. However, extensive evaluation demonstrated that not only was it ineffective overall but that for some young people it actually increased their risk of substance use.

> 'I think to have had more open conversations when I was younger, and more levels of freedom, would have changed my whole outlook by the time I'd got to university. So, you know, rather than saying, even as a 16/17-year-old, "No, you're not going there, you're not going to your friend's house, you're not going to that party because they'll be drinking," and so on, perhaps if they'd said, "Yes, you can go, we'll pick you up at 11. Does that sound fair?" Just to be more open around the topic, and saying, "There's probably going to be alcohol there, so if you are having a drink, just stick to one or two, don't go crazy." I feel like a balanced attitude growing up would have given me a healthier relationship with alcohol, and not to feel like suddenly when I moved away to university I'm let loose, I can do everything I want to.' **Raz**

- *Shock tactics.* You know your child, and for them it may be enough to tell them a tragic story, or show them a shocking photo, and they'll never, ever risk going anywhere near any sort of substance themselves. However, teenagers do soon realize those worst-case scenarios are, thank goodness, rare. The more they see and hear about the positive drug-related experiences of peers – even if airbrushed, filtered or fictional in reality – the less likely they are to let that well-intentioned parental scaremongering stand in their way.

> 'I was always brought up to know they weren't a good thing to do. I know it's quite cliché, but when you see a homeless person on the street, I was always told, "Oh, that's because of drugs." It did deter me for a long time. So, we did speak about it, but we didn't ever have a big sit-down chat about it.' **Luke**

- *Facts, facts, facts.* Accurate, up-to-date, relevant information is such an important tool for a teen to bring to those decision-making situations, but remember how hard it is for adolescents to manage choice and risk safely, however much they know. Facts will only get most of them so far. See below.

The drug conversation – what to include

- *Accurate, up-to-date, relevant information.* It's not the only thing they need, but they do need it. Find reliable sources of information (see the end of the chapter), look at these yourself, and together (and do remind them their friends may not be the best place to turn to).
- *A life skills approach.* Having the skills to bring that knowledge to bear when they're making decisions is a vital component of making safe choices about drugs. As well as all the resilience

stuff of Part 1, scenario-based conversations can help with this: 'So, if you were ... and someone said ... what could you do?'

- *An interactive approach.* This is a topic of conversation that can tempt a parent into lecture mode, but again, remember Part 1, and how to do all that active listening and mutual engagement.

- *Challenging social norms.* Young people often hugely overestimate the extent to which their older peers are getting up to stuff like taking drugs and getting drunk, and these false perceptions of what's normal behaviour can shape their own decisions. Stress to them that whatever age, across the board, most young people are doing neither.

Non-verbal drug conversations

Our teenagers are watching us, and listening, and learning all the time, and there's lots we communicate well beyond a conscious conversation about drugs, through our own relationship with substances. Whether it's alcohol or nicotine, coffee or chocolate, medicines on prescription or over the counter, we're modelling attitudes to our children that can shape their own for good or ill. There's nothing inherently wrong with pouring a glass of wine at the end of a stressful day, and if you frame it within a narrative that makes it clear you're aware of the down sides and risks, you're making sure moderation and management is in the forefront of your mind, then that can be positive messaging for your teenager. If you're needing that wine to cope, then that's different. Just be aware of what your own choices are saying, and what you're saying about them.

Different types of drug use, different conversations

People young and not so young use drugs in many different ways, and for just as many different reasons. There's always a beginning, and always an end, but there's not one, single, predictable journey from that first time of trying something. If young people do say 'yes' to drugs, then for most it's a brief foray into occasional use, experimenting with friends now and then for a while, before moving on, and generally coming away unscathed. For some this may become a more regular thing that they do – perhaps every weekend, perhaps more often – and although most will also stop at some point, some may move from here into addiction.

> 'The first time I tried it was at a party. It made me feel like I fitted in. There was a lot of people a few years older than me, and it's always a little bit intimidating being in a room full of people who are older than you. I started feeling confident and chatty and stuff, and I liked that, but as well they all looked like they were having a better time than me. So, it was just something I didn't really think about. I just thought I'll do it, and just went for it.' **Luke**

There are differing risks to each of these types of use, and regardless of how often or few times you take something, especially if it's an illegal drug, those risks can be unpredictable and significant. My younger son, Dan, died when he was 16 taking MDMA, and his story is the narrative thread that I wove through all the information, insights and practical advice for parents I crammed into my book about young people, drugs and decisions, *I Wish I'd Known*. Thankfully, Dan's experience is rare, but it's just that order of worst-case scenario that plays out in every parent's panic as soon as drugs are mentioned. Death or descent into dependency. But if you suspect or know your teenager is using drugs, remember Part 1, take a deep breath, try not to let your imagination leap straight to disaster, and focus on the conversation in hand. But how can you tell if your child's using drugs?

'My parents were none the wiser for a long time – I'd probably say about six months. I've never been one for going and isolating in my room – I've always spent a lot of time watching TV with my family – but them six months I was going up earlier and earlier so that I could be on my own to take drugs in my room. I was coming downstairs for a drink, and, like, I was really chatty and my eyes would be dilated, which is something they didn't notice. I was really sweaty as well 'cos cocaine makes you sweat a lot. So, I think there were those kind of warning signs … It's only when I found myself in massive debt and I couldn't pay it off myself, that's when I had to tell my mum.' **Luke**

SIGNS OF DRUG USE CAN INCLUDE …

Occasional use

- Unusual smells, pupil dilation or constriction, sore or runny nose
- Changes to their behaviour, for example being unusually energetic, euphoric, talkative, chilled, aggressive, agitated
- Loss of coordination, drowsiness, slurred speech

Regular use

Any of the above on a more regular, frequent basis, plus …

- Changes to sleep patterns, increased lethargy, unexpected changes to weight or build
- Changes in friendship group, especially if new ones include people known or suspected to use drugs
- Drop in performance and behaviour at school
- Irritability, anger or aggression
- Depression, anxiety or panic attacks

Addiction

Any of the above, plus ...

- Changes in personal care and hygiene, social isolation
- Too little money, possessions of value or money going missing
- Persistent lateness at school, poor attendance or truancy
- Loss of interest in previous activities
- Unpredictable behaviour or self-harm

The occasional use conversation

So, your suspicions are aroused, or your fears are realized. What do you do? What do you say? How do you say it? If they've come home under the influence, the best time to talk isn't when their faculties aren't fully functional. If you can, keep your cool, register with them your awareness of their condition and your concern, and let them know the conversation is parked for now, but won't be so for long. That also gives you time to get your own emotions in check, and find the calm head you need, so you can have a conversation that won't shut doors but will enable you to talk honestly and openly (ideally). If you have your suspicions, check them out first before jumping in, because it could be something else. What have you noticed? What are your concerns?

You can start with concerned curiosity in either case, and do your best prompting and listening. It's likely they'll feel your disappointment, or fear your anger, and they may get defensive, but find out, if you can, what they're taking so you can make sure they understand its risks. Find out too, if you can, what their motivation was, and what was going on for them – and help them to understand this themselves if they're not actually entirely clear. How do they see this panning out going forward, in relation to risks, decisions, strategies, friends, working through scenarios. And what about sanctions? Were boundaries broken with consequences that they'll be expecting, and that you need to decide how to act on?

The regular use conversation

'It was all around then I changed schools and moved into a different friendship group, so rather than having mates where literally all we did was go and play football, I went to having so much time on my hands, that it was just kind of like, I dunno, it just became the norm for our group to do drugs every Friday, Saturday, Sunday.' **Ryan**

Many of the signs of drug use becoming more regular can be down to different causes, so a curious conversation is called for again, which can focus on what you've noticed, and why you're concerned, asking if they're OK, how they're feeling, if anything's going on, without making any assumptions, or jumping to any conclusions. If you know drugs are definitely involved, however, that conversation can be more direct and your concerns more explicit. All the advice just above applies here, too. Try to stay calm, and do all your prompting, listening, eliciting their understanding of the risks they're taking, finding out what's going on for them and encouraging them to reflect on their motivation, and that of the people they're doing this with.

'It would've been better if my mum had asked what was going on for me. Yeah, just why, just questions coming down to my level, and just listening, 'cos that's one thing that never really happened for me was to be able to talk to someone. It would always be arguments, just arguments, just shouting, and if she started shouting at me, I would shout back, and then it'd just blow up. And I'd leave the house and go to my mate's and do even more drugs. I know it's hard to not shout, though.' **Ryan**

One of the worries with more regular use can be a confidence that's often misplaced, and that may mean that risks are underestimated, overlooked or disregarded. It's important they have a good understanding of the substance-specific risks as well as more general ones. You might want to revisit the boundaries you'd set, and re-establish or renegotiate these in the light of this new behaviour. It's possible they won't be entirely honest about an intention to stop, but they may be quite open about the fact they don't feel it's an issue – 'Everyone's doing it! You just don't understand, Mum/Dad' – and it's vital your boundaries take this into account. It's also crucial that you make sure they have accurate harm reduction information and advice (see the end of the chapter), however uncomfortable that might feel, so they do at least know what can be done to limit the risks they're taking.

'I feel I could have gone to my mum when I was at university and said look, "I'm a bit worried I'm drinking a bit too much," but I think there was still that level of fear around her reaction, and then would it just make her put more restrictions on me when I went home for holidays, or would she be checking up on me? So, I think that was in the back of my mind when I decided not to reach out.' **Raz**

The addiction conversation

'It happened so quickly I didn't see it as a problem, 'cos I never thought I'd get into that sort of lifecycle. And then, boom, I'm doing it every day of my life, like out of nowhere, and I'm just becoming dependent. Yeah, I think that's one that I struggled with, just 'cos it happened so quickly.' **Ryan**

Addiction isn't so much to do with how much or how often someone is using a substance, but how much control they have over their use of it, whether they're able to stop or cut back despite the harm it's causing them and the impact it's having on their life. There are certain neurological changes that happen when someone is experiencing addiction, and these can mean an honest conversation can be hard to come by.

> 'My mum bought a blood-pressure machine, knowing that cocaine makes your blood pressure really high, so she was doing my blood pressure more or less every day to see what it was like, and for a long time I was still in denial. I was telling her that I wasn't taking cocaine and that my blood pressure was just high. She believed me as well. She wanted to believe me, I guess, so she did.' **Luke**

The brain becomes wired around needing and using that substance, and pathways of reward and reinforcement are strengthened, while access to the sensible prefrontal cortex is even more challenging than it already is in adolescence. Prolonged drug use can alter a person's behaviour, and you may find them saying hurtful things they'd never have said before, or lashing out in anger, or withdrawing.

> 'Drugs do all sorts to you. They make you angry and stuff, and that's not the person that I am at all. It definitely changed me into a completely different person.' **Ryan**

If you've been worrying about some of the signs above, you do need to talk. Look up some of the resources listed at the end of the chapter, get information and find out what help is available locally. Try to find a time to talk when they seem more calm, engaged and 'themselves'. As always, keeping your own emotions in check is key, and again you can start with what you've been noticing, why you're concerned, finding out what's going on with them, doing all your best listening and keeping that conversation open.

'My mum and dad reacted very differently. My mum got really upset. She felt guilty because she didn't notice that I was using drugs, and 'cos I didn't talk to her. She was saying, like, "I'm your mum, you can tell me anything," but it's not that easy because it's a lot of shame and embarrassment and guilt, and the fear of letting people down.

'My dad was really angry. He's always been anti-drugs, so for him to hear that his son was using drugs every day in his house, he was really angry. He knows what damage it can do, but as well, I could have brought trouble to his door, because the drug dealer I owed all that money to knew where I lived.' **Luke**

What if they don't think it's a problem?

'I think I knew it was a problem when I tried to stop and I couldn't. I tried to go a day without picking up and I couldn't. But for a long time, I just kind of let that go and accepted it was who I am.' **Luke**

Because of the way addiction affects the brain, it's quite possible they won't be able to see it's a problem at first (or for a while), or that they might need help, but here are some questions you could think through together that could help you both:

- Are they prioritizing it over things they used to do or value? Has doing it disrupted their life and their relationships?

- Does doing it make them feel better, and, if so, in what ways? How important has it become to their sense of self?

- Do they find themselves doing it more often and for longer periods of time than they meant to?

- How anxious or uncomfortable do they feel if they can't do it – or if they just think about not doing it?

- Are they continuing to do it even though they know it's causing them harm? Do they intend to stop, or cut back, but find they keep going back to it, or doing it even more?

Getting help, having hope

A teenager can be more vulnerable to addiction than an adult, because their brain is going through such a critical process of change. Talk about getting professional help if this isn't something you feel you can unravel together. Teenage addiction can also be more difficult to overcome – but it can be done, and has been by Ryan, Luke and Raz. Hold on to hope, and help them to believe they can find a path to freedom.

What about you?

As with all these tough conversations, make sure you look after yourself, find your own safe spaces and your own support networks. Your child needs you to be there to come back to, and to stand solid, and solidly with them, and believe that together you can get through this. And take to heart what Ryan has to say:

> 'Don't blame yourself as a parent, 'cos that starts bringing on anxiety about why's he doing it and what am I doing wrong and what can I be doing better and stuff, and it just makes it all worse. So yeah, don't blame yourself, 'cos it's not your fault.'

And finally ...

> "Cos of what I've been through, now me and my mum have the most open conversations in the world. Like, we're really open with each other, and I think that's the way I really like it. It's a lot better of

a relationship. We talk about anything. We discuss things that we would never have dreamed of talking about before all of this. My dad's a lot easier to talk to as well, because he understands more now of what I've been through. My relationships now are a lot stronger than they've been in years. Yeah, I wouldn't change what I've got at the moment.' **Luke**

FINDING OUT MORE

Online resources

Adfam: https://adfam.org.uk **DrugFAM** www.drugfam.co.uk **Scottish Families Affected by Alcohol and Drugs (SFAD)** www.sfad.org.uk UK-based charities providing information, advice and support for family members affected by a loved-one's substance use.

Crew2000: Scottish harm-reduction charity www.crew.scot.

Talk to Frank: UK government-funded website for young people www.talktofrank.com.

We Are With You: UK drug, alcohol and mental health charity https://www.wearewithyou.org.uk/.

Books

Dr Owen Bowden Jones, *The Drug Conversation* (RCPsych Publications, 2016)

Elizabeth Burton-Phillips, *'Mum, Can You Lend Me Twenty Quid?': What Drugs Did to My Family* (Piatkus Books, 2008)

Dr Suzi Gage, *Say Why to Drugs* (Hodder & Stoughton, 2021)

Fiona Spargo-Mabbs, *I Wish I'd Known – Young People, Drug and Decisions: A Guide for Parents and Carers* (Sheldon Press, 2021) Supplementary materials to the book, including a guide for parents of neurodivergent children, are also available to download from https://library.johnmurraylearning.com.

11

TALKING THE TOUGH STUFF OF EATING DISORDERS

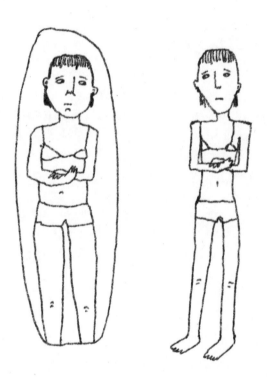

'I hate the way I am, and wish I had never changed. I wish I was still happy and loved my life, but I don't and I can't change that. I don't really see any proper future for myself, although I used to. I just try to think about each day as it comes, and get through it. I really hate the way I am now, especially as I have put on weight. I feel utterly out of control, and lost in a big world.'

Sophie (aged 15)

'Parents are crucial. They're the only people that are going to hold on to that hope all the way through. The unconditional love of a parent is everything. And it's that patience and that perseverance with eating disorders which is absolutely crucial.'

Jenny Langley

WHO'S WHO?

Sophie is 30 and grew up in North London, and **Sue** is her mum. Extracts of an essay Sophie wrote at school when she was 15 are included, as well as our conversation.

Jenny Langley is Lead Facilitator at New Maudsley Carers Kent, co-author of *Caring for a Loved One with an Eating Disorder: The New Maudsley Skills-based Training Manual* (Routledge, 2018) and author of *Boys Get Anorexia Too: Coping with Male Eating Disorders in the Family* (Lucky Duck Books, 2006), which includes the story of her son Sam who developed anorexia at the age of 12.

What do we mean by ...?

Eating disorders are mental illnesses that involve disordered eating behaviour. They have their own particular painfulness for parents, because feeding our children, and feeding them well, is one of the first and most fundamental parts of our job. However, eating disorders are illnesses, and complex, and although they appear to be focused entirely on food, they're not, or not anywhere near entirely.

> 'Part of the thinking behind the eating disorder, although I don't remember being consciously aware of it till much later (after years of therapy), was that I feel guilty for existing, which comes out in various ways, so, like, for example, I feel guilty for taking up space (hence losing weight), and I feel guilty for using up resources (especially food) and taking up people's care (so I feel I only deserve care if I'm ill enough).' **Sophie**

Most people can and will recover, but living with an eating disorder, and loving someone with an eating disorder, can be complicated and confusing, and cause chaos within families. They can make communication challenging for many reasons, not least because they involve so much secrecy and duplicity, but also, for many, it can seem as if the eating disorder takes over the child they know and love, takes on a life of its own and very much has its own voice in any conversation.

> 'I think I was in secondary school when I first started doing diets and stuff, and then skipping meals. I was probably around 13 or 14. And then, when I started the next year at school, I had probably about three months when I ate maybe four or five meals the whole time. I'd get up early, pretend I'd had breakfast – get some crumbs on a plate, get a knife with butter on it – then give away my packed lunch at school, and then dinner I'd be out every day. I'd just be, like, "Oh yeah, it's Guides and we're eating this week," or Air Cadets, we're eating this night, this kind of stuff, and just telling Mum I was eating at all these different places.
>
> 'My weight really plummeted, and that was when I got pulled in to the nurse at school.' **Sophie**

What it's not ...

- *It's not (just) about food.* It's not (just) about eating, or weight either; it's (almost) always about something else altogether, about which behaviours relating to food have become a way of coping. This is why there's so much secrecy, and fear of being found out, and having it taken away. Restoring regular eating is crucial in terms of both physical health and brain function, including emotional regulation, and facing foods that are feared is a huge part of recovery, but without addressing what lies beneath it all, none of this is likely to work, and all of it is likely to get worse.

> 'We need to acknowledge that this is a coping strategy. It can really help parents to think about the benefits the eating disorder gives to their child. Why are they holding onto it with such ferocity and tenacity? Your child isn't being wilful. They've found a coping strategy that's working for them at the moment.' **Jenny Langley**

'One of the reasons I struggle to gain weight is because being low weight is the only visible sign to others that I'm not OK. I'm not good at showing my emotions or asking for help, so if I stay low weight, people are more likely help me or not expect too much from me. It's why I struggled so much when I did gain weight, but I was still bingeing. People around (including doctors) all said I was doing really well and recovering, but my behaviours were the same and everything inside my head was still the same, too. The larger body didn't match with the mess in my head. It just made me increase the self-harming as a way of continuing to use my body to show that things were still not good. So being forced to gain weight in hospital didn't fix anything, it just shifted where I displayed my symptoms.' **Sophie**

- *It's not a fad or a phase.* Don't ignore your concerns if you have some, or just hope it will pass. If it's an eating disorder, then early diagnosis and treatment can make recovery much less protracted and painful. Medical checks and interventions may also be needed. If your fears are unfounded, then checking them out won't make anything worse.

'It's really important parents understand the medical risks to their child [see websites at the end of the chapter]. Getting a medical assessment early on is really important with a restrictive eating disorder. The doctor will do all of the physical measurements – heart rate, blood pressure, weight, height, all of that – so that gives you a baseline, so then at least when you go to your doctor a week later or a month later they'll see what's moved from that baseline. You need to know that trajectory. And, really importantly, it's all about writing everything down.' **Jenny Langley**

- *It's not always visible.* Not in body size or on the scales at least, nor in altered behaviours relating to food, as far and for as long as they can be hidden. You may see a rapid loss of weight in your child, but the majority of people with eating disorders remain within a normal healthy weight range, or become overweight, and many maintain a relatively stable shape and size, or hide fluctuations beneath carefully selected clothing.

Me: When did you notice, Sue?

Sue: It wasn't until the school called us in, when she was 14 or 15. I think before that happened we were oblivious. She's a very clever girl, and we were totally fooled.

Me: And did you find ways to hide your weight loss, Sophie?

Sophie: Not really. I kind of wanted that reassurance that I had lost weight. You encouraged me at first, Mum, because I was the top end of normal.

Sue: I'd lost quite a lot of weight around that time, and I was pleased with myself for doing so – so that won't have helped, because we were literally friends together going, 'Yeah, we've managed to lose weight!' So certainly, it flipped from me being pleased to me being worried for you. But before that I hadn't noticed.

Sophie: But at that point I never got below normal. I went from right at the top of normal to right at the bottom of normal. It wasn't till I was over 18 that I actually ever dropped to below normal, but doing that in three months was not ideal! And then the bingeing started after that, so, you know, that wasn't ideal either.

- *It's not just girls.* Up to a quarter of people with eating disorders are thought to be male. The stigma around eating disorders and around male sufferers means it's hard to know for certain, but it's safe to say boys are by no means immune.

- *It's not a choice.* Although the most obvious thing for someone risking their health, and potentially their life, by not eating, is surely just to eat, this is a serious mental illness, and it's far from being that simple.

'I became tormented by my brain. One half was telling me to eat, that I was being stupid, but the other half was telling me not to eat, that I was too fat to be allowed food. I hated it and was very confused.' **Sophie (aged 15)**

'Eating disorders are not a choice, they just happen to people, so you can't just choose to stop. Imagine if you had this voice in your head that went crazy at you every time you even looked at food. It's excruciating. If you had that bully in your head, you'd do anything to keep them quiet.' **Jenny Langley**

- *It is – but it's also not – your child.* Your child may say some terrible things to you, and behave in ways you would never have imagined possible. Parents can feel their child is lost and gone for ever, but any awfulness isn't your child, it's the eating disorder, taking an (almost always temporary) control.

'It's not disobedience or being naughty. It's not about deliberately upsetting the people who love you. It needs treatment, not punishment. It really helps if parents treat it with more compassion instead of anger and frustration.' **Sophie**

'The main thing you can do is avoid arguments at all costs. The minute you have an argument with someone with an eating disorder you tend to get caught up in a battle with their eating disorder voice, and you're never going to win that argument. So the most important thing, always, from the minute you suspect an eating disorder, is to stay calm and to use a low voice. A raised voice feeds straight into the eating disorder argument.' **Jenny Langley**

- *It's not their fault.* It's an illness. They may feel it's their fault, and others may too, and that won't help, so they need you to know that it isn't, and to make sure other people understand that, too.

- *It's not your fault either.* You'll almost certainly be convinced it is, but there's no real evidence parents cause eating disorders, and in fact they play the most vital role in the frontline of care, support and bringing a teenager through, and hopefully out the other side. Feelings of guilt and responsibility can be very hard to shake off, but they're also debilitating, and your energy is needed, and much more usefully spent on supporting your child and the rest of the family, and also yourself.

'To start off with, parents will be talking to family and friends who know nothing about eating disorders, and sadly people will often say all the wrong things. They'll make you feel ashamed. They'll make you feel guilty. So, very often when parents come together with other parents who also have children with eating disorders, it's the first time they've been able to talk openly about what's going on in their house, to people who understand what's going on.' **Jenny Langley**

What are the signs and the symptoms?

There are four main eating disorders: anorexia, bulimia, binge eating disorder and Other Specified Feeding or Eating Disorders (OSFED). However, people may not have all the symptoms of any one disorder, they may have symptoms that overlap several, and their symptoms, and consequently their diagnosis, may change over time. Have a look on the Beat Eating Disorders or F.E.A.S.T. websites for more information and details.

'The big, big warning signs are an increase in perfectionism, going on a diet, upping the exercise and becoming more moody. These are things to look out for. Then literally every day you'll start to notice something else, so my big tip for parents is start writing down any changes in behaviour – write it all down. Food, mood, weight, shape, exercise.

'But so many parents say they just didn't see it coming. It's so difficult for parents, because what happens to begin with is that they see their child is eating more healthily, which seems like a good thing. They see their child is doing more exercise, which is a good thing. So to start with, that child is getting so many affirmations from everyone around them, and that can itself be the trigger into a full-blown eating disorder, and it can happen in a week. So we can talk about warning signs, but you have to take a step back and accept that sometimes you just don't see it because it happens so quickly.' **Jenny Langley**

That said, there are many general signs that may (or may not) indicate an eating disorder – too many to list in detail – but some of the main ones are:

- preoccupation with food and eating, and altered attitudes and relationship with food
- secretive and self-conscious behaviour around food
- changes in weight, and/or weight fluctuations
- body image concerns
- excessive or compulsive exercise
- irritability, anger and mood swings
- tiredness, feeling cold
- social withdrawal and isolation
- low self-esteem, anxiety, feelings of shame and guilt.

For some young people an eating disorder may not be the only way they've found of coping with difficult emotions. Some also self-harm. Some use substances. Some attempt suicide. None of these are inevitable, but need to be on the radar of a parent with a teenager who's found at least one unhealthy coping strategy they know about.

'My mum was called into school and told about everything, so she became much stricter about food. I still had no lunch, but I was forced to have breakfast and dinner. I hated this time, so to deal with it I cut myself even more. As I had to eat more I decided I had to exercise more to make up for it.' **Sophie (aged 15)**

The first conversation(s)

So, you've noticed some changes in your teenager's behaviour that you're concerned could be the sign of an eating disorder. What do you do? What do you say? How do you say it?

'The first conversations need a softly, softly approach. The minute you say, "I think you have an eating disorder," you've shut the door to further communication, and you're likely to drive them underground. So it's all about noticing what's going on for that person. Calmly notice the signs that you're seeing – "I've noticed that you're tired and cold. I've noticed that you're cutting down on your food." A really good tip is to say, "I've noticed you're not quite yourself, and I've booked an appointment with the doctor just to have a physical check-up."' **Jenny Langley**

Once you have that diagnosis – or even if you don't (this can sometimes still be hard to come by) but you've done your research, and know you've got good grounds for concern – then your eating disorder journey begins. For your child this will have begun perhaps long before, but this is the start of you travelling this road together, and it's one that can swallow up so much of your – and your family's – energy, time, patience and hope. It needs the right help and advice, it may need medical intervention and you both/all need good, solid support.

'I always say to parents the eating disorder of course paralyses you – you are frozen with fear that your child's never going to get better – but you need to step out of that paralysis, and become the warrior, not the worrier. Think about the Saint Bernard – in the face of any avalanche, the Saint Bernard is there, solid, calm, compassionate, never going anywhere. It's that unconditional love that's so important.' **Jenny Langley**

You may need to find your own Saint Bernard, especially at the beginning, for those times when the oncoming avalanche feels just too overwhelming for you to withstand yet again. But most parent find that the more they adopt this role, the better they get at it. Have hope.

Why can talking be particularly tough?

There are dynamics specific to eating disorders that mitigate strongly against a calm conversation, but as with all these issues, talking is vital. Here are a few of the factors at work.

- *Denial.* Expect this, especially at the start. They may genuinely not think they have any issues around food. They may not think what they're doing is that bad. They may be terrified you'll try to take it away, and make them stop.

> **Sue:** In those early months you wouldn't have told me 'I feel I'm anorexic' because you were still trying to hide it.
>
> **Sophie:** Yeah, I was. I wanted to be thin enough still, and I didn't want someone to stop me being thin.

- *Lying.* Eating disorders are secretive, and sufferers go to ingenious, imaginative and sometimes quite extreme lengths to avoid detection. Expect your child to lie, and to try to deceive you in multiple ways, but know this comes from fear, and illness, not because they don't value honesty or your trust.

> 'I told my mum that we were having social outings, cookery nights etc. at Guides and Air Cadets, so I didn't have to have dinner most nights. It felt weird because I had never been good at lying, but I suddenly found it easy, because I felt it was vital that I was believed.' **Sophie (aged 15)**

- *Resistance.* If this is the way they're coping with something too big for them to bear, then someone trying to take it away will feel incredibly threatening. Cooperation may be hard-won, and your best negotiation skills required to make any headway.

'Dad tries to bully me into recovery even now, and it doesn't help. I just say, "Screw you". You can't bully it out of someone. If you fight me, I fight back straight away, like, I'm straight on the defence.' **Sophie**

'It's all about the strength of the relationship, not the strength of the argument. So all the time parents need to think, "Am I connecting with my teenager or am I actually pushing them away?" And if you feel you're pushing them away, then get out a blank piece of paper and start again, because pushing them away is exactly what the eating disorder voice is wanting – "Your parents don't understand you. I'm your only friend." So always think, "Am I still connecting?"' **Jenny Langley**

- *Strong emotions.* Expect to be hated, and to hear hurtful things, but try not to take it personally. They don't really mean it – there's a lot going on for them. There's the fear that comes from the threat of this being taken away, and the fear they may have that their eating is actually out of control, especially if they're bingeing. There's the effect on their mental health, the heavy load of guilt and shame, the impossibly low self-esteem and of course the pain of the problems that lie behind their eating disorder. Prepare to weather a storm.

Me: So why did you hate your mum, Sophie?

Sophie: Because she was trying to control me, and feed me. Like, for example, you went through my pockets at one point, Mum, because I used to hide food there, and you made me turn them all out after a meal one time.

Me: Did you feel that was you or the eating disorder talking?

Sophie: I dunno, yeah, it was definitely the eating disorder side of me that hated her. The rest of me didn't.

- *Effects on the brain.* On top of all the regular changes going on in any adolescent brain, a brain in a body that's undernourished will take more of a hit. This can affect a teenager's social cognition, decision-making skills and their emotional regulation and expression, all of which are already challenged. It might seem to change their personality altogether, but it's not them, it's their eating disorder.

> **Me:** So presumably Sophie at that early stage you didn't want to talk to your parents because you wouldn't want anyone to stop you?
>
> **Sophie:** No, I definitely didn't want anyone to stop me.
>
> **Me:** And from the point when you found out, Sue, were conversations OK, or were they difficult?
>
> **Sophie:** We fell out BIG time! I hated you with a passion. I wanted to move out. I couldn't stand to be around you. We had massive arguments. We had screaming arguments.
>
> **Sue:** I don't remember that at all. I remember things like in Germany when we were on holiday, and going round that amusement park together just you and me – we left the boys with Dad, do you remember? – and we had a lovely time together, and this was right in the middle of this stage, so ...
>
> **Sophie:** I don't remember that at all.
>
> **Sue:** You don't remember it? You see, isn't it strange? I've got exactly the opposite.
>
> **Sophie:** Once I was ill, the only thing I remember about holidays was food.

The mealtime conversation

Dinner is served, you're all at the table, and the eating disorder is sitting there too, alive and kicking and not showing any signs of cooperation or compliance. Again. The stakes are getting higher. The risks are rising. It's impossible not to feel this has become a battleground, with your child and that plate of food in front of them the victor's prize (or the loser's punishment). What can you do?

'The biggest piece of advice at mealtimes is to keep calm and avoid arguments at all costs, which is really hard when we know the eating disorder voice is going to trying to get your child to not eat anything, but the minute you raise your voice, the minute there's any hint of criticism, that voice is going to flare up in their head. And don't talk about food, weight or shape at the meal table. Don't get into in a circular argument about how many calories are in this or that.

'To do this you need to be talking about something else. Distractions at the meal table are really powerful. That takes preparation, and that means sitting down with your child and having that conversation. What would help to get you through a meal situation? Is it having funny YouTube videos on? Is it all of us playing a game?

'To get through the meal itself you do whatever you can, and every family is unique. Some families find that if they just go "One more bite, you can trust us," that helps to keep the eating disorder voice quiet. Another family will find that if there's an element of choice – 'Three potatoes or a cup of rice?' – that'll work. So it's very much family by family working out what helps for them. You've got to have that conversation with your child in advance, of course, and away from the meal table, so preparation is key.

These are some practical tips, but don't beat yourself up if it doesn't work. To start with you do get trapped in having an argument. Parents are very good at feeding their healthy child, but they're not good at feeding their very, very sick child. It's so hard – it's the hardest thing – and you feel awful when you don't manage it.'
Jenny Langley

Me: What would have helped conversations in that difficult time from your point of view, Sophie?

Sophie: I dunno. I think less of a battleground between us would have helped.

Sue: Me not checking through your pockets, not checking your room ...?

Sophie: I think, maybe, making agreements, like asking me which bits I could manage, rather than you telling me, 'You are going to eat all of this,' or whatever. So going, 'OK, I'm not going to fight on the breakfast, but can we eat the vegetables at dinner?' you know, that sort of thing. The second Mum starts trying to control something I fight back against it, whatever it is.

Me: So, sort of negotiating an agreement between you rather than imposing something?

Sophie: Yeah, I think so. And, like, little baby steps maybe? There's a slightly higher chance of me agreeing if I was involved in that decision-making process, I think. The times when it's helped has been when it's come from me. And it's certainly helped our relationship as well.

The ongoing conversation

All of those Part 1 conversational strategies and skills will help with talking the tough stuff of eating disorders, but there are also some specific suggestions that may help in addition to these. One is to keep the focus as much on non-food-related matters as possible, and hold on to life outside the eating disorder. Make time, if you can, either just to hang out, or to do things together you both enjoy, and that make your child feel good about themselves.

'My advice to parents would be to sort of try to not fight, in a way. Like, I feel every time we talked it ended in an argument. Kind of be there to talk about other stuff, and sort of, you know, don't make it about the food, because it probably isn't about the food, and if you start trying to fight the food it just ends up in a battle, whereas if you kind of sit down and go, "Is anything going on?" or just talking generally, I think it's more likely to get a response.' **Sophie**

Also, if there are two of you parenting your teen together, try to find a united position. It's not at all uncommon for two parents to hold very different views on how this can best be dealt with, and your child's eating disorder may well work away at any division between you, and play one off against the other. Talk and listen to each other, as well as to others you trust, and try to find some common ground you're both comfortable in, because this will be the best help to your child, and to each other.

What about you?

As with all of these Part 2 issues you do need to look after yourself. This is often a long haul. Find your own safe spaces and trusted people to sit with and go through your fears, hurts and frustrations, away from the conversation with your child. Do your research, find your support, connect with others going through similar stuff. You need to take care of your own emotional and physical wellbeing, not just because you need to stay strong to help your teen get through this, but because you matter, too.

Hold on to hope

This is so important, though it may be incredibly hard at times. Recovery is usually a protracted process with many backward as well as forward steps, but most people do get there, and of those who don't, most find ways to live with, and cope with, their eating disorder. You need to hold on to that hope for your child, but you may need someone to hold on to hope for you, too, for those times when it slips from your grasp. Hope is so important for you both.

'Parents can hold the light for their child, even when they're in a really, really dark place. Most people with eating disorders have a stage when they say, "I'm not going to recover, I don't want to get better," and that's really hard for parents. But it's important for parents to know that most people with eating disorders will say this, but most will also go on to make a full recovery. So, you can hold on to that light for them. It's about focusing on what's going well for your child. It's about belief in their abilities. You're providing a scaffold and a safety net for what's wrong with them but you're also providing that visualisation of happier times ahead. That's so important.' **Jenny Langley**

And finally ...

Sue: I do still worry that, once I wasn't confronting the eating disorder, then I think I went too much the other way, and I felt like I was almost encouraging it, and I think that balance is difficult for parents. I can't remember the name they used for it in the training we did.

Sophie: Enabling?

Sue: Yes, maybe enabling. I sort of made a decision: I'm not going to interfere with it because I'm only making it worse. I just want to enjoy being friends. But I worry I'm making it worse from the other direction.

Sophie: The only thing I remember them saying is about being a dolphin, nudging along beside you. Your parent's swimming along beside you, and when you sink then they nudge you back up again. And I'd say that's what you do.

Sue: Would you? I feel like I'm almost making it too easy for you.

Me: But maybe you're just being a dolphin?

Sophie: I certainly see you more as a dolphin ...

FINDING OUT MORE

Online resources

Beat Eating Disorders: A UK charity providing information, resources and support for anyone affected by an eating disorder www.beateatingdisorders.org.uk.

F.E.A.S.T.: A US-based non-profit (Families Empowered And Supporting Treatment for Eating Disorders), F.E.A.S.T. is a global community of parents and those who support parents www.feast-ed.org/.

National Eating Disorders: A US non-profit organization dedicated to supporting individuals and families affected by eating disorders www.nationaleatingdisorders.org/.

New Maudsley Carers: A UK organization providing downloadable worksheets and videos for parents and carers as well as online workshops https://newmaudsleycarers-kent.co.uk/.

Talk ED (formerly Anorexia & Bulimia Care): A UK charity providing care and support for anyone affected by an eating disorder www.talk-ed.org.uk.

Books

Jenny Langley, *Boys Get Anorexia, Too* (Paul Chapman Publishing, 2006)

Dr Pamela Macdonald, *How to Help Someone with an Eating Disorder: A Practical Handbook* (Wellbeck Balance, 2021)

Jane Smith, *The Parents' Guide to Eating Disorders* (Lion Books, 2011)

12

TALKING THE TOUGH STUFF OF SELF-HARM

'You don't ever forget that feeling of it. It's really weird,
like, it's such an adrenaline rush and kind of such
a ... it becomes a niggling thought in the back of your
mind. And, like, still to this day it's something that
I really struggle to not listen to, because it can get so big
sometimes, and it's just ... it becomes all you can think
about, and something sometimes you just can't ignore,
like, the voice in your head that's going, "You need to do
it, you want to do it, it's the only way." You get to a point
that you feel so numb and you're, like, nothing matters
anymore. This is the only way to kind of get out.'

Sofia

WHO'S WHO?

Sofia is 21 and is at university in the south of England. Outside term time she lives in London with her mum, **Pat**.

Jane Smith was CEO of UK charity Anorexia and Bulimia Care from 2004 until 2020 (now Talk ED). She is author of *The Parent's Guide to Self-Harm* (Lion Hudson, 2012) and *The Parent's Guide to Eating Disorders* (Lion Hudson, 2011), written both as a specialist and as a parent with lived experience.

Note: I'm using the term 'self-harm' in this chapter, also commonly referred to in the United States as 'non-suicidal self-injury'.

What do we mean by ...?

Self-harm happens when someone deliberately hurts or injures themselves. For obvious reasons, this can be very distressing for parents. We're full of overpowering instincts to protect our children from harm, and to stand in the way of anyone who hurts them, so learning this is something they're doing to themselves can be extremely tough.

'You've spent your life as a parent putting plasters on things, not wanting them to fall and hurt themselves, and then to know that they're deliberately doing this themselves, it's incredibly hard. But the hurt serves another purpose. It manages the situation of how they're feeling about themselves, and the struggles they're facing – and of course as a parent you don't understand that to begin with. All you can see is that they're harming themselves, and you want them to stop.' **Jane Smith**

Sofia: Do you remember the first time? It was because school had rung, 'cos they could see it in PE. Mate, you were traumatized! You took a picture of my arm. That was not good.

> **Pat:** I do remember being traumatized, and it was just, like, I just couldn't believe it, because I had no idea. It was a total shock.

Self-harm can take various forms. You may think first of cutting, but it can include anything from scratches and bruises to burns or overdoses – basically anything anyone does to deliberately hurt themselves. Some people may just do it once or twice, while for others it can be something they keep coming back to. Injuries may be minor, but could be serious, and can unintentionally risk their life, so this is something that does need to be handled with great care.

> 'The first time I was kind of young. Basically, Mum had this cutter thing, where you cut pieces of paper with it, like a piece of plastic, but I didn't use like the razor part, I used the plastic part. I was too afraid to use sharp things, but also using blunt things, it kind of hurts more, so it makes you feel, like, more alive.' **Sofia**

Self-harm is always a sign that something else is wrong. It's the way your child is coping with whatever that might be, and though it may be hard to understand, it does mean there's always reason for concern, and not just about the obvious 'what' of the wounds, but the 'why' that's hidden behind them. It may be something that might seem quite small to a parent – worrying about an exam or a friendship in crisis – or it could be a much more deep-seated issue, but whatever it is, at the moment your child is unable to find a better way to cope.

Why talking self-harm can be tough

It's very hard for children and young people to talk to a parent about the fact that they're intentionally hurting themselves. It's something they're probably going to considerable lengths to conceal, to protect their private method of dealing with difficult things. It's something about which they may feel some shame and guilt. Opening up honestly will take a lot of courage and trust on their side, and a lot of sensitivity and patience on yours, but being someone they feel they can turn to is so important, as always.

'The shame you do feel afterwards, I don't know what the word is … it's awful. You feel very isolated and very alone, like, "Why do I feel like this? And why doesn't anyone understand why I feel like this?"' **Sofia**

There are myths and misconceptions about self-harm we can all as parents hold in our heads that can get in the way of open, honest and fruitful conversations. Run through the following: don't be too hard on yourself if one or two resonate, but note them and put them out of your own head if they do.

'One of the first assumptions many of us make is that self-harming is a bid for suicide, and although it can be, mostly it isn't, and it can lead to panic and anger due to the fear around that. At the other end of the scale is that it's a copycat activity. Sometimes parents can tend to be a bit dismissive of it on this basis, and say, "Oh well, everyone's doing it," which makes the child feels belittled or dismissed, or like they're being stupid. Sometimes parents assume it's only "difficult" or "other people's children" do this, and so that can convey disgust and disdain which doesn't help conversations. Or sometimes they think by intervening in some way, talking about it or whatever, they could be making this worse, so they'll just keep quiet. And I think also it's a case of not understanding that there's a process towards recovery or overcoming self-harming, so the "Just stop it!" isn't at all helpful, or doable actually, and realizing that your child might not be at the stage of wanting to stop, even though you're desperate for them to do so.' **Jane Smith**

Why self-harm?

There are many reasons why people self-harm, and understanding what these are for your child is important in order to support them, and to help them find a route through. As well as uncovering the issue that's motivated this as a coping strategy in the first place, there's also finding out the specific way this is helping them cope, what the benefits are for them and how it makes them feel better.

- *Relief.* Self-harm can be a way to release difficult thoughts or emotions, providing a vent when these build up so much they just don't feel they can hold them inside any longer.

- *Distraction.* Hurting yourself can clear your head if, again, it feels too full of anxiety or trauma or negative thoughts. It focuses the mind on the pain on the outside and away from the pain on the inside.

- *Control.* If young people feel their life is chaotic, and they're powerless to exert the influence they want to over things that are affecting them or the people they love, then self-harm can give them something they feel they can control amid all they can't.

'I don't know, like, looking back on it, it seems so dumb, but at that point it feels like it's the only thing that you can do. I had a lot of troubles at home with my dad … Yeah, like, obviously Mum and my sister were amazing, but my dad was horrible. He was a lovely person, but when he was drunk, he was a horrible person, and I started to feel a bit like, "Why do I get to live in this while other people seemingly have normal lives?" I was even cross with Mum, 'cos I was like, why is she making us live in this house? And she always threatened to leave, and we'd never go. I just found that really difficult to live with. I felt like I didn't have anything to control, and I had just, like, so much frustration. The only thing I could control was how I physically felt.' **Sofia**

- *Physical rather than emotional pain.* For some young people, physical pain makes sense in a way the pain they're feeling inside doesn't, and it can validate their emotional state.

- *Punishment.* Causing themselves pain or injury can be a way some young people, including perfectionists, punish themselves for a perceived failure, and it can feel to them an appropriate response to their sense of worthlessness, poor self-esteem or for getting things wrong.

- *Connection.* Sometimes, if someone has experienced trauma, they can switch off, or tune down, their feelings to reach a degree of sufficient numbness to cope. Self-harm can enable them to feel more connected or 'alive'.

- *Pain relief.* There are physiological reasons why physical pain can provide relief from emotional pain, although it's a very short-term measure, as with all the above. When we experience an injury our body releases endorphins which are a natural painkiller. They also help us think more clearly and feel more relaxed and calm.

What signs might you see?

Most young people who self-harm go to some considerable lengths to prevent anyone around them from knowing, especially a parent, who might panic, or be angry, or disappointed, or try to make them stop. And a busy parent can easily overlook what clues there might be, or put them down to the difficult stuff of being a teenager.

> 'You might notice them becoming more withdrawn or depressed, spending more time in their rooms, although this is often hard to notice as teenagers often do this anyway, but you kind of know, don't you, if something's not right?

'Look out for them spending more time than usual in the bathroom or shower – this is often the only private and lockable room in the house. Boys getting into fights or more fights. Covering up – maybe wearing long sleeves even in summer so they're not showing marks.

'If you think they may be self-harming, then I'd be looking in their wastepaper bin, looking out for things like blood on tissues, you know, looking out for signs. But try not to go snooping or following your child round the house, listening outside their door or the bathroom door.

'You might actually see scratches, cuts or burns, or bruises often on arms or thighs. These can often be explained away as accidental, so you might notice something, but your child says, "Oh no, it was the cat," or whatever. They're very good at covering up, because they know you're going to be worried, and they'll fear you questioning them, but also they need it as their own secret coping mechanism, and they know that parents are probably going to try to stop them.' **Jane Smith**

What to do if you have concerns

If you do have concerns, as always, trust your instincts. You're the person who knows them best. It may not be self-harm, but if your parental radar is on alert, then there'll be a reason.

- *Do your research.* Do some discreet observation at home; build up a picture and look for patterns. For the time being keep medicines and razors discreetly hidden (though this isn't fool-proof to a determined teenager). Use the resources signposted below to find out about self-harm – the reasons, the risks and how and where to find help if it's needed.

- *Find a good time and place.* Where and when will you both be relaxed and receptive? Would it help to take some time out together? Do your best gentle questioning, careful listening, keeping those channels of communication as safe and wide open as you possibly can.

'Beware of launching in straight away with your fears about them and "accusing" them or becoming emotional. Just a general open-ended question, you know, "How are things going? I've noticed you're not yourself. Is anything the matter?" And they'll probably go, "Oh nothing, nothing ..." and you might have to try lots of times, keeping the lines of communication open, trying to understand what is at the root of their change of behaviour.' **Jane Smith**

- *Keep your emotions in check.* Keep the tone non-judgemental and calm, reinforcing your unconditional love for them whatever is going on, whether they feel they can talk at that time or not, and keeping the conversation open for when they might be ready. Think through what your own feelings might be if your child does disclose self-harm.

'I remember Dad seeing one of my self-harm marks by accident and he went absolutely ballistic. He went mental! "How dare you do that to your body? What do you think you are doing? You're so stupid! Wait till your mother finds out about this. Why were you trying to keep it away from me?" And it was, like, really like, "Ohhhh my gosh!" I got banished to my room. He was, like, "Go away! Go to your room!" I was terrified. He didn't talk to me for the rest of the day and, like, waited until Mum came home and then he made me talk about it in front of him and Mum, and basically it was like, "You're really stupid to have done that," which, obviously, didn't make me stop, and I just felt very alone, very, yeah ... very ashamed. I just remember, like, going to bed and crying myself to sleep.' **Sofia**

- *Expect resistance.* There may be many reasons why your child may not be ready or willing to talk to you, and pushing the subject too hard, or at all, may make them back off and shut down. Be sensitive to the moment, test the waters and bide your time if you need to.

'You might get denial, anger, tearfulness, arguments, somebody who's completely "closed" and not willing to talk. Realize that these are typical reactions. Being calm and showing love and concern might enable your child to talk to you, but don't give up if your first few attempts to talk don't go well. Try again another time or place.' **Jane Smith**

- *Find a proxy.* If it's clear there's an issue but they can't talk to you, ask them if there's someone else they feel they could talk to who they (and ideally you) trust, such as another family member or family friend, someone at school, a counsellor or your family doctor (try to find one in the practice you feel would understand).

What to do if you know

'It's really important for parents to make their child feel safe and not feel ashamed for doing something like that, 'cos you do feel immense guilt afterwards. So, to know, like, it's OK that you're feeling how you're feeling. You're not a weirdo, you're a not bad person for doing it, you know. It's just that you've got to a point where you feel you couldn't do anything else.' **Sofia**

If you've pieced together a pattern of clues, the dawning of realization will have given you some time at least to prepare your response, but if it's an out-of-the-blue phone call from school, an unintentional glimpse of an undeniable sign or they've been brave enough to tell you themselves, that's a very big deep breath moment for you.

'If they tell you, "Yes, I'm struggling with this, and you're going to go mad, but actually, I find I get some relief from cutting my arm," you're going to want to burst out into, "What?!" and "Why? Why would you do this?" But just try and think, they've come to you and something's really up for them at the moment, so actually, forget your shock and horror for the moment, take that out somewhere else, and say, "OK. I'm really sorry to hear that. Can you tell me more about the issues, and also about the self-harming." Try to understand where your child is on their "journey" of self-harm – is it new to them or has it been going on for a while?

'Show them that you really want to listen and hear from them. Let them have the floor. Don't interrupt and say what you think and what you fear. All this allows them to come to you again if they're in distress, or worried about a wound that hurts them or something, and of course if they want your help to reduce the self-harming, if they're at that stage.' **Jane Smith**

What (to try) not to do

It's always important to keep communication open between you and your teens, but especially if they're at risk and struggling, it matters more than ever you do your best not to shut the channels of conversation down. This can be easy to do, however, so here are some understandable 'don'ts' to avoid.

'Don't get angry with them, which can often be the result of your fear and panic. Don't dismiss or belittle it either, because even what might seem like relatively minor self-harming will have a root issue that is really troubling your child. Don't blackmail them emotionally to "just stop" by telling them how much this affects and hurts you or anyone else they care about. Don't tell lots of people – keep it as confidential as you can for their sake, to maintain their trust, and avoid lots of questions and judgement.'

'Don't "police them" and stalk them, and try not to imagine they're self-harming whenever they are out of sight. It's really easy to just worry, worry, worry all the time. And don't make their self-harming the only thing you talk about. That's really easy to do too, because it's on the tip of your tongue all the time you're with them.' **Jane Smith**

Ongoing conversations

- *Keeping talking, keeping listening, keeping calm.* All the best advice of Part 1 is especially important with the tough stuff of Part 2, when the burdens are that much heavier, and the barriers to good communication can be much more complicated. As well as creating safe spaces to talk, explore ways they feel you could help, if you can, and if they'll let you.

'It's something like just listening, and saying, "Whenever you're ready and feel like you're able to talk to me about it, I'll be here. There's completely no judgement. You feel how you feel for a reason and your feelings are valid." And then once you've started that conversation it can be, like, "What are the steps I can do to kind of see that you're starting to get to that bad point again? And what can I do to help you, if there is anything?"' **Sofia**

'Especially if it's an older child, I would ask them, "What help would you like, and what part would you like me to play?" As self-harming is a coping method and an immediate response to the emotions your child is feeling, you may be able to work with them during these times of heightened distress and emotion to choose other methods of calming themselves, and find some distraction techniques. See if they can let you know when they feel triggered to self-harm, because usually it comes like a growing wave, and if they can identify when that moment is coming, you can help to steer them into alternative actions or feelings. What is it that helps them? Different things will work for different people. Breaking the cycle of self-harming for those for whom it has become a ritual and planned can reduce the occurrence.

'It's really key to help them identify the root cause, and perhaps help them to untangle it, and if possible even find some strategies to deal with that issue. People who self-harm often just can't process their thoughts or problem-solve, and one of the things we may be able to do as parents is to help them find some sense and order.

'You might be able to talk about some ground rules with your child, like being open to talking about wound care and telling you (or someone they've designated) if a wound has become deep or infected and needs attention. One of the other ground rules could be not leaving signs of self-harming about for younger siblings to see – or even older ones, actually – which can be really upsetting.

'Of course, if they say, "Leave me alone," you may have to explain why you can't do that, and talk about the risks, and the unintentional serious, even life-threatening harm.' **Jane Smith**

Try to make sure, though, your conversations don't always gravitate back to self-harm, as Jane has said, and that you do things together as a family, and you remember your wonderful, unique and precious child is still there, and keep reminding them of this, too.

'It's really important to remember that the child you love is still there, you know? They haven't become a difficult, horrible person who does things that you wish they didn't. They're just preoccupied with their concerns and have developed an unhealthy "solution" for coping, which obviously upsets and worries the hell out of you. Remind yourself and them of all their wonderful qualities – how kind they are, how thoughtful ...' **Jane Smith**

- *Talking safety.* There are obvious risks involved in self-harm, and although you do want to leave those conversational spaces open to come back to when they're ready, there are also times when you need step in and get them the help they need. You may need to find out how bad it is, whether immediate medical help is needed, and if so, whether that's something you can deal with at home, or if they need taking to a doctor or hospital.

Pat: Your number-one priority as a parent – I'm sure all parents are the same – is to safeguard your children – obviously, you know, doing that through love and respect and all the rest of it, but yeah, that's going to be your number-one priority, and that's why you need to kind of understand what level you're talking about – even if you don't want it at the time, but actually, medically, do you need intervention of some sort?

Sofia: Oh no, definitely. And I think, like, at that point, if you know it's something more serious, you obviously use your power as a parent – like, "I'm not doing this to be horrible or to cause you more shame or anything like that, but this is serious, this is something that needs to be looked at." You need to be constantly reassuring, which I know is very hard, but constantly going, you know, "It's OK. The doctor will have seen things like this before. Don't worry."'

- *Reducing risks.* Although it's counterintuitive for a parent who just wants their child to stop, talking harm reduction is also important until they're ready to do so. There are ways they can reduce the risks in the short term, like knowing where major arteries are, and also minimize future consequences, for example from scarring. See the resources below for more information.

- *Taking time.* Patience is an enormous challenge for a parent who knows their child is at risk. It may pass quickly for them, but it may not. Whatever lies behind their self-harm might take some time to unravel, and at the moment it's how they cope.

'I think being very calm is the key, not rushing it, although you want the answers now to make sure that, like, your child's OK. But rushing them will just push you farther away from them. It's just about taking it slow, and make sure you are taking it at their speed, at their time, although I know it's very worrying, but you've just got to understand that they are going through something very traumatic and very hurtful and there's such a deep feeling that it's really scary. And yeah, just they'll come to you when they feel like it's right.' **Sofia**

If they feel pressure to stop before they're ready, while the underlying issue is still there, and before any other strategies are in place, they're much less likely to open up to you again, they're more likely to conceal it better, you're less likely to be able to help and they may turn to more extreme and risky means to manage.

Sofia: It's kind of like the biggest pill to swallow is the fact that you can't just stop them.

Pat: Yeah. When you find out you just want to make them better, you just want to fix it, but it's not fixable like that, and that's really frustrating as a parent. You want to sort it all out – well, certainly I wanted just to sort it all out.

Sofia: Well, that's the type of person you are. I think the problem with Mum – and I mean this in the nicest way possible – the problem with Mum is she problem-solves everything. And sometimes you don't want to go and hear a solution, you just want to talk about it.

Pat: I am, I'm very practical. I'm just, 'Right, what shall we do then?' But that's just me – but I'm sure that loads of parents would feel the same way, so to know that you might have to wait for your child to open up and give you the information that you need, that's really hard, you know?

• *Keeping things on the radar.* A parent also needs to keep the issue quietly on their radar because, as Sofia said at the start, for some young people self-harm sticks in their heads and can call to them long after it seemed that particular voice had been silenced.

Pat: Say they haven't done self-harm for quite a while, I think it's really important to understand that you should still be quite aware that potentially it could come back. It might never go away, so be aware of that and don't think, 'Oh, right, it's all fixed now. She seems much happier, great.'

Sofia: Er, yeah, I mean, literally up to about, what, three weeks ago, I felt like it, but I know now it's such a temporary feeling. I think accepting how you're feeling was the biggest thing for me, to help me to get over it. It's like, OK, yeah, I'm going to feel not very good for the next couple of days, but I'm going to try and do little things that help me.

Pat: But it'll pass.

Sofia: It's going to pass.

Self-harm and suicide

Self-harm can, of course, be very serious, and even fatal. This may be unintentional, such as accidentally taking too large an overdose, or cutting a major artery, but the connection with suicidality needs to be in parents' minds, too. Self-harm isn't the same as suicide, and indeed self-harm is a means of coping, whereas suicide can seem the only option when coping no longer feels possible. However, suicidal thoughts and attempts are significantly higher in teenagers who self-harm, especially those who do so frequently, and some of the risk factors are the same for both. See Chapter 13 to understand better how to go about these especially tough conversations.

What about you?

Your teenager will need you to remain calm, patient and supportive, but there'll be some powerful emotions around for you, and as this may continue for some considerable time it's important you find support for yourself, look after yourself and check in with yourself regularly. You can feel very isolated, so is there a friend you can trust? What are the things that can help you let off steam or let out fear and frustration? Your feelings are valid and need their space.

'You feel you've failed if your child is feeling that way. You feel you must have done something wrong, because why would they do that? You hide it almost. You don't want to tell people that your child has difficulties, but actually as soon as one person opened up, I found others had, too, and that made me feel better, 'cos I know that person's a good parent, and yet their child still ended up doing that. **Pat**

'Consider getting some counselling for yourself, or as a couple if you have a partner. Apart from the support it offers you, it can help you be consistent in your approach as a family and increase the support you can offer your child.' **Jane Smith**

Hold on to hope

Sofia: The counselling I got in the end did really help. I think I still would have stopped anyway 'cos I wanted to, but it would have been a lot harder.

Pat: Yeah, you're very strong willed – that's in Sofia's character. So, if Sofia wants to do something she'll do it. If she doesn't want to do something, she *will* make a way to not do it.

Sofia: *(laughs)* So true!

Help them to hold on to hope, even if you're struggling to do so yourself. They can get through this, it won't always feel so bad and you'll be there for them all the way.

'Enable them to think towards the future, the next chapters in their lives. Give them hope. It can be very hard for parents. You can't see if there's a light at the end of the tunnel. You've no idea. For some people self-harming is a flash in the pan, for others it's very long term, but it's important to have hope as a parent, and to pass that on to your children: "You will get through this. You will get through these feelings. You will get through this period of unhappiness. Life isn't always going to be like this." Giving them hope that life will get better.' **Jane Smith**

And finally ...

Pat: I felt ... I felt that you grew really strong, Sofia. You got absolutely brilliant at really standing up to your dad at times, and telling him, you know, 'No go!'

Sofia: I decided to not let my aggression in because it was physically hurting me by me actually hurting myself, and it was mentally hurting me, so I decided not to hold my anger against him in anymore. And I started arguing back to him and catching him out in his arguments. And he loved me, but he hated me because I ...

Pat: Because you stood up to him.

Sofia: I caught him out on things, like I could ... what's the word? It's like I held up a mirror to his face and showed him his true self, and I wasn't going to back down. And that's why I've become quite a feisty outspoken person, where I tell people exactly how I feel, which is not the best sometimes, I have to admit, but it's way better for me.

FINDING OUT MORE

Online resources

Adolescent Self-Injury Foundation: US non-profit providing advice for young people and parents, including a hotline https://www.adolescentselfinjuryfoundation.com/.

Calm Harm app: Award-winning app developed for UK teenage mental health charity stem4, designed to help people manage or resist the urge to self-harm. It's available in the UK, US, Canada, Australia and 'rest of the world'. https://calmharm.co.uk/.

Selfharm: UK charity providing online self-harm support for teenagers https://www.selfharm.co.uk/.

Self-Injury Support: UK charity providing support for girls and women affected by self-harm, trauma and abuse https://www.selfinjurysupport.org.uk/.

Books

Pooky Knightsmith, *Can I Tell You about Self-Harm? A Guide for Friends, Family and Professionals* (Jessica Kingsley Publishers, 2018)

Jane Smith, *The Parent's Guide to Self-Harm* (Lion Hudson, 2012)

13

TALKING THE TOUGH STUFF OF SUICIDE

'He keeps saying stuff like, "The way I think isn't normal, is it?" I said, "What makes you think that?" and he said, "Well, is this it? Is this life? Is this all there is to life, because it's a bit rubbish. Are you happy with just, like, getting up and going to work, and coming home again, and not much else?" So, I think he just gives himself a hard time, like, why is he not more content? Why is he not happier? Why do those thoughts of suicide crop up every so often?'

Teresa

WHO'S WHO?

Teresa and her son **Jamie** (25) live in North Wales. Jamie has recently graduated from university. **Mischka** (27) lives in the east of England and works in IT.

Kelly Thorpe is Head of Helpline Services at PAPYRUS Prevention of Young Suicide, a UK charity dedicated to the prevention of suicide and the promotion of positive mental health and emotional wellbeing in young people https://www.papyrus-uk.org/.

I've also included additional extracts from the stories of **Luke**, **Tamara** and **Lois** from earlier chapters.

What do we mean by ...?

Suicide needs no defining. We know what it means, and it's a word parents dread having to use in any relation at all to their children. It literally is a matter of life and death, and if it touches a family, it can leave parents lost in vast oceans of fear, confusion, guilt, shame and also, often, anger.

There are many dimensions to suicide, and the dynamics at work in each of these are complex. There's thinking about suicide, talking about suicide, attempting suicide and, ultimately, dying by suicide. Thankfully, the numbers attached to each of these get significantly smaller as we move along that list. However, every suicide attempt must be taken seriously. Every utterance that strays even close to suicide must be taken seriously. And if you have the tiniest suspicion your child may be having suicidal thoughts, it's something you must fight your fears and talk to them about, clearly and directly, and listen with great compassion.

What it's not ...

- *It's not (generally) about wanting to die.* It's about feeling no longer able to live with the pain they're experiencing. It's also the case that most people swing between wanting to live and wanting to die. The instinct to live is a powerful one to overcome.

- *It's not a choice (or it doesn't feel like one).* A sense of entrapment is one of the most commonly experienced factors in people who feel suicidal. They're imprisoned in a place of impossible pain, and unable to see any other escape.

> 'It was when I got into the biggest amount of debt ever for drugs, and my mum had already said, "I can't afford to pay off your debts anymore. If it comes to it again, you're done." I just didn't think there was any more help out there for me. So, I took a load of cocaine, took myself off to the river, tied my legs up with a scarf, and pushed myself back in, because for me I couldn't see a way out. But I started to get fearful when I was underwater, thinking what I was leaving behind and stuff like that. So, I pulled myself out, and just kind of pushed myself up onto the riverbank and untied my legs. I drove home and told my mum. She was really upset. She was heartbroken.
>
> 'It was late at night, and I knocked on the door and it was my twin brother who opened it, and he burst into tears, and my mum came running downstairs. It was a really sad moment. But that's the moment where I really started reaching out for extra help, and I really started my recovery journey. And luckily enough, I'm still here today, and I'm living a majorly better life ...' **Luke**

- *It's not selfish.* In fact, for many, it's an act of ultimate selflessness. They feel they're relieving those they love most from the burden they believe they've become to them. For others, they may have had to cut off their emotions in order to cope with their pain, and in doing so also their empathy. Selfishness doesn't come into it.

Tamara: I'd oscillate between feeling suicidal and wanting out, to feeling nothing at all. Why do other people still have emotions? Everything's pointless. I felt weirdly, sort of, I don't know if arrogant is the right word, but I felt that everybody was stupid for not feeling the way I did. Now, looking back, I think I was not in a good way! Like, if anyone was in that way, I'd encourage them to get help immediately. But I just found it strange that people thought life was worth living.

Lois: That was when I was sleeping in your room, and I remember you saying to me, 'You can stay here but it doesn't matter what you do, I will do it. I will die. It doesn't matter if you're sitting there.' It was awful. I don't think you remember all those things?

Tamara: No, but I look back and think I must have been so awful to be around, and it must have been so terrible for other people. I don't like to think of myself as a nasty ...

Lois: No, you're not nasty. No, it's an illness.

Tamara: Yeah, it's an illness, and I thought I was right. I just thought, 'Yeah, my way is true. Just other people thinking there's a point to life, they're just stupid. You're all missing this key bit of information.' I think it was like an automatic coping mechanism, and in some ways it's liberating at first, because you think, 'I feel nothing.' It's better than feeling something. And then as it goes on you realize that's really bad.

- *It's not manipulative or attention-seeking.* As with self-harm, this is a sign that our child is in pain. Thinking this risks suicidal thoughts or acts being trivialized and underestimated, which puts that person at greater risk of coming to harm. They do need our attention, and also our compassion and care.

- *It's not caused by any one thing.* There may seem an obvious factor, but suicide is complex. There will have been a maelstrom of stuff on the inside, stuff on the outside and stuff often going way back in the past, that's reached a pitch of intensity. That said, there are certain risk factors, which we'll come on to.

- *It's not inevitable.* Suicidal thoughts don't inevitably lead to suicidal acts, and if someone has experienced thoughts, or even acted on them, it doesn't mean they will again. For many people suicidal risk is short-lived, and when it isn't, there are protective and preventative measures that can reduce the risk.

- *It's not your fault.* It's impossible not to blame ourselves as parents. But even if you can point to things you could have said and done differently – and we can all find those for anything when we look – the causes of suicide are so complicated. Self-compassion and self-forgiveness are just as crucial for parents as they are for struggling, suicidal teens.

What can put some more at risk?

Although the causes are complex, studies have shown there are certain factors that can, in combination with all sorts of other elements, place some people more at risk. Knowing what some of these are can help parents know when to keep their eyes and ears on the alert. Mental illness is the most obvious, though not all suicidal people are depressed or mentally ill, or vice versa. However, there is an undeniable relationship, especially with major depressive disorders, schizophrenia, bipolar disorder and substance use disorders. Self-harm can become suicide, although, as we've seen in Chapter 12, this is far from inevitable. Bereavement and especially exposure to the suicide of others may increase risk, especially if it's someone close to them. A strong indicator of future suicidal behaviour is previous suicide attempts, although for many it happens just once. Lastly, trauma, especially in early life, can create some of the greatest risks.

'So, basically, my dad sexually abused me from when I was five till I was 11, and now I know he was controlling me, like, my whole life, and it only really stopped when he died a couple of years ago. So, for me it's all complicated, 'cos it's, like, when you're under that control you don't understand that you are. I wasn't even aware that weight was there till it went when he died. I'd always been told my entire life by my dad I was worthless, and eventually you start believing it.

'When I went to university I got into another abusive relationship, with this guy, Ed. I didn't know just how much I was under his control, but it got worse, to a point he wasn't allowing me to actually go to university to study, so I was missing virtually every lecture, every seminar. It's like there were just days when it was, "OK, just take me. I can't do this anymore." Most of my suicide attempts were at university.

'To start off with it was never, "Right, I can plan this," it was, "This needs to happen right now." I tried so many times, and it really drove me mad that none of them worked. I was in a coma for one, and when I came round the nurses were like, "You were incredibly lucky to survive that," and it was, "Dammit. I didn't want to." I was really upset that I'd actually woken up. The only thing going through my head was, "OK, now I need to plan this more carefully."

'The last one was the one I'd planned most thoroughly. There's no way that would have failed. I'd got to the point where I literally had no hope at all, and I had no desire to live, because I knew what Ed was doing, and I couldn't see how I'd ever get away. If it hadn't been for the accident that morning, I know I wouldn't be here. I still don't remember much about it, but apparently I was crossing the road and didn't see a car coming. I still hate the fact that that car put me on life support when none of my suicide attempts had. I know it sounds weird, but I'm still embarrassed by that.' **Mischka**

What are some of the signs?

'When Jamie was around 14 he kind of noticeably, I guess, started to experience difficulties in managing his emotions – lots of what you may imagine as teenage behaviour happening at that point, lots of anger, and the relationship between the two of us was quite fraught. He'd become really withdrawn, just in his room, not interacting very much, and then that escalated, and the withdrawal got quite extreme. His self-care and his cleanliness were quite a worry as well.' **Teresa**

So many signs of these Part 2 struggles are hard to distinguish from the everyday, evolving teenage experience, but there are certain things to be sensitive to, coupled with concerning changes in their behaviour. Listen out for any signs of feeling trapped, being a burden or experiencing 'tunnel vision' blocking out any alternative options, or the sort of perfectionism that makes them feel they have to live up to an impossible standard for others. Kelly outlines some more:

'Signs can include things like using self-harm to cope, drug and alcohol use, withdrawing from activities, making almost throwaway statements, you know, "I can't cope anymore, I don't want to be here anymore," which doesn't necessarily mean that they're experiencing thoughts of suicide, but the advice for parents is to notice changes in behaviour, especially when they're coupled with a stressful event. If there's any change, even if it's a change for the better, it's a change, and any change is worth exploring.' **Kelly Thorpe**

What do you say? Where do you start?

'I knew something was very, very wrong; I just didn't know what to do about it. Every time we tried to have a conversation, it ended up in just bursts of anger and quite abusive outbursts from him. I was at the end of my tether as well, and I'd get quite angry. It was really distressing.' **Teresa**

- *Do your research.* If you do have concerns, before you start, do your research, and prepare yourself using all the tools of Part 1– all your best open questions, active listening, keeping calm, validation, affirmation, empathy – but also being on the alert for any immediate action needed to keep them safe.

'We call those little subtle changes, or subtle signs, invitations. So, they're invitations to explore, and maybe if those verbal ques include any identifiers of feeling helpless or hopeless, and that kind of thing, ask the question about suicide. It just gives you the invitation, doesn't it? Not many teenagers will jump up and down and say, "Hey, I'm feeling suicidal." Sometimes they will, but it's more likely they're going to be giving those invitations so that they don't have to find the words. It just invites you as a parent to explore it, to help them find those words.' **Kelly Thorpe**

- *First, ask them if they're thinking of suicide.* Asking your child directly whether they're thinking of ending their life is incredibly hard for a parent, but it has to be done, and as clearly and simply as possible.

'Parents worry that asking the question directly will make the situation worse. It's absolutely impossible to do this, but it's like treading on eggshells, isn't it? You don't want your child to die, essentially, and you want to keep them safe, but the best thing to do, is to just ask the question, because otherwise you're not allowing yourself to be a safe space for that child to come to, and that's exactly what you want. You want to be that safety net, don't you? "I'd rather know then we can deal with it together. I want to be on your team. Let's work on this together." You need to ask it directly and clearly, so you know one hundred per cent what it is that you're dealing with.' **Kelly Thorpe**

Fears it will give them ideas, or make things worse, are completely understandable, as is not wanting to face the possibility your child's answer may be 'yes'. However, there's no evidence that asking the question raises the risk, and in fact it's more likely to be protective, and prevent them from turning their thoughts into actions. It could give them the chance to reconsider this as a route ahead. It could help them find the help they need. As we've said before, you're the expert on your child, and if you have a concern, there'll be a reason. If it's nothing to do with suicide, then that will be a relief, and it's opened the floor to talk about anything else.

'I started doing a bit of research, and I found PAPYRUS's website and I rang them. What I was looking for was someone to tell me whether he was suicidal or not. I was cross with them when they wouldn't do that on the phone for me, but they did advise me to have a conversation with him openly about suicide, because I hadn't ever asked about whether he was thinking about ending his life. I'd asked him all kinds of other things, you know – whether he'd been subject to abuse, whether he was being bullied – but yeah, there was something niggling at me which I can't really explain, almost a gut instinct, I think, that he was feeling suicidal, but I needed somebody else to tell me that.

'So, they encouraged me to have the conversation, but I was, like, "This isn't going to work. I don't think I can do it, not with how aggressive and emotionally charged he is." It took me another few weeks, I think, before I plucked up the courage, and I couldn't describe to you directly what I said but it was very long-winded and all around the houses, when it could have been a very simple, "Are you suicidal?" The reaction I got was horrendous – really intense and aggressive – and that's when the withdrawal increased to its worst. I was very angry with the advice I'd been given. I was, like, "I knew this would happen. I knew we'd just made it worse by talking about it."

'I think it was a couple of weeks after that, I'd been out and come back in, and he was sitting on the sofa – which was really unusual –

and he was crying – which was also really unusual – and he said, "What you asked me a couple of weeks ago, well I am." And I was like "Oh my word!" It's probably the best and worst thing I've ever heard, all at the same time. Because I think it's such a privilege if your kids are actually able to tell you something like that, but it's also terrifying. You're, like, "What the hell am I meant to do with this? How am I meant to keep this kid alive?"

'But I think for anyone who's got that gut instinct that's telling them that something isn't OK, just ask the question directly, you know: "I'm really worried about you. I might have got this wrong, but it's because I care about you. Are you thinking about suicide?" I actually feel very lucky that Jamie's still here because I didn't have the confidence. I was worried about the impact it would have on him. Worried about making the situation worse, but it's like grabbing the nettle. It's horrible in that moment, but it doesn't last very long, and then you know what you're dealing with and you can do something about it.' **Teresa**

- *Second, ask them if they have a plan.* If they have, that increases the likelihood they might act on it, and the more clearly formulated it is, the more likely it is to happen. If they have a plan, and access to the means, and they're not sure whether they can keep themselves safe, it's vital you get them help immediately.

'An easy mistake – and this is quite natural – is with parents whose child has a particular suicide method, the parent will try to get all of that item out of the house, in order to keep that child safe. Reducing access to means is really important. It's a crucial part of any suicide safety plan, but it's finding those baby steps, and seeing what that child can do for themselves, because if you're reducing access without that collaboration, then nothing has changed, has it? The thoughts of suicide are still there, and I haven't done anything about it. And the more we do things for them, that's quite disempowering. What we want in terms of suicide prevention is to empower them, because things feel so out of control, so let's try and give them some control back. So, it's that negotiation and collaboration.' **Kelly Thorpe**

285

- *Keep calm.* This is always a challenge with these Part 2 issues, and perhaps never more so than here, but it's also perhaps never more important. Their own emotions are going to be turbulent, or numbed, and they need a steady, safe pair of hands to be there for them. They'll also be gauging how much you can cope with hearing, and deciding how much they'll be able to share.

'When parents call with concerns, or their child has made a suicide attempt, first of all we unpick how that parent is feeling, and that's quite an emotionally charged conversation. It's important for parents to have that space where they can be honest, they can be angry, they can say exactly how this situation left them feeling, because you don't want to do that with your children. So, it's about getting that out in a safe space before we're able to move on and figure out what kind of support and advice would be best for them in that moment.' **Kelly Thorpe**

- *Get help.* What this looks like for you and your teen will depend on so much, but getting them to a doctor or another professional you trust will understand is important if you can, even if it takes some negotiation.

'We were able to kind of figure out a way forward that worked for the two of us. I wanted him to speak to a doctor and he wasn't up for that at all, but we were able to compromise, like, "If we do go and see the doctor, can I speak on your behalf?" And he said, "Yeah." I said, "But I need you there with me. I'm not just going to say it all – we need to do half and half." So, we did.' **Teresa**

Keeping talking, keeping listening

'It was difficult in the early days. I kept ringing PAPYRUS, you know, "What do I do next? What do I do in this situation? How do I have this conversation?" How do I keep him alive, essentially? It was only

by getting more support from them at that point, in terms of having those conversations and negotiating and collaborating with him, that I was able to navigate it. I don't think I'd have been able to do it myself. And it's hard because, you know, those thoughts of suicide didn't go away even though he took control over them, and life sometimes gets in the way a little bit and makes it harder to cope.'
Teresa

This may have been a passing moment in your teenager's life, but it may not, and you may need to be prepared for many conversations to come. Some will go well, others won't, most will probably fall somewhere in between, but, however it goes, communication is key to a teenager coping and coming through this. Whenever and however you can connect and talk, it really will have the potential to make a positive difference.

'It's sometimes going back to the beginning – "Did you attempt to take your life? Was that a suicide attempt?" Because sometimes children and young people aren't quite sure. Sometimes they might say, "It was self-harm, but it wouldn't have mattered if I'd died." So, the more that you take it right back to the beginning, it actually helps you have that conversation moving forwards.

'Where you're able to plan for a conversation it's helpful, but quite often you're not going to get that opportunity. It's going to hit you in the face, isn't it? Whether it's a suicide disclosure or whether it's a suicide attempt, you can't plan for that. I think you've just got to try your very best in those moments really. But actually, be proud that you're able to have those conversations with your child, be they planned or unplanned. You've got a space to make a difference in that case, haven't you?' **Kelly Thorpe**

What can help?

- *Collaboration.* This is at the heart of everything that will help, whether with you, the school, healthcare professionals, or anyone else. Your child needs to have ownership of their recovery, and needs you on their team, enabling them to do this.

> 'He consistently had a plan for suicide, which was the same thing, same risk. So, we kind of had to work together to figure out a way of helping him feel a bit safer from that. So, at first it was very simple things like, "When you are feeling like that, how would you feel about just leaving your bedroom door open?" It was tiny steps almost, taking it right back to basics in terms of what he could manage, and that seemed to really help.' **Teresa**

- *Compassion.* Showing compassion is so important (even if you're frustrated or angry or scared), as is helping them learn to be compassionate towards themselves. Suicidal teenagers often carry a load of guilt and shame, which can be very much part of the suicidal mix.

- *Connectedness.* A sense of isolation is common among people who feel suicidal, so do all you can do to nurture, encourage and help them build connectedness – with you, of course, and, if possible, with even just one other person. Pets can help hugely, too.

- *Control.* As mentioned above, letting them have some control wherever possible is a vital part of recovery, even if it's those baby steps. That parental urge to stand in the way of the oncoming train is never more powerful than in the face of possible suicide, but without letting them take as much of the reigns as is safe, their recovery will be harder.

- *Giving hope.* Suicidal people tend to have significantly fewer positive thoughts about the future even than people with depression. Help them find even the tiniest grain of something that strengthens that swing towards life.

'An understandable mistake a parent can make is where they can push for those reasons to stay safe – you know, "I'll be devastated if anything were to happen to you. What would your sister do without you?" – but it's helping them to come up with those answers for themselves. A great way of doing that for a parent would be, "You're feeling suicidal, but what's kind of spurring you on to stay safe? What is it every day that keeps you fighting?" And that's where you get those connections to life, however big or small, which then gives you the permission to move on to staying safe. "So, you've told me about that course you want to do, or the dog, whatever it might be. It sounds like staying safe is important, so we ned to do that." Young people need to be empowered around why they might want to stay safe.' **Kelly Thorpe**

- *Keeping calm.* In this situation, keeping your emotions in check is incredibly challenging (and not always possible), but it's so important to do this, for all the reasons outlined above. You do, however, need somewhere safe, away from your child, to vent.

'I don't think you ever get your response quite right do you? [*Laughs*] You know, the emotional attachment makes having these conversations difficult, and then managing your reactions is even more difficult because you've got so many emotions running around. You worry for them, and I had my own emotions about me as well. I was, like, "Oh, I've failed this child. Why is he feeling like this? It's my fault ..." So, it was like being side-swiped from all angles with these emotions, so I think I've not always managed them the best. You know, I've reacted in total shock. I've reacted with my own tears and things like that. Luckily, I've been able to have those conversations with him as he's got older and apologize for some of that. You know, "I'm glad that you were able to bear with me and keep coming back to me, because it was really hard for me to hear those things."' **Teresa**

- *Getting help.* What this looks like will be different for every teen and every family, and is likely to change over time.

Your child may remain unwilling to engage with anything professional – or be unable to access anything even if they're willing – but with or without formal support, and wherever they might best locate all the informal things that help them, ongoing listening and looking at options are both things to embed sensitively into your conversations.

'The idea of speaking to someone about the way he felt at that point was a no-go area for him, but weirdly, as he's got older and over the recent months, he has actually talked about accessing therapy for himself. He did go on to get a diagnosis of autism when he was 17, which I think gave him a bit more understanding in the way he ticked in comparison to other people, and I think that helped. He got some really good support, and he was able to go back to college and started studying something he really enjoyed rather than the academic stuff, and he went to uni and he graduated at the end of last year with a music degree.

'It doesn't kind of take away those thoughts of suicide, or that emotional distress that he can feel, and he still can often feel like that. And there have been suicide attempts after, but I'm very lucky, I feel, that he was able to speak to me about that in the immediate, following that impulsive action.' **Teresa**

- *Hold on to hope.* We've already talked about how healing having positive thoughts for the future is for a teenager struggling with suicidality, but hope is so important for their parents too. This is serious, but hold on to the fact that for almost all those who have suicidal thoughts, and even those who act on them, this isn't the end of any story, just a particularly painful chapter, and sometimes only a paragraph.

'It took me a long time to recover from the accident, but because of that I got a proper counsellor who's amazing and I'm still seeing her, and my dad died, which lifted this huge weight, and I got a new job and made friends with Amy, who's helped me so much. I can't find the words to explain it. Just something like ringing me – was it last week? – when I said I was emotional, that'd it'd been a really tough day. None of my friends have ever picked up the phone if I said I was struggling ...' **Mischka**

What about you?

As always, you need to take care of yourself, because this will take its toll, and that toll could be crippling. Find your own safe spaces, trusted people and ways to let off steam, and nurture your own wellbeing and health. Your child needs you to be OK, and so do you.

'We speak to lots of parents who have children who have survived a suicide attempt, and the emotions of the parents are often very similar to those of their child, either really angry or relieved. It's so important that parents have that space to talk openly and safely about what they've been through, because it's terrifying for the two of them, particularly if they've not got any ongoing support.' **Kelly Thorpe**

And finally ...

'Those early stages were really hard, but it gave us the opportunity to figure that path out in terms of what we'd both be happy with. I think, yeah, from there on in, rather bizarrely, it brought us closer together, because we didn't have that before, really. It was always just like, I don't know, like an authoritative mum and a child that doesn't want to fit into those societal norms almost, but yeah, it definitely brought us together, and I think it's made the strong relationship we have now.' **Teresa**

'For me it's still kind of weird that I don't have the suicidal thoughts, because they were so frequent, so now they're not there, it's kind of, "Oh, I don't know how to do this." 'Cos yeah, the self-harm is there, but it's not suicidal. I've got more confidence in me now. I still can't describe who I am, but I know I'm getting there.' **Mischka**

FINDING OUT MORE

Online resources

#chatsafe: Tools and tips to help young people communicate safely online about suicide and self-harm https://www.orygen.org.au/chatsafe.

National Suicide Prevention Lifeline: National network of local crisis centres providing free and confidential emotional support around suicide https://suicidepreventionlifeline.org/.

PAPYRUS: UK suicide prevention charity providing information and advice for young people, parents and professionals https://www.papyrus-uk.org/.

Books

Rory O'Connor, *When it is Darkest* (Vermillion, 2021)

Linda Pacha, *Saving Ourselves from Suicide* (AutumnBloom Press, 2019)

FOR YOUR BOOKSHELVES

In addition to all of the books referenced in each of the chapters of Part 2, here is a list of books I found useful in writing this one:

Blakemore, Sarah Jayne, *Inventing Ourselves: The Secret Life of the Teenage Brain* (Transworld Publishers, 2018)

Brooks, Ben, *Every Parent Should Read This Book: Eleven Lessons for Raising a 21st-century Teenager* (Quercus Editions Ltd, 2021)

Candy, Lorraine, *'Mum, What's Wrong with You?': 101 Things Only Mothers of Teenage Girls Know* (4th Estate, 2021)

Clarke-Fields, Hunter, *Raising Good Humans: A Mindful Guide to Breaking the Cycle of Reactive Parenting and Raising Kind, Confident Kids* (New Harbinger Publications, 2019)

Colombus, Katie, *How to Listen: Tools for Opening Up Conversations When It Matters Most* (Kyle Books, 2021)

Drummond, Alicia, *Why Every Teenager Needs a Parrot: Tips for Parenting 21st-Century Teenagers* (Let's Talk Ltd, 2013)

Duffy, John, *Parenting the New Teen in the Age of Anxiety* (Mango Publishing Group, 2019)

Faber, Adele, and Elaine Mazlish, *How to Talk So Teens Will Listen and Listen So Teens Will Talk* (Piccadilly Press, 2005)

Fortune, Joanna, *Fifteen-Minute Parenting: The Teenage Years* (Thread, 2020)

Jensen, Frances E., with Amy Ellis Nutt, *The Teenage Brain: A Neuroscientist's Survival Guide to Raising Adolescents and Young Adults* (Harper Thorsons, 2015)

Komisar, Erica, *Chicken Little, the Sky Isn't Falling In: Raising Resilient Teens in The New Age of Anxiety* (Health Communications, Inc., 2021)

Morgan, Nicola, *Blame My Brain: The Amazing Teenage Brain Revealed* (Walker Books, 2013)

Pandit, Vivek, *We Are Generation Z: How Identity, Attitudes and Perspectives Are Shaping Our Future* (Brown Books, 2015)

Perry, Philippa, *The Book You Wish Your Parents Had Read (and Your Children Will be Glad That You Did)* (Penguin Life, 2019)

Stillman, David, and Jonah Stillman, *Gen Z @ Work: How the Next Generation is Transforming the Workplace* (DAS Creative LLC, 2017)

Thompson, Dominique, and Fabienne Vailes, *How to Grow a Grown Up: Prepare Your Teen for the Real World* (Vermillion, 2019)

Williamson, Ian, *We Need to Talk: A Straight-Talking Guide to Raising Resilient Teens* (Vermillion, 2017)

ACKNOWLEDGEMENTS

A book always owes its existence to so many more individuals than its author, and this book perhaps more than most, because it's a book full of voices. My role as its author has been very much that of a careful curator of words not my own. This is a book built on conversations and owes an enormous debt of gratitude to all the many, many teens and twenties, and parents of teens and twenties, who generously gave me their time to chat. It's one of my favourite things to do, and I did it for hours and hours, gathering such a rich abundance of insight, experience and advice. For anonymity's sake, they all have alter egos here, and in some cases altered details, too, but they know who they are, and I hope they know how useful their words will be for others, and how much this gift is appreciated.

I'm particularly thankful to all the young adults and parents among these who've been willing to revisit some very difficult places to share their experiences of the toughest of stuff for Part 2 of this book, for the sake of other families. Their honesty and generosity have given this book so much.

I'm also enormously grateful to all the specialists who've contributed their expertise, insights and advice to this second part of the book. Not only have they given their own words and wisdom, but they also checked mine were saying what they needed to say.

And this leads on to a very big thank you to Emma Hazelgrove, who not only transcribed hundreds of hours of recorded of conversations (which, as anyone who's done this knows, takes many hundreds of hours to do) but also organized lots of the admin relating to these, and through it all has never tired as my number-one cheerleader.

And almost last, but never least, my ever-patient editor Victoria Roddam at Sheldon Press. Victoria not only believed there was a second book in me after the first, but also believed I could find my way into it, out of one that was quite different. Huge thanks are due for her faith, and for guiding me gently and wisely all the way.

Finally, thanks to my family. To my dear husband, Tim, for not minding my not getting much done other than writing a book for far too long. And to my dear son Jacob, for chatting with me all of his life, and for letting me write down some of these chats for this book.

INDEX

#NeverAgain, 7

abuse, 189, 194–8
acceptance
  of diversity, 7–8
  of mental ill health, 214
adolescence
  benefits of, 28–30
  brain functions, 53–4, 55–64
  difficulties of parenting through,
    30–1
  stages, 31–5
apologizing, 161–2

belonging, 38–9
body image, influence of social
  media, 20–1
body language, 84–5
boundaries
  online content, 22–3
  privacy, 134–6
  rebelling against, 123
  screen time, 17
brain functions, 53–4, 55–64
  affected by eating disorders, 252

catastrophizing, 143–5
changing world, 3–14, 24
  attitudes towards gender and
    sexuality, 174–5
  relationships and sex, 202
  risk-taking behaviour, 64
'Circle of Truth', 95
climate change, 6
coming out, 177–81
communication see conversations

communities, 138–9
  supporting LGBTQ+ teens, 184
confidence, 65–7, 73
conflicts, 35–6, 140–5
  avoidance of, 145–7
  emotional, 69
  over priorities, 18
  repairing after, 160–3
consent, 188, 189–91, 201
control, 147–9
  and self-harm, 262
controlling behaviour in
  relationships, 197
conversations, 76–80
  coming out, 177–81
  conflict avoidance, 145–7
  connectedness, 98–9
  curious, 92, 233–4
  about drugs, 225–30, 233–7
  about eating disorders, 249–55
  about emotions, 110–13
  forced, 136–40
  getting the message across, 82–4
  giving space for, 93–5
  going wrong, 103–4, 127–8,
    140–5
  importance of silence, 94
  important issues, 87–8
  initiating, 80–2
  listening to parents, 125–6
  listening to teens, 88–91, 95,
    100–1, 131
  about mental health, 209–12
  miscommunication, 107–8
  non-verbal communication, 84–5
  openness, 25–6

opportunities for, 95–7
about self-harm, 260–1, 265–72
about suicide, 282–7
co-parenting, 157–9, 166–7

disappointment, 123–4
discipline, 147–52
diversity, attitude changes, 7–8
drugs, 223–5
  addiction, 235–8
  conversations about, 225–30,
    233–7
  denial, 237–8
  different types, 231–2
  parents as role models, 230
  professional help, 238
  resources about, 239
  warning signs, 232–3

eating disorders, 242–7
  conversations about, 249–55
  denial, 250
  getting through mealtimes,
    252–4
  hope of recovery, 255–6
  resources about, 257
  secrecy, 243
  warning signs, 247–8
educational pressure, 47–9
emotions, 110–13
  connection between parent and
    child, 72
  and eating disorders, 251
  and self-harm, 265
  self-regulation, 67–70, 152–6
  and suicidal feelings, 289
  teens protecting their parents
    from, 124–5
escalation, 140–3
escape plan, 62
existential worries, 10–11

family, extended, 138–9
fears for the future, 10–11, 47–8
financial worries, 10–11
forgiveness, 160–3
friendships, 37–9
  influence of peers, 57–63
  sharing difficult issues, 167–8

Gen X (1965–80), 5–6
Gen Z (1995–2012), 5, 6–13
gender identity, 170, 172, 173–6
  adjustment for parents, 183
generational differences, 3–14, 24
  attitudes towards gender and
    sexuality, 174–5
  in relationships and sex, 202
  understanding of social media,
    19, 21–2
global financial crisis (2008), 10
grooming, 194–8
growing up, parents' acceptance of,
  128–30

honesty, 120–2
hormones, 32, 40–1
hurtful comments, 155
  and eating disorders, 251

information overload, 18–19
internet
  access to adult content, 22–3
  growing up with, 12, 14
  safety, 23

'Just Say No' campaign, 228

keeping in touch, 6

lectures, 85–6
legislation, generational changes, 8
letter-writing, 87–8

letting go, 128–30
LGBTQ+ community, 171–3
  coming out conversations, 177–81
  resources, 185
  support, 184
limbic system, 40, 53–4, 55, 63
listening
  parents to teens, 88–91, 95,
    100–1, 131
  teens to parents, 125–6
lying, 120–2
  about eating disorders, 250

mass shootings (US), 7
menopause, 41
mental health, 205–7 (see also eating
  disorders; self-harm)
  attitude changes, 9
  conversations about, 209–12
  hope of recovery, 219, 220
  of parents, 214–15, 219–20
  professional help, 217–18
  resources about, 221
  signs of problems, 207–8
  and suicide, 280
  trying to fix, 212–14
  unwillingness to discuss, 209–10,
    215–17
messy rooms, 104–7
miscommunication, 107–8
mistakes, learning from, 63–4
mobile phones
  always online, 12–13
  Gen X managing without, 6

non-verbal communication, 84–5,
  104

oestrogen, 40–1
online gaming, 18
  violent content, 22

online/offline distinction, 12–14,
  21
organizational abilities, 104–7

panic, 154
parental controls, 23
parents
  differences between, 157–9
  as role models see role modelling
    behaviour
peer influence, 57–63
perspective, 103–4
'phygital', 12
physical wellbeing, 65, 115–16
pornography, 22, 193–4
prejudices towards LGBTQ+
  community, 175, 182–3
pressure
  educational, 47–9
  from parents, 48
priorities, conflicting, 18
privacy, 134–6
problems
  developing skills to solve, 70–1
  trying to fix, 50–1, 132–3,
    212–14
progesterone, 41
protest movements, 7
puberty, 32, 41–4
punishments, 150–2

rebellion, 122–3
relationships, 187–8 (see also sex)
  giving advice about, 45
  grooming, 194–8
repairing relationships, 160–3
risk-taking behaviour, 32, 54–7
  changes through time, 64
  with drug use, 235
  peer influence, 59–63
  protection from, 64–5

role modelling behaviour
  around drugs, 230
  emotional self-regulation, 69–70
  physical wellbeing, 65

screen time, 14–18, 115
self-care, 168
self-esteem, 65–7, 166
self-harm, 259–60
  alongside eating disorders, 248
  conversations about, 260–1,
    265–72
  hope of recovery, 273
  providing support as a parent,
    268–72
  raising concerns, 264–5
  reasons for, 262–3
  resources about, 274–5
  and suicide, 272
  warning signs, 263–4
sex, 187–8
  consent, 188, 189–91, 201
  conversations about, 46–7
  grooming, 194–8
  pornography, 22, 193–4
  terminology, 188–9
sexting, 191–2
sexual assault, 189, 199–201
  resources about, 202–3
sexual harassment, 189
sexuality, 170–1, 174–5
  adjustment for parents, 181–3
  coming out, 177–81
siblings, 166, 269

sleep, 114–16
social acceptance, 57–63
social connections, 73
social media, 19–21
  understanding of, 19, 21–2
step-parents, 159
stigma about mental health, 9
stress, 49–50, 109–10
strictness vs. leniency, 147–9
suicidal feelings, 217, 277–80
  conversations about, 282–7
  hope of recovery, 290–1
  professional help, 286, 289–90
  providing support as a parent,
    287–90
  related to self-harm, 272
  resources about, 292
  risk factors, 280–1
  warning signs, 282

teenage years (see also adolescence)
  benefits of, 28–30
  difficulties of parenting through,
    30–1
terror attacks, 11
testosterone, 41
text messages, 140
Thunberg, Greta, 7
transgender identity, 175–6
trust, 117–19

Winnicott, D. W., 160

Yousafzai, Malala, 7